To Heather for sending me down this road

CONTENTS

ACKNOWLEDGEMENTS

I'd like to thank the Sorbonne Nouvelle for its support during my studies, in particular Professor Franck Rebillard. Thanks to the Journalism Department at London College of Communication for sending me around the world to share my research. Special thanks to the individuals in Paris and beyond who gave their time to me during this process.

INTRODUCTION

When I moved to Paris from Philadelphia in 2008, I had never read a TripAdvisor review. I had never Googled a blog about Parisian life. I was only vaguely familiar with YouTube, launched just three years earlier. Instead, I came armed with a recent edition of the *Lonely Planet* guide, gifted to me by my former boss, and a university diploma fresh from the press. I worked at an American study abroad campus by day not far from the Eiffel Tower, but on the nights and weekends I wrote stories about trips in Paris, itineraries, places to visit, and general news for a platform called Associated Content. It was a service, since acquired by Yahoo, that allowed me to upload my stories and earn a few meager dollars from the comfort of my apartment. The more views I got, the better the pay, and there was always the possibility that a publication would purchase my story from the site. I was, as far as I was concerned, becoming a travel journalist.

I wrote about a recent trip to Philadelphia just prior to my departure. I penned a piece about Air India cancelling their low-cost route between Paris and Newark. These articles went up on the website, seen by a few dozen eyeballs before disappearing into the abyss of the internet. I may have earned about twenty US dollars for all my efforts, but I was determined. I wanted to keep writing. I hoped to move beyond user-generated content, to become a 'real' travel journalist which meant working for one of the big brands like *Condé Nast Traveler*, where I had interned as a university student in New York. I scoured job sites, sending out résumés left and right. It wasn't until I began my masters nearly two years later that I got my break interning for an American travel journalist in Paris. All of a sudden, I was working on the *Fodor's* travel guide. Through this journalist I met other writers who knew other editors, and my network grew. By the time I left Paris in 2016, I had worked for travel guides and websites around the world and could more confidently call myself a travel journalist, seguing into London where I continued to work with other brands on travel-related projects.

Looking back on the last ten years, I believe that the route I took may look unfamiliar to many aspiring travel writers. With Instagram influencers, blogs on every major publication's website, and easier access to creating quality podcasts, I'm not sure that I could have relied on following the same path I did a decade earlier. At the time though, it made sense to me then. Raised on daily papers, stories above the fold, *Reader's Digest*, and *Time* magazine, print was all I knew. My journalism education at university was not yet designed to tackle questions of user-generated content or online publishing, and teachers praised me for landing stories in print, like my first story in the *New York Post* when I was a senior. In school, however, we never mentioned travel journalism, at least not as a viable career option. The only travel writing class I could find focused on works by Gustave Flaubert and Jamaica Kincaid, sequestered in narratives and not journalism. Venturing out on my own, however, I learned very quickly that digital publications were where I should be looking. The big papers were still there, still accepting pitches, but there was a whole online frontier that was only just being colonized.

Ten years later, travel journalism is still evolving. Like most evolutionary shifts, however, these changes do not happen in isolation. Both the tourism industry and the journalistic profession are responsible for the news practices and expectations facing travel journalists today. It is increasingly difficult to discuss this niche form of media without understanding the forces at work behind it, shaping it, and adapting it to a digital environment where its practitioners and audiences mingle concurrently. This book is a look at this environment and these players, to help journalism students understand how travel journalism faces a unique collection of challenges in a digital age, and how they can respond in a professional arena.

Journalism, travel, and the web

Online journalism is no longer a novelty. Multiple studies haven driven home the idea that newspapers and other print media are navigating the web, figuring out how to maintain their editorial authority while grappling with social media and user-generated content (Bruns, 2005; Domingo et al., 2008; Peters and Broersma, 2017). While digital advertising accounts for more than one third of all advertising in the US, it is clear that audiences are increasingly moving online to consume their information, while glossy magazines and newspapers often take a back seat (Pew Research Center, 2016). What this means for the industry is unclear, as the 2017 Digital News Report from the Reuters Institute revealed that 16 per cent of respondents are willing to pay for their news, up from 9 per cent. Audiences are moving online, but they may be beginning to value paid content more than before – how will these changes affect travel media?

For travel journalists, the challenge goes beyond simply maintaining audiences willing to pay for their content. The combination of online travel agents and booking sites like Expedia along with review sites like TripAdvisor has upended the gatekeeping role of travel professionals – both agents and journalists – as well as the financial model of travel publications. Travelers report beginning their research online, oftentimes using a search engine to guide them, while some click directly to a preferred travel website based on brand knowledge or past experiences (Pirolli, 2016). A lot of new media, however, is only broadening traditional word of mouth recommendations and advice that travelers have relied on for years (Litvin et al., 2008). How journalists fit into this ecosystem, however, is an ongoing question as more and more voices join the mix.

Consumers, however, can now research and book their trips without *ever* consulting travel professionals or professional printed media, a departure from travel journalism's unofficial beginnings in the nineteenth century when a bustling guidebook industry and travel agents like Thomas Cook led tourists. Brick-and-mortar travel agencies are under threat from online travel agencies, though some analysts predict slower growth for online sales now that the market is nearly saturated with sites like Orbitz or aggregators like Kayak (Patel, 2016).

Despite all of this uncertainty, legacy brands like *Lonely Planet, Travel+Leisure,* and *National Geographic Traveller* remain active, while new magazines, like *Afar* and *Monocle* appear to thrive in a multi-platform environment. Travel media is slowly adapting, and over the past two decades, has not always done so gracefully, as detailed by *Skift* senior writer Andrew Sheivachman. In a 2017 article on *Skift*, a leading travel industry news website, Sheivachman wrote that travel brands 'did a poor job of appealing to readers on new platforms, despite their outsized influence and recognition among travelers'. News producers have taken steps, albeit slowly, towards integrating new tools and practices into their work (Paulussen, 2011, p. 63). Travel journalism has only recently come to terms with these changes. With gradual integration on social media, smartphone apps, and online video alongside their print publications, however, many of these travel brands are keeping afloat. At the same time, new online publications are cropping up all the time.

We can then conclude, rather bluntly, that travel journalists use the internet. No simpler statement could summarize the environment in which I researched and wrote this book. While it is a given today that journalists use the web to research, publish, and disseminate their work, in addition to a multitude of other practices, the unique profile ascribed to travel journalists over the years has not fully adjusted to the web, while both academics and professionals continue to examine these changes. The following chapters will look in more detail about how they are adapting to the web and the challenges that their profession is facing.

The consumer orientation of travel journalism has seemingly ceded much of its influence to review sites and commentaries, forcing us to question the value of the travel journalist as an expert critic. The entertainment aspect flourishes on blogs and Instagram where images and stories whisk readers away more freely and instantly than a magazine or newspaper might. The journalistic ethics under which travel journalism should operate have been thrown into peril over recent years, with 'fake news', 'sponsored content', and 'paid influencers' among the many hurdles that are forcing a re-evaluation of the profession. While not the first time that journalism has faced a moment of transition, travel journalism's already tenuous status as a serious profession is teetering precariously with so many online advances.

Throughout the following chapters, I seek to explore the new demands and practices facing professionals today. While by no means entirely unique to travel media, these changes affect travel journalists in specific ways that we can discuss here, without generalizing about journalism more broadly in a digital age. Through interviews with travel journalists – as well as bloggers and travel information consumers themselves – this book introduces how social media and search engine optimization affect writing and topic choice (Pirolli, 2016). There are other demands heaped on travel journalists – providing their own photos, uploading onto content management systems, and promoting their work – that complicate the lives of established travel journalists. I want to demonstrate how, currently, some professional journalists resist many of these changes and are leaving social media and other Web 2.0 innovations to the non-professionals, but not without acknowledging the need to follow suit. It is also worthwhile to pinpoint how professionals perceive the work of non-professionals, to understand both their praise and concerns for user-generated content. Travel journalism is at a crossroads, and its practitioners are still scratching their heads about the best route to follow as they re-evaluate their roles.

This snapshot, however, is not set in stone. Travel journalism is still arguably in a transitional phase, maybe even a permanent one, and these technological innovations will likely become normalized as bloggers and other digital natives rise up in the ranks of media sites (Witschge, 2013). As both media consumption and tourism become increasingly integrated with the web, these changes will be less intrusive and more the norm in the near future, until the next hurdle presents itself. Travel journalism is still grappling with the potential of the internet, but both legacy media and digital first sources of travel information are finding ways to maximize this potential to attract audiences and deliver compelling, useful, and engaging journalism in a way that, ideally, would generate revenue for practitioners.

Why study travel journalism?

Before getting into how all of these things are changing, it's fair to ask why we study travel journalism at all. Numerous authors have already laid a framework for justifying these claims, but it bears repeating. Travel is an important industry, accounting for over 10% of the global GDP in 2016, according to the World Travel and Tourism Council (2017). The group also reports that tourism accounts for one in ten jobs worldwide, meaning many humans depend on tourism for survival. According to the UN World Tourism Organization, tourism receipts in 1960 amounted to 2 billion USD, but destinations worldwide earned a staggering 1.22 trillion USD in 2016 (2017a). How destinations are represented arguably impacts to some extent how the tourism sector will fare, and journalists traditionally have been the mediators between destinations and tourists. Of course, tourism offices play their own role as destination marketers, with advertisements and campaigns targeted at increasing interest. Even these marketers, however, understand the benefits of the media in promoting their messages and work with the travel press and guidebook industry.

While the media facilitates this continually growing industry, the number of potential tourists is also increasing. Worldwide, the number of international arrivals has skyrocketed to 1.235 billion people according to UNWTO (World Tourism Organization, 2017b). BRIC nations – Brazil, Russia, India, and China – have been an emerging market for nearly the last decade, with China leading international spending. Among these travelers, fewer and fewer require visas to travel. Combine growing populations of travelers with more low-cost options for transportation, and it's increasingly clear why the UNTWO projects steady growth in the industry. While low-cost carriers like Ryanair and easyJet in Europe, jetBlue in the US, and a slew of others offer inexpensive short-haul service, 2012 saw companies like Norwegian Air offering competitive prices for long-hauls. Suddenly flights from London to Los Angeles were available to more modest budgets. While low-cost travel alone is not the catalyst for the uptick in tourist numbers, it's one clear example of how things are changing in the early twenty-first century.

As prices drop and borders become more permeable, however, other walls have potentially hindered tourism in certain regions. In 2016, a referendum vote for Brexit created uncertainty for tourism within the United Kingdom and the rest of the Europe. In 2017, the much-mediatized travel bans in the United States were allegedly responsible for a dip in tourism during the first quarter of 2017, according to a *New York Times* article (Glusac, 2017). Terrorism likewise played a part in stunting growth, albeit it temporarily, in France after the 2015 attacks in Paris (Rodionova, 2016). Similar attacks – Brussels in 2016, Nice in 2016, Germany in 2016, London in 2017, Stockholm 2017, Manchester 2017, Barcelona 2017 – have shaken the West and may deter hesitant tourists. Travel journalism, however, can play an important role in contextualizing these incidents and keeping them in perspective – and they can do so online more quickly than ever.

As commercial tourism becomes more commonplace, the possibilities for twenty-first-century travelers are seemingly endless. Digital innovations have seen Google Maps replace folded paper cartography. Airbnb now rivals traditional hotels. Online travel agents are chipping away at brick-and-mortar travel agencies, which have not yet disappeared altogether. The *post-tourist* described by Urry and Larsen has more opportunities than ever before to mix kitsch, touristy experiences with those that resonate as more authentic (2011). At the same time, journalism is facing an ongoing and well-documented identity crisis, especially as the World Wide Web introduced self-publishing possibilities that continue to allow tourists to become information providers to global audiences through social media. Whether it's on a personal blog, in a YouTube video, or through online forums like those found on TripAdvisor or Reddit, non-professionals can work alongside professionals to produce relevant and useful information for anyone with an internet connection. The intersection point of these two industries, travel journalism, is the object of study in this book. It's timely to ask what the value of travel journalism is at all, given that so much travel-related content is available online. More importantly, it is important to understand *what* travel journalism is in the first place, if there is, in fact, a difference between all of these information providers, and I argue that such distinctions have blurry boarders.

Studies on travel journalism in the early twenty-first century are increasingly visible in journals and academic publications. While Greenman's 2012 *Introduction to Travel Journalism: On the Road with Serious Intent* acts as more of a how-to than a study of the topic, numerous works by Folker Hanusch and Elfriede Fürsich culminated in a 2014 collaboration, *Travel Journalism: Exploring Production, Impact and Culture*. In it, the authors correctly assert that, despite years of not being taken seriously, '[i]t is precisely the significance of leisure in contemporary society that makes the study of tourism and travel journalism such a fertile field for research' (p. 3). Lyn McGaurr's 2015 work introduced further empirical studies to the profession's study, while authors like Ben Cocking and Andrew Duffy have published many recent articles based on their own research of travel media. Add these pioneers to a long list of other disciplines – travel writing, tourism studies, journalism studies, audience studies, etc. – and it becomes clear that there is a general interest to understand how tourists inform themselves and what the consequences are on the industry. These questions are rooted in a deep history of writing and informing over the centuries, linked to exploration, colonization, and representation of foreign peoples and places. Travel writing and tourism 'can become instruments of political, military, scientific, and economic power as well as of racism and sexism, themselves tools of power exercised over others' (Roberson, 2001, p. xx). Travel journalism today is still a part of these processes, even if it is being produced or consumed on a smartphone.

Lifestyle media and beyond

The interest in travel media is not unique in and of itself, but demonstrates a continuing interest in broadening the horizons for journalism studies. Most journalism study has focused on a civic orientation and preserving democracy, something which many authors have challenged recently (Zelizer, 2013; Peters and Broersma, 2017). Breaking away from the civic or watchdog function of journalism, however, has only recently gained steam in journalism studies. Newer handbooks about fashion journalism in the UK (Bradford, 2015) and international journalism in France (Marthoz, 2008) demonstrate a need to differentiate the goals and practices of specific types of journalism. While arguably a common thread runs through all journalism – a devotion to the truth, an empowerment of the reader – how we get there isn't always the same. A political reporter and travel journalist have as much in common as a podiatrist and a neurologist. Both are concerned with the body overall, but their goals are targeted and unique. Both journalists want to inform and empower their readers, but perhaps to very different ends, and thus different means. Recent research, however, suggests looking more at addressing emotion, identity, and consumption in journalism research, which resonates with existing interpretations of lifestyle journalism (Hanitzsch and Vos, 2018).

Through journal articles and a ground-breaking collection of work edited in 2013, Folker Hanusch has largely been responsible for introducing an academic frame of reference for the more consumer-oriented lifestyle journalism, under whose umbrella term we find travel journalism. According to Hanusch, lifestyle journalism is 'a distinct journalistic field that primarily addresses its audiences as consumers, providing them with factual information and advice, often in entertaining ways, about goods and services they can use in their daily lives' (2014, p. 4). Lifestyle journalism, as Hanusch explains, can have implications on economy and national identity, especially as leisure culture continues to expand, but it largely goes overlooked by academics. While formerly considered frivolous, as Sjøvaag suggests in her study of Norwegian newspapers, 'these lower journalistic genres are also undergoing specialization that can ultimately contribute to legitimizing journalistic practices that are largely criticized for operating uncomfortably close to the economic field' (2015, p. 112). Lifestyle news is increasing in legitimacy while political and other hard news genres seem to be losing face to fake news, brand publishing, and new pressures from social media.

One example, while small, clearly demonstrates how lifestyle media can have real-world effects. In 2004, reports in the French press revealed that each year some 100 Japanese visitors to the French capital are stricken with what became known as 'Paris Syndrome'. A form of extreme culture shock, symptoms begin with depression and sometimes end with suicide attempts and hospitalization before being sent home to Japan. The source of the shock, according to reports by the *Libération* newspaper, was a discord between what Japanese magazines showed as a picture-perfect Paris and the reality faced once these visitors arrived in the city. Japanese lifestyle media did not accurately represent Paris and its people, and the results were visible as Japanese tourists repatriated to Japan during their vacations. Whether the blame falls entirely on the media or not is of course up to debate – best left to media effects theorists to argue. Still, it demonstrates that lifestyle media – and not just the more 'serious' reporting of politics and business – plays a very real role in our lives.

With this in mind, it's fair to underline the need to embrace a more interdisciplinary nature of journalism. We can't consider just one journalism, just as there is not one study of law or medicine. A multidisciplinary approach will allow students and researchers to explore how specific types of journalism operate. Within journalism education, these realities are already visible. At New York University's journalism department, undergraduates are required to double major, to have an area of expertise that may guide their journalism career. Some study biology to be health reporters, some study economics to be business journalists, and I studied French language and culture in hopes of becoming a foreign correspondent – ultimately, I wasn't far off my mark. Other schools worldwide are also embracing multidisciplinary approaches to journalism education. At the London College of Communication, the master's in Arts and Lifestyle Journalism addresses the specific demands of this consumer-oriented media. Students at the Sorbonne Nouvelle have one of the world's first master's in cultural journalism, addressing practices specific to producing magazines or reviews. All of these developing diplomas highlight a need to dissociate journalism from simply being a vector of democracy and understand that, especially in a digital age, it serves many purposes unforeseen by journalists of previous centuries.

Goals

Journalism education, however, is not just about learning to produce quality content. Students, through dissertations and critical essays, seek deeper understanding in their work, underscoring the theories and ideas that shape their chosen profession. I hope this book can be used as a springboard for students studying travel journalism in the future. This book sets out to introduce new ways of interpreting and examining travel journalism, based on research with real travel journalists and other content providers. The goal is not to learn how to become a travel journalist per se, but rather to understand how travel journalism positions itself in an ever-changing digital environment, confronted by new actors and new expectations. For students of the profession, it will open up discussions about how to reinterpret a travel journalist's work, to look beyond the twentieth-century norms and consider new possibilities and practices introduced by technological innovations. The lessons, however, are not all unique the travel journalism and can be extended to other lifestyle journalists as well.

This book is not a writer's handbook or a style guide, nor is it about how to pitch or publish stories. Instead, read it as an ethnography of travel journalists in the early twenty-first century, as a snapshot of this profession in a digital age that will, ideally, lead to a better understanding of the expectations and challenges facing today's travel journalists.

I've set out three goals for any student of journalism, whether preparing to research the profession, practice it, or like many of us, do both.

Identify

First, I want readers learn to identify the practices, ethics, customs, and norms of their profession. Any reader of this book should already have a background in journalism, a working understanding of the profession either as a student or a practitioner. The idea is to identify now a common vocabulary among travel journalists to engage with the occupation *professionally* and not just by calling oneself a travel journalist. A professional ideology only exists insofar as all members of the profession share the same values and ideals. While these values and practices may extend well beyond those described in the following chapters, and may likewise change over time, the first step is to acknowledge that there is something to identify in the first place.

Understand

Identifying common practices, however, is meaningless without understanding where they come from and why travel journalists engage with them. For some thinkers, practice precedes theory. 'Some intelligent performances are not controlled by any anterior acknowledgements of the principles applied in them', philosopher Gilbert Ryle writes (1949, p. 30). You may already be an accomplished journalist when it comes to reporting and writing. But is that enough? Thinking critically about the work that a travel journalist does, why we discuss things like disclosure, and what we offer that maybe social media users don't, are all essential to preserving the legitimacy that journalists seek. This legitimacy, in turn, is what keeps audiences patronizing the brands that ultimately pay the travel journalists' salaries.

Challenge

Finally, I want readers of this book to challenge the journalistic profession – more specifically as it relates to travel, but looking more broadly as necessary – and to question whether normative practices and values continue to function as we think. As both the media and tourism industry evolve, so will audiences. As I suggest incorporating conversations around constructive journalism and the sharing economy within travel journalism, I hope future innovations will also be up for debate. Continually challenging and questioning the profession is one of the best ways to avoid complacency, especially for researchers and practitioners who, upon confronting changes, often tend to become nostalgic for the way things were.

Methodology

This book is the result of years working in travel media and concurrent Ph.D. research carried out at the Sorbonne Nouvelle in Paris. Working in media since I began contributing to a local county paper in the United States when I was 16, I have been able to write and create content for publications like *CNN Travel, Time Out,* the *DK Eyewitness* guidebook series, and *Travel+Leisure,* among others. My professional experiences, while not indicative of the whole travel journalism field, have allowed me to witness many of these evolutions first-hand. Working as a travel journalist in Paris and London, I have interacted with editors abroad, relied heavily on social media at times, and developed my own routines that all illustrate how travel journalism is changing with the internet.

Furthermore, stemming from my doctoral work at the Sorbonne Nouvelle, my research spans several years of interviews with practitioners and content analysis of English-speaking travel journalism. I studied professional practice, to understand how travel journalism – set apart from journalism more broadly – might embody its own set of professional ideals. As Waisbord discusses, journalism is often criticized as a profession for impeding the very democratic ideals it purports to uphold. While professional journalists seek 'basic ethical principles that define occupational behaviour,' these ethics remain ambiguous, with the goal of professionally-minded journalism still focused on public service (Waisbord 2013, p. 125). Travel journalism, however, is not uniquely anchored in these, goals, and, as Waisbord challenges these normative views on professionalism, the real goal of identifying professional practice becomes evident. Professionalism, he states, 'is about how an occupation engages in relation with other fields and seeks to maintain distinction and legitimacy' (2013, p. 129). My research, therefore, attempts to identify what distinctions travel journalists have developed online to understand how they maintain legitimacy in the face of so much online content. What does a travel journalist offer, for example, that a TripAdvisor thread or blog post might not?

To that end, my research involves in-depth interviews and follow-ups with over thirty content providers, following indications in several research manuals (see Beaud and Weber, 2010; Lindlof and Taylor, 2011). These individual included travel journalists, bloggers, editors, and online forum contributors who helped make sense of what sorts of content they create and why they create it. How do they find their stories? How do they imagine their audiences? How do they respond to certain ethical questions? These authors were mostly American, Canadian, British, and Australians living or working in Paris at the time, who published for English speaking audiences. Some were editors of travel websites, some were freelancers for major broadsheets, and some were contributors to online publications only. Some wrote travel guides, some blogged about food, and others spent their days responding to travelers in online forums. They all have one thing in common – a desire to share information with tourists. Beyond that, their practices and principles reveal some marked differences between groups, allowing me to explore the norms that contribute to the boundaries of travel journalism (Singer, 2015). Throughout this book, authors are identified by their roles when quoted. Furthermore, some of the research for this book involves a content analysis of these authors' works as well as specific case studies on other samples of travel journalism that are explained when necessary.

Because the goal was to explore and understand professional practice – or actually, define its facets in the first place – speaking with practitioners was the most effective way to begin these conversations. Of course, the results are perhaps a bit biased, coming from a Western, Anglophone perspective. Still, because travel journalism is not necessarily dependent on democracy to function, focused more on the consumer, it's not inconceivable that these conversations could resonate across the socio-political spectrum.

Chapter by chapter overview

To begin these conversations, this book is divided into three parts addressing three areas of travel journalism. In Part I: Travel Journalism as Profession, I explore the underpinnings of travel journalism not just as a craft or occupation, but arguably as a profession. In Chapter 1, I will sketch out a history of travel journalism, which, while too ambitious for one chapter, will illustrate the key changes over the centuries that have led us to the current iteration of the travel journalist. It will help readers understand why we talk about changes today that may not be obvious, especially to students who did not witness them. In Chapter 2, I will move towards a framework for a professional ideology among the travel journalists interviewed. By understanding the different expectations between travel and non-travel news workers, it becomes clearer what a travel journalist offers audiences more concretely. In Chapter 3, I tackle the question of news, a defining feature of journalism. I question how travel journalists interpret the idea of news in their work, which doesn't always involve the same standards as their counterparts at the business or international desk.

Part II, Travel Journalism in Practice: Challenges and Changes, takes on the bulk of the contemporary practices for travel journalists online, thematically introducing the challenges and changes for professionals in a digital age. Chapter 4 sets out to explore the economics of this niche form of media, highlighting how the media is adapting to the web to fund its practitioners in innovative, though questionable ways. Chapter 5 addresses interaction with audiences. In this chapter, I revisit the notion of authenticity in travel to discuss with journalists how they interpret and respond to tourists' expectations. Chapter 6 is a nod back to Greenman's book, exploring how writing styles have changed online. Travel journalists need to reflect critically on clichés and stereotypes for global audiences, while SEO guides much of their writing for better or worse. Chapter 7 dives into the topic of social media, specifically addressing how travel journalists use it to their advantage, and why they are reticent to do so. Chapter 8 takes a different look at travel journalism to introduce how the internet has allowed more remote professionals, especially among expats. In it, I discuss how the commercialization of expats as a new wave of travel journalists can help to remedy, if even partially, these issues, while facing its own challenges. Chapter 9 ends Part II with the idea of self-branding, to dialogue with practitioners to see how they use the internet to engage with entrepreneurial journalism, much like bloggers have been doing for years.

Part III, New Interpretations and Opportunities, takes a step back from practices to look at new or alternative ways of thinking about travel journalism online that may not have been discussed yet in an academic setting. Chapter 10, for example, suggests that travel journalists can now take a constructive approach to their storytelling, especially since the web offers instantaneous publication unlike ever before. Inspired by the work of Danish research Cathrine Gyldensted, I'll look at how constructive journalism, a newer current of journalistic interpretation, played a role during the 2015 Paris attacks. Chapter 11 introduces the idea of representation, going beyond questions of 'othering' to ask instead how the internet allows for more debate and potentially more accurate or nuanced representations of foreign cultures than before. In particular, it will show how a site like TripAdvisor, when used in tandem with traditional media, can potentially respond to shortcomings in journalistic endeavors. Chapter 12 ends with a look at the sharing economy – emblemized by websites like Airbnb – which has segued into the media world. With its new magazine, *Airbnbmag*, published in 2017, Airbnb has turned both the tourism industry and the travel media on its head, and this chapter will examine the publication more closely to see what it provides in the way of journalism.

Again, a reading of this book will allow a practitioner or student of travel journalism to think more critically about their profession. Such reflections are more important for the media than ever before. In an age where fake news divides unions, enthrones radical leaders, and generally disrupts our daily lives, trust has eroded between information providers and audiences. Travel media is no different. Fake hotel reviews, fluffed-up sponsored content, and opinion-soaked assessments often parade as fact, leading tourists astray. It's a slight exaggeration, but with over 10 per cent of the global GDP depending on a healthy relationship between travelers and destinations, we can't afford to leave all of the mediation to chance.

References

Beaud, S., and Weber, F. (2010). *Guide de l'enquête de terrain*. Paris: La Découverte.

Bradford, J. (2015). *Fashion journalism*. Abingdon: Routledge.

Bruns, A. (2005). *Gatewatching: Collaborative online news production*. New York: Peter Lang.

Domingo, D., Quandt, T., Heinonen, A., Paulussen, S., Singer, J. B., and Vujnovic, M. (2008). Participatory journalism practices in the media and beyond: An international comparative study of initiatives in online newspapers. *Journalism practice*, 2(3), 326–342.

Glusac, E. (2017). International tourism to the U.S. declined in early 2017. *New York Times*. Retrieved from https://www.nytimes.com

Hanitzsch, T. and Vos, T. (2018). Journalism beyond democracy: A new look into journalistic roles in political and everyday life. *Journalism*, 19(2), 146–164.

Hanusch, F. (Ed.). (2014). *Lifestyle journalism*. Abingdon: Routledge.

Hanusch, F., and Fürsich, E. (2014). On the relevance of travel journalism: An introduction. In F. Hanusch and E. Fürsich (Eds.), *Travel journalism: Exploring production, impact and culture* (pp. 1–18). Hampshire: Palgrave Macmillan.

Lindlof, T. R., and Taylor, B. C. (2011). *Qualitative communication research methods: Edition 3*. Thousand Oaks, CA: Sage.

Litvin, S. W., Goldsmith, R. E., and Pan, B. (2008). Electronic word-of-mouth in hospitality and tourism management. *Tourism management*, 29(3), 458–468.

Marthoz, J. (2008). *Journalisme international*. Brussels: De Boeck.

Patel, N. (2016, February 10). Online travel agents. The Henry Fund, Henry B. Tippie School of Management. Retrieved from https://www.biz.uiowa.edu/henry/download/research/Online_Travel.pdf

Paulussen, S. (2011). Inside the newsroom: Journalists' motivations and organisational structures. In J. B.Singer, A. Hermida, D. Domingo, T. Quandt, A. Heinonen, S. Paulussen, and M. Vujnovic (Eds.), *Participatory journalism: Guarding open gates at online newspapers* (pp. 57–75). Chichester: Wiley-Blackwell.

Peters, C., and Broersma, M. J. (Eds.). (2017). *Rethinking journalism again: Societal role and public relevance in a digital age*. Abingdon: Routledge.

Pew Research Center (2016). *State of the news media 2016*. Retrieved from http://assets.pewresearch.org

Pirolli, B. (2016). Travel information online: Navigating correspondents, consensus, and conversation. *Current Issues in Tourism*, doi:10.1080/13683500.2016.1273883

Pirolli, B. (2017). Travel journalists and professional identity: Ideology and evolution in an online era. *Journalism practice*, 11(6), 740–759.

Roberson, S. (Ed.). (2001). *Defining travel: diverse visions*. Jackson: University Press of Mississippi.

Rodionova, Z. (2016, Aug. 23). Paris loses £644 as tourists steer clear of the city after terror attacks. *Independent*. Retrieved from www.independent.co.uk

Ryle, G. (1949). *The concept of mind*. London: Hutchinson.

Singer, J. (2015). Out of bounds: Professional norms as boundary markers. In M. Carlson and S. C. Lewis (Eds.), *Boundaries of journalism: Professionalism, practices and participation* (pp. 21–36). Abingdon: Routledge.

Sjøvaag, H. (2015). Hard news/soft news: The hierarchy of genres and the boundaries of the profession. In M. Carlson and S. C. Lewis (Eds.), *Boundaries of journalism: Professionalism, practices and participation* (pp. 101–117). Abingdon: Routledge.

Urry J., and Larsen, J. (2011). *The tourist gaze 3.0*. London: Sage.

Waisbord, S. (2013). *Reinventing professionalism: Journalism and news in global perspective*. Cambridge: Polity Press.

Witschge, T. (2013). Transforming journalistic practice: A profession caught between change and tradition. In C. Peters and M. Broersma (Eds.), *Rethinking journalism: Trust and participation in a transformed news landscape* (pp. 160–172). New York: Routledge.

World Tourism Organization. (2017a). *UNWTO annual report 2016*. Madrid: UNWTO.

World Tourism Organization. (2017b). *UNWTO tourism highlights: 2017 edition*. Madrid: UNWTO.

World Travel and Tourism Council. (2017). *Travel and tourism economic impact 2017* Retrieved from https://www.wttc.org.

Zelizer, B. (2013). On the shelf life of democracy in journalism scholarshop. *Journalism*, 14(4), 459–473.

PART I

Travel journalism as profession

1

A TRAVEL JOURNALISM HISTORY

Introduction

Two of humankind's oldest pastimes – besides anything related to survival and propagation – are traveling and storytelling. Originally a nomadic species, we only settled down some 10,000 years ago – a mere blip in our history. Human travel has had direct impact on politics, trade, and religion long before the earliest recorded accounts, with archaeological excavations revealing how people and goods moved around the ancient world (Gosch and Stearns, 2007). The caves of Lascaux in southwestern France depict some of the earliest examples of storytelling with images dating possibly as far back as 20,000 years, but there's no telling how far back oral storytelling reaches. What's clear is that we've been moving and narrating for a long time and, despite a change in how we do it, these urges have not wavered throughout the millennia. In fact, today, more people are traveling than ever before, with over a billion international travelers each year and countless domestic travelers shuffling around for business and pleasure. At the heart of all of this movement is the information needed to perform it, which itself has transformed drastically from the days of troubadours and hand-crafted letters. Today's holiday makers and nomads are better equipped with an overabundance of information at their fingertips from the stories of those who have already been there – but it wasn't always the case, of course.

Travel journalism is just one of these many sources of information, and the one that, arguably, instils some notion of trust that others may not. Before leaping into a discussion about its virtues and pitfalls, it is important to understand how travel journalism fits historically into the greater media landscape. One of the major difficulties in situating it, however, is its complex, poorly defined history as a profession. No comprehensive work exists that traces the roots of professional travel journalism, for two concrete reasons. First, travel *writing*, as a genre, has existed for centuries in numerous iterations, including personal letters, ship logs, and longer works of prose. This doesn't take into account the paintings, photography, and eventually video that also function to represent foreign people and places. Second, journalism, itself difficult to define, has only existed as a recognized profession for the past 100 or so years in much of the Western world, with social and legal definitions varying from country to country. This chapter seeks to trace the development of travel writing as an amateur pastime through its evolution as a professional activity, leading to a renaissance of amateurism in the twenty-first century with the proliferation of the internet. While it is impossible to pinpoint the moment when travel journalism was born, it will clarify how the genre developed with cultural and societal changes, reflecting transformations in travel habits through the centuries. This understanding, in turn, should help clarify the discussions to follow on the profession in a digital age, at least in the western world.

This chapter will offer just that, a look at the beginnings of travel narratives, tracing the relationship between writing styles and the tourism industry. It will arrive at the more recent development of journalism as a profession, considering links between travel writing and journalism, before moving on to more contemporary, twenty-first-century changes brought on by the internet, social media, and a continually changing economy. The goal is not to highlight every branch of travel writing that exists – that's another book all to itself – but rather to understand how the very idea of travel journalism appeared in a historical context, and to grasp how the travel journalists of today and tomorrow are fitting into this narrative. It is a complex history with no real beginning and no end in sight, as an increasingly mobile population will no doubt make way for more tourism-related content and stories throughout the twenty-first century.

Travel writing beginnings

According to Tim Youngs, 'Travel writing consists of predominantly factual, first-person accounts of travels that have been undertaken by the author-narrator' (Youngs, 2013, p. 3). This simple definition encompasses everything from a letter written by a medieval pilgrim to a more contemporary blog post written by a millennial to contemporary forms of what academics define as travel journalism. At its heart, most travel writing was, and perhaps still is, a personal, amateur affair, something destined only for the writer or a few acquaintances. Historically, there was no travel press in ancient Egypt or Greece to diffuse narratives to the masses. Youngs furthers this idea, saying that travel writing is a unique hybrid category, itself borrowing from different styles and genres, including scientific writing, autobiography, and diaries (2013, p. 6). Generally, tourists knew who they were writing for, and rarely was it for other anonymous tourists, since a complex commercial travel industry only developed relatively recently in human history.

The earliest travel writing, however, can be traced back to ancient cultures, including Egypt and Mesopotamia. While far from anything resembling modern journalism, these ancient texts, not unlike blog posts of the twenty-first century, have a common thread running through them, namely a basic human curiosity for the unknown (Blanton, 1997, p. 2). While some travel stories, including *The Epic of Gilgamesh* in Mesopotamia and Homer's *Odyssey* in Greece, focus on the more fantastic or imagined notions of travel, not all texts were as fictional. Many voyages motivated by political and commercial interests are enshrined in several texts, including the journeys of an Egyptian general, Harkhuf, around 2300 BCE. His narrative detail his many months of journey through sub-Saharan Africa, with descriptions of the goods and gifts he returned to the pharaoh (Gosch and Stearns, 2007). Harkhuf is often identified as the first long-distance explorer in history through the record he left on his tomb (Weaver, 2015; Youngs, 2013).

It wasn't until around 460 BCE that the Greek writer Herodotus emerged as a more modern recorder of history. Today, in his accounts, *The Histories*, readers receive a more narrative account of the writer's travels around the Mediterranean, including his observations of the Persian Wars (Hartog, 1988). Interestingly, Gosch and Stearns note the lack of any practical information woven into Herodotus' journeys, with no references to how he moved about or paid for his travel, which would frustrate today's *Lonely Planet* reader (2007, p. 30). Still, moving slowly from fiction towards facts, the author and his reflections are markedly absent from the volumes, taking on a more objective role (Blanton, 1997, p. 6). The Romans continued keeping records of travels across their empire, while the excursions of Paul the Apostle are clearly documented in a secular reading of a little-recognized travel narrative, chapter 27 of *Acts of the Apostles* in the Bible (Gosch and Stearns, 2007). As Christian persecution eased up in the fourth century, pilgrimages to Jerusalem and the Holy Land led to other recorded accounts – 526 between 1100 and 1500 AD (Youngs, 2013, p. 24). One of the first female travel writers appeared around 400 AD when the nun Egeria completed a pilgrimage around the Holy Land, writing of her travels for women back home. In her letters, she introduces practices that form the basis for more modern travel writing: descriptions of the exotic as well as her own voice and reflections throughout the narration. As Blanton describes, she interacts with her environment, introducing individuals that she meets and asking questions about what she observes (Blanton, 1997, p. 7).

Throughout the Middle Ages and into the Renaissance, however, a thirst for exploration pushed humans further abroad and overseas in search of new lands and trade routes, and it wasn't just Europeans who were setting sail. Spurred by new technology in shipbuilding, an end to Mongol rule, government-sponsored trips abroad, and mercantile endeavors, Russian, Chinese, and African explorers ventured further than ever before (Gosch and Stearns, 2007, p. 162). While research into non-Western travel journalism may very well yield a different tale, Europe's story is a well-documented one. As diplomacy, empire, trade, and discovery lured people further away from their homes, western travel writing grew to encompass these new habits, as well as to address evolving readerships with the increase of literacy following the invention of the printing press. Journalism as we know it today, however, was still not on the radar by the Renaissance, with few early newspapers circulating at all through Europe until the onset of the Enlightenment.

From exploration to experience

As explorers crossed the globe, they recorded their treks, and travel writing took on a more scientific approach, like the stories of explorer Marco Polo. In the widely popular book alleged to be the accounts of his travels, Polo spoke often of the Other, looking at indigenous people as objects of study. His stories circulated through Europe, introducing Westerners to foreign cultures in a way that objectified them as subjects of study. In one story, Polo was reported to describe local drink, breaking it down to basic elements, saying, 'The greater part of the inhabitants of the province of Cathay drink a sort of wine made from rice mixed with a variety of spices and drugs. This beverage, or wine as it may be termed, is so good and well flavoured that they do not wish for better' (Wright, 1899, p. 220). While more modern travel writers may actually ask the locals about the beverage, Polo keeps his distance, describing from afar. While previous writers also shared impressions of foreign people, these explorers discussed them in detail, albeit in a removed fashion (Blanton, 1997, p. 7). Moreover, Polo was one of the first writers to provide advice for future explorers, a practice that would become mainstream in the following centuries through commercial travel guides (Youngs, 2013, p. 29). Stories by Marco Polo in the fourteenth century and Christopher Columbus in the fifteenth century ushered in a wave of factual, almost disinterested reporting on their travels, bringing a more scientific view to exotic lands. As newspapers and gazettes began to appear throughout Europe in the seventeenth century, many travel logs and accounts found a place in their pages. Through the eighteenth century, these writings, at least in France, were destined even for literary journals, which also attracted a large readership, according to Yasmine Marcil. Such writings, she explains, illustrate to what point journalism about travel and discovery played a role in the literary press in France, suggesting an entertainment quality to these narratives that still exists today (Marcil, 2007).

Through the eighteenth century, however, travel writing took another step towards what we might consider travel journalism's precursor. As individuals began to travel more for pleasure – think of the Grand Tour undertaken by young European men – writers who documented their travels began sharing more reflective writing than ever before. Blanton describes how the changing motivations for travel writers evolved over the centuries, and how it became 'the kind of writing that foregrounds the narrator in an attempt to sentimentalize and/or glorify the narrator's experiences in hostile environments. Here the inner world is stressed over the outer world. A traveler's thoughts, reactions, and adventures are of paramount importance' (1997, p. 13). While Harkhuf, Egeria, and even Marco Polo may have hinted at these ideas in their writing, by the eighteenth and nineteenth centuries such travel writing became commonplace. A look at Gustave Flaubert's letters and diaries from an 1849 trip to Egypt, published after his death, offers a glimpse into this type of writing. He wrote:

> But the first days, by God, it is such a bewildering chaos of colours that your poor imagination is dazzled as though by continuous fireworks as you go

about staring at minarets thick with white storks, at tired slaves stretched out in the sun on house terraces, at the patterns of sycamore branches against walls, with camel bells ringing in your ears and great herds of black goats bleating in the streets amid horses and the donkeys and the peddlers.

(Flaubert, 1972 [1849], p. 79)

The focus on the experience, on the differences, on the sensations, are all of primary importance in this description, which describes vividly how the author is bewildered and dazzled by the visit to Egypt. This more self-indulgent writing, however, blossomed as another type of travel text popularized itself through the middle of the nineteenth century: the travel guide.

Industrialization and modern tourism

Through the nineteenth century, the Grand Tour slowly gave way to increasingly commercialized travel, requiring a more mainstream form of communications for a new class of tourists. This industrialization of tourism came about thanks to technological advancements, notably the steam engine and railroad, culminating with commercial air transport in the mid-twentieth century. As railroads and steam boats became commonplace, more individuals could travel easily and comfortably, giving rise to a larger leisure class. Socio-political changes also help explain the shift towards mass travel. For example, after the Napoleonic wars in the early nineteenth century, the English began to visit continental Europe en masse again. Entrepreneurs like Thomas Cook in England exploited these new trends, opening travel agencies during the second half of the nineteenth century (Buzard, 1993, p. 46). This innovation arguably marked the beginning of mass tourism that would expand throughout Europe through the rest of the century. At the same time, more and more travel stories appeared in publications by both American and European writers exploring Europe, including Mark Twain, Charles Dickens, and Frances Trollope (Buzard, 1993; Bertho-Lavenir, 1999). While they mostly provided entertaining or reflective accounts of their own travel, these authors contributed more to literature than to any form of journalism, but their potential to inform readers about faraway places maintained a link between the genres. Slowly, however, travel and informative writing began to intersect more formally for mass audiences during the 1800s as a new industry of travel handbooks took root.

While European and American newspapers were still developing, the idea of a travel section had not solidified fully by the nineteenth century. Papers did, however, focus on travel issues more and more by the late nineteenth century. The American newspaper of reference, the *New York Times*, for example, began publication in 1851. From its first issue it covered travel-related issues, including the arrival and departure of steam boats. It wasn't until 1896, however, that editors began publishing a Sunday magazine, including articles dedicated to consumer travel, which planted seeds for the popular Sunday travel section (archives, the *New York Times*). Newspapers weren't necessarily interested in catering to leisure

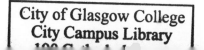

travelers prior to mass tourism, when marketing campaigns became more interested in reaching audiences.

Before the press invested in tourism-related topics on a consumer level, the guidebook industry set the tone for a growing travel media industry. In order to respond to the growing hordes of tourists, the late nineteenth century saw the advent of the modern travel guide. Travel manuals existed before the nineteenth century, like the *Conseil aux Touristes* (*Advice to Tourists*) written in 1793 by Hans Ottokar Reichard. Whereas this early book catered to a certain kind of upper-class traveler, educating more on etiquette and decorum than on what to experience, the new travel guide industry focused on specific locations and what to do there. These guides also helped users navigate the commercial offers advertised by the growing railways (Bertho-Lavenir, 1999). Travel agencies also offered their own publications. Thomas Cook, for example published a magazine entitled *The Excursionist* in the UK beginning in 1851 (archives, Thomas Cook). The idea of a specialized travel press began to develop at this time, embracing the commercial aspect of an adolescent tourism industry going through a growth spurt.

Travel guides were, arguably, the most fundamental ancestors of modern journalism. They have continued to exist throughout the evolution of travel media, adapting to the new environment as needed. They have introduced much of the format for travel websites today, which fundamentally offer similar information aimed at tourists organizing their trips. While the styles and platforms have changed, the goals are largely the same. By the nineteenth century, steam engines and boats made commercial tourism possible for a larger segment of the population, though it remained largely an elite activity. Automobiles and aviation would eventually open the world up to even more people, creating truly international commercial tourists, and these consumers were thirsty for information on how to reach their destination and what to do once there. European authors began to adapt their travel writing through the innovation of the commercial guidebook. Whereas before, much of their writing focused on personal letters and recommendations rarely destined to be read by the public, a new class of writers spearheaded by John Murray sought to standardize travel writing for the masses. By the mid-1800s, the guidebook had developed not only to share stories and anecdotes, but to assist individuals engaged in a whole new world of travel. As Catherine Bertho-Lavenir points out, these books and guides taught tourists what to admire while traveling, but also how to get themselves there (1999, p. 41). Whereas narrative writing may have entertained and inspired, these guides rose to inform and educate.

Murray called his publications 'handbooks', which reflected their pocket-size format and utility, and they were quickly adopted by other publishers. Most famously, Karl Baedeker in Germany printed his own books inspired largely by Murray's, creating a famous rivalry throughout the nineteenth century. Buzard describes their contribution, writing:

> Murray and Baedeker had invented an imperious and apparently ubiquitous authority small enough to fit in the tourist's pocket. They preceded the tourist,

making the crooked straight and the rough paces plain for the tourist's hesitant footsteps; they accompanied the tourist on the path they had beaten, directing gazes and prompting responses.

(1993, p. 75)

In his second edition of *A Hand-Book for Travellers on the Continent*, Murray lays out the handbook's editorial mission clearly, writing, 'The writer of the Hand-book has endeavored to confine himself to matter-of-fact descriptions of what *ought to be seen* at each place, and is calculated to interest an intelligent traveller, without bewildering his readers with an account of all that *may* be seen' (Murray, 1838, p. v). He takes a notably journalistic approach, 'preferring to avail himself of the descriptions of others' (p. v) and describing how he has 'taken much pains to acquire the most recent information from the best authorities' (p. vi). The prefaces to various editions all underscore the possibility of errors and inaccuracies, often asking readers to notify the publisher of any changes that need to be made – a precursor to the digital collaboration made possible in the twenty-first century with advances in Web 2.0.

As the guidebook industry began to boom, both Murray and Baedeker reached out to other writers and began mass-producing guides without actually writing the books themselves (Buzard, 1993, pp. 73–74). Their ability to streamline the process and mass-produce their guides led to a standardization of the travel experience. As Buzard describes, 'Baedeker and Murray set a style of bureaucratic efficiency that would render individually produced guidebooks idiosyncratic and obsolete' (1993, p. 31). Travel media became a big business that would only expand over the coming decades as guides appeared in dozens of languages around the world.

By the 1900s, new players were entering the field. Thomas Cook's own set of guides reached the market. His guides followed Murray's almost verbatim, as in the guide to Algeria and Tunisia, where the preface indicates that 'the object of this book is to inform the traveller how to reach Algeria and Tunisia and where to go when he gets there' (Cook and Sons, 1908, p. iv). The guide also calls for readers to notify the editors of any misinformation in the guides, just like Murray's guides half a century earlier. Other publishers followed these models. Michelin launched their guides at the turn of the century in France. In the US, Eugene Fodor extended the offer in 1936, adding more recommendations and personal anecdotes to his guides. Automobiles become increasingly popular, leading to more individualized travel, and consequently to a more personalized approach by travel media. Media continued to evolve, with new technologies and innovations in mobility. Individuals had more purchasing power after World War II, and commercial air travel created a more mobile population. Leisure travel boomed, and with it a series of glossy magazines appeared, targeting wealthier consumers, like *Travel +Leisure*, published by financial and travel company American Express. Other titles like *Town and Country* and the more recent *Condé Nast Traveler* covered an even more luxurious side of travel. The *Rough Guides* and *Lonely Planet* appeared later in the 1970s and 1980s, catering to a new breed of budget travelers and backpackers that developed gradually (Pearce, 1990). Travel media was fragmenting, following market trends and consumer patterns, with brands attracting advertisers who wanted to tap into certain audiences (Morgan and Pritchard, 2000, p. 61). In the same way that newspapers diversified for various audiences – be it based on political leanings or social class – travel publications specialized according to an ever-diversifying population of travelers.

What today I – tentatively – label 'travel journalism' had rooted itself firmly in western media and by the end of the twentieth century was sprouting branches in different directions. With it came new practices and norms – including sponsored press trips and advertising opportunities – that are some of the features distinguishing travel journalism from other types of news reporting that don't necessarily rely on commercial experiences for their stories. As sources of information for consumers and as advertising space for airlines, hotel chains, and other industry actors, the travel media blossomed through the end of the twentieth century.

Travel guides and magazines were filling a new need in society, but they were just one part of travel writing as an industry, with more journalistic leanings. Travel writing, more broadly, however, became more widespread among all classes throughout the twentieth century. Youngs explains that as more and more commercial tourists were crossing the globe, one unique, authoritative voice became less necessary, because these travelers were going out and testing hotels, restaurants, and historic sites, sharing their thoughts with others. Conversations about travel and word of mouth recommendations were becoming more commonplace, no longer reserved for an elite (Youngs, 2013, p. 50). As such, travel writing in general became more subjective, breaking from the standard, clear-cut writing that Murray and Baedeker engaged in with their guides. As more people began writing, however, information became simultaneously less trustworthy – a paradox inherent to travel journalism that, as I'll discuss, accelerated with the internet. Travel narratives – think of writers like Bruce Chatwin or Bill Bryson – differed from guides in that they offered more whimsy and wanderlust than practical guidance or information. As Holland and Huggan write, 'The ambiguity surrounding travel narratives – the uncertainty, at given moments, of whether the writer is telling the truth – is part of their appeal; the stories they tell are no less compelling if they happen to be mendacious' (Holland and Huggan, 2003, p. 9). Despite this uncertainty, they still contributed to the conversations taking place about destinations among consumers.

Travel journalism – still a nebulous concept – began to take shape as a way to distinguish itself from the many narratives which blended fiction with travel, to help travelers create and fashion their own experiences. As Greenman writes, travel writing involves the author looking in a mirror, while travel journalism requires the author to look out the window (2012). Such a distinction, however, doesn't fully capture what sets travel journalism and writing apart. Perhaps more importantly, professional groups began to develop throughout the twentieth century in an attempt to demarcate the borders of travel journalism and travel writing. Most of these changes followed the professionalization of journalism, itself an early twentieth century adaptation in much of the western world. Travel writers followed suit and established organizations to give themselves a presence. The Fédération Internationale des Journalistes et Ecrivains du Tourisme appeared in 1954. The British Guild of Travel Writers began operating in 1960. In 1991 the North American Travel Journalists Association was formed. All of these groups supported travel journalists with networking possibilities and ethical guidelines for their work, helping to legitimize the profession further. The main idea here is that by the twentieth century, there was a parallel evolution of professional journalistic gatekeeping and commercial travel that began to intersect. Travel journalism was becoming a watchdog of sorts for the blossoming travel industry in the same way that political correspondents developed norms and ideologies relative to democratic governments. Western journalism, by the end of the nineteenth century, began to adopt notions of objectivity and factual reporting that became hallmarks of the profession (Allan, 2010). Similar ideals filtered into travel sections and magazines. *Condé Nast Traveler*, for example, still prides itself on publishing articles that have been reported independently, free from the constraints and influences of destination-sponsored press trips and invitations. Many newspapers and magazines – and today, websites – still refuse stories that were produced in the context of sponsored travel or press trips, raising ethical questions that I'll deal with later in this book.

It remains impossible, however, to identify an exact moment that marks the birth of travel journalism, should one exist, but it was slowly emerging as writers in North America and Europe began fighting for professional recognition. As they were stepping up as journalists, establishing their credibility, new mass audiences were developing as consumers of tourist experiences. Throughout the twentieth century, publications catered to these new audiences, and gradually 'travel journalism' established itself as a credible – if not enviable – profession to both the media and tourism marketers. Curiously, much of its critical and consumer-oriented reporting is at direct odds with the news values developed in the early twentieth century, but set apart as a subsection of lifestyle journalism, travel journalism developed its own particular identity in the media industry. Lifestyle journalism, at its heart, 'focuses on audiences as consumers, providing them with factual information and advice, often in entertaining ways, about goods and services they can use in their daily lives' (Hanusch, 2012, p. 1). Lifestyle topics include food, fashion, arts, and of course travel, but relatively little academic work has focused attention on this type of journalism as opposed to more civically-oriented journalism. I will explore these contradictions and departures from professional norms throughout this book, but first it's important to approach a more recent history to comprehend how travel journalism and media have grown with the rise of the internet.

A shift in perspective, from author to anonymity

Travel writing and narration, well before journalistic practice developed, exhibited varying and ever-changing perspectives. The author was not always a central figure in the writing, and, as Blanton writes, historically, 'the narrator's thoughts and reactions are all but hidden' (Blanton, 1997, p. 3). She discusses ships' logs, for example, which may have been more factual than narrative. By the eighteenth century Descartes introduced ideas that opened up conversations about writers' emotions, which begin to become more prevalent (Blanton, 1997, pp. 11–12). By the nineteenth century the travel narrative had become a literary genre unto itself, according to Bertho-Lavenir, who cites texts by French authors Stendhal, Hugo, Dumas, and Flaubert, writing, 'We know what the traveler saw and what he felt, if the vantage point was beautiful or if the sun was scorching' (Bertho-Lavenir, 1999, p. 44). These literary evolutions put into question the role of the author, who was no longer simply describing, but actively participating and expressing reactions along the way. This changing perspective opened up debates in the nineteenth century on the difference between travelers and tourists – a dated debate that still rears its head today in the industry. The idea of a noble traveler and a mundane tourist developed, often related to class and travel style. For example, group travel, popularized by companies like Thomas Cook in the nineteenth century, was considered touristy, while individualized travel, accessible to the wealthier, carried the more illustrious label of travel. Part of being a traveler was the idea of a personal conquest, more than simply visiting a location (Blanton, 1997, p. 107). It was in this context that Bertho-Lavenir explains, 'The traveler is that which the tourist is not. The traveler is aristocratic, the tourist is plebeian. The traveler discovers, the tourist follows. The traveler lives an intimate and intense experience; the tourist goes in groups and steps in the footsteps of others' (1999, p. 403).

This notion of personal travel was reflected in many of the travel guides named for their intrepid followers. As Buzard explains, 'this was rational administration with a human face' (Buzard, 1993, p. 48). Murray in England, Baedeker in Germany, Joanne and Michelin in France, Fodor in the United States – all were supposedly based on a central figure and voice. They were the original influencers of their day. Throughout the twentieth century, the role of the author became increasingly important as the travel writer – and eventually, journalist – became a real authority. In the tradition of the nineteenth-century handbook writers, some writers like Rick Steves built travel-related empires while celebrity travelers like Anthony Bourdain comment for major media outlets like CNN. But with the internet, these roles have changed.

From the beginning of the twenty-first century onward, travelers have invested their trust in faceless, nameless, often entirely anonymous voices found on sites like Yelp and TripAdvisor. This relationship between traveler and anonymous reviewer is both spectacular and frightful. Oftentimes, it works, but sometimes the reviews get it wrong or expectations are shattered for the worse. If I can put a pin in any judgement values on these sites – which I, too, use – it's the larger picture that interests me here. Why do some people skip the edited, professionally curated guidebook in favor of a stranger's opinion who may or may not share similar values or experiences? It is a fantastic phenomenon to study, and one that will be addressed through the following chapters. More than a trend begun by Amazon that will fizzle out, reviews are the lifeblood of hotels, Airbnb, tour companies, restaurants, and other actors in the tourism industry. How will the perspective of the professional journalist adapt to this reality? Of course, not every traveler is relying on TripAdvisor, but increasingly user-generated content is taking precedence over established brands, with Airbnb gaining more attention than hotel booking sites and hotel brands, for example (Emarketer, 2017). To understand these phenomena, we must first look at how the internet has impacted travel media in the past few decades.

Industry shake-up

Almost as soon as travel journalism seemed to be settling into a rhythm, the internet changed the beat. Studying twenty-first-century travel media is a difficult endeavor due to seemingly endless and rapid innovations. While a few notable works on both sides of the Atlantic address how lifestyle media is changing with the web, there are numerous factors that have yet be explored (e.g. Hanusch and Fürsich, 2014; Greenman, 2012; Beauscart and Mellet, 2012). First, however, it's important to understand briefly how travel journalism developed with the internet. The first travel websites began to appear in the 1990s as the World Wide Web became commonplace. Booking sites like Travelocity and Expedia both began in 1996, and the latter spun off from Microsoft in 1999. Last-minute package deals were sold on lastminute.com from 1998 onward, and the then-fledgling review site TripAdvisor.com was officially launched in 2000. With the introduction of free blogging software like Blogger in 1999 and WordPress in 2003, travel-themed blogs created by individuals began to gain attention, increasing in leaps and bounds since the first unofficial travel blog was published in 1994. For the first time in history, anyone who traveled had the tools to reach large audiences with their unfiltered and unedited stories instantly. Suddenly, it appeared as if everyone could be a potential travel journalist – or, less arguably, everyone with an internet connection could easily become a travel writer for a large audience.

At the same time – coincidentally or not – guidebook and magazine sales were suffering (Clampet, 2013). Between 2005 and 2012, guidebook sales in the UK fell by 45 per cent (Strachan, 2013). In the US, a similar trend saw guidebook sales fall 40 per cent between 2006 and 2012 among the five top publishers (Clampet, 2013). Turmoil is a word that helps encapsulate travel media's state in the early 2000s. One of the most successful guides, *Fodor's*, saw a 45 per cent drop in sales between 2006 and 2013 (*The Economist*). While the guidebook industry has since rebounded – if ever slightly – on these losses with investments in e-books, smartphone apps, and a bolstered online presence, it is interesting to note how it experimented with new online players. For example, the American travel guide *Fodor's*, begun in 1936, bought by Random House in 1986, has been a standard in travel publications in the English-speaking world. As TripAdvisor climbed in popularity, editors at *Fodor's* integrated user reviews into their guides in 2011, bringing TripAdvisor off the screen and onto the printed pages of their books. The partnership was a way for the legacy brand to remain relevant online, while it gave the new online player an aura of legitimacy, a stamp of approval from a trusted brand in travel. As some researchers suggest, user-generated content is complementary to these professional sources of information, offering perspectives and resources that journalists may not have (Robinson, 2011). In travel media, unlike in political or community reporting, it becomes difficult to know what exactly a professional journalist provides that a well-informed traveler cannot. This ambiguity, however, did not stop most travel magazines and newspapers from creating their own websites, with additional content, blogs, and eventually videos appearing online, in tandem with their printed versions.

Some travel brands have capitulated to the demands of migrating online. The popular dining guide *Zagat* ceded to acquisition by Google, where its content became folded into new initiatives by the internet giant. American travel guide *Frommer's* was bought by Google in 2013 and sold back after several months, returning the brand to the Frommer family. In 2013, *Lonely Planet* switched hands from the BBC to an American company, NC2 Media, which has since led to the brand creating a stronger presence as lonelyplanet.com. While the website was relaunched in 2016, it's interesting to note that printed publications still remained valuable to these brands, and *Lonely Planet* launched its magazine for the US market in 2015, joining eleven other international versions of the printed periodical. All of this industry change, however, underscores the uncertainty of travel media in a digital age. While legacy media brands are learning how to migrate online, digital-first sites have popped up, bringing content to web users. Eater, Spotted By Locals, The Matador Network, Culture Trip, Thrillist, The Culture Trip, and Eurocheapo, among countless others, bring tailored travel content to audiences online, building up their brands exclusively online and through social networks. These websites, focusing on niche groups of travelers or interests, model themselves largely on legacy media, but have also embraced the potential to integrate instantaneous content, online video, and direct links to commercial offers like hotel bookings or restaurant reservations.

From a commercial perspective, the internet has further complicated the situation of travel media. Now, information and booking sites are all but indistinguishable. From TripAdvisor to the Telegraph in the UK to Lonely Planet and to all of the web-native brands, these media sites allow consumers to book hotels and experiences directly through their sites. Whereas before TripAdvisor only provided user reviews and Lonely Planet only provided information, both are now portals for travel experiences, including third party trips and excursions developed specifically for a certain site. Prior to the internet, commercial interests were related to selling ad space, books, and magazines, but travel websites are now equally concerned with having customers book tickets and reservations directly through their websites, adding another layer to the already muddled field of travel journalism. Are travel journalists simply advertising agents at this point? I argue against this notion, but a deeper conversation about their role as critiques and evaluators in relation to marketing powers is a necessary step forward in understanding this profession.

New paths for travel journalism

In this environment, studded with apps and printed guides, innovation and tradition, travel journalism has the potential to be as rich as ever. At the same time, however, increased internet use and lower costs of entry have allowed user-generated content and new media ventures to compete for eyeballs, siphoning off audiences into an ever-atomized world of travel information.

While legacy media continues to migrate to the web, rethinking their offers, competition from commercial sites producing their own travel information is an ever-looming threat to travel journalism. Expedia UK, an online travel agency, has been publishing consumer news in its City Diaries blog since 2014. More drastically, beginning in 2016 home-sharing site Airbnb began publishing guides based only on recommendations by its hosts. In 2017 the company partnered with Hearst to publish its first printed magazine, *Airbnbmag*. These evolutions relate to the new sharing economy made possible – at least on a large scale – by the internet. These innovations join the decade-long rise in social networks – from Facebook to Foursquare, from Twitter to Instagram – which has allowed consumers to seek direct word of mouth recommendations from other users in a destination.

Have these new sites superseded the need for the specific travel publication, edited by journalists, to tell individuals where and how to travel? This question remains central to this book, which, ultimately, has no easy answer. Every tourist is different, so it will remain impossible to know what each person values, trusts, desires, and consumes. What is clear is that travel journalism still very much has a role in this environment, and the following chapters will address this role, how it is changing, and how it is adapting to online tourism. We need to consider how travel journalists distinguish themselves and what value they bring to consumers, as well as how they engage in reporting that may have consequences not only for tourists, but for the destinations and people that they are visiting. Questions of professionalism, ethics, responsibility, and trust will arise in the following chapters as I strive to capture how travel journalism is evolving with technology, propelling it through the twenty-first century.

References

Allan, S. (2010). *News culture*. UK: McGraw-Hill Education.

Archives of The New York Times. Retrieved from www.nytco.com/who-we-are/culture/our-history/#1835-1880

Archives of Thomas Cook. Retrieved from www.thomascook.com/thomas-cook-archives/

Bertho-Lavenir, C. (1999). *La roue et le stylo: Comment nous sommes tous devenus touristes*. Paris: Editions Odile Jacob.

Beauscart, J.-S., and Mellet, K. (2012). *Promouvoir les œuvres culturelles: Usages et efficacité de la publicité dans les filières culturelles*. Paris: Ministre de la Culture et de la Communication.

Blanton, C. (1997). *Travel writing: The self and the world*. New York: Twayne Publishers.

Buzard, J. (1993). *The beaten track: European tourism, literature, and the ways to culture, 1800–1918*. Oxford: Clarendon Press.

Clampet, J. (2013, March 4). Lonely Planet and the rapid decline of the printed guidebook. Skift.com. Retrieved from https://skift.com/

Cook and Sons (Eds.). (1908). *Cook's practical guide to Algeria and Tunisia*. London: Thomas Cook and Sons.

Emarketer (2017, May 30). Airbnb traffic surges, surpassing other brands. Retrieved from https://www.emarketer.com/

Flaubert, G. (1972 [1849]). *Flaubert in Egypt: A sensibility on tour* (Ed.) F. Steegmuller. New York: Penguin.

Gosch, S., and Stearns, P. (2007). *Premodern travel in world history*. London: Routledge.

Greenman, J. (2012). *Introduction to travel journalism: On the road with serious intent*. New York: Peter Lang.

Hanusch, F. (2012). Broadening the focus: The case for lifestyle journalism as a field of scholarly inquiry. *Journalism Practice, 6*(1), 2–11.

Hanusch, F., and Fürsich, E. (Eds.). (2014). *Travel journalism: Exploring production, impact and culture*. Basingstoke: Palgrave Macmillan.

Hartog, F. (1988). *The mirror of Herodotus: The representation of the other in the writing of history*. No. 5. Berkeley: University of California Press.

Holland, P., and Huggan, G. (2003). *Tourists with typewriters*. Ann Arbor:University of Michigan Press.

Marcil, Y. (2007). Le lointain et l'ailleurs dans la presse périodique de la seconde moitié du XVIIIe siècle. *Le Temps des Medias*, 1(8), 21–33.

Morgan, N., and Pritchard, A. (2000). *Advertising in tourism and leisure*. Oxford: Butterworth-Heinemann.

Murray, J. (1838). *A handbook for travellers on the continent: Being a guide through Holland, Belgium, Prussia, and Northern Germany, and along the Rhine, from Holland to Switzerland*. London: John Murray and Son.

Pearce, P. L. (1990). *The backpacker phenomenon: Preliminary answers to basic questions*. Townsville, Queensland: James Cook University of North Queensland.

Robinson, S. (2011). Journalism as process: The organization implications of participatory online news. *Journalism and Communication Monographs*, 13(3), 137–210.

Ryle, G. (1949). *The concept of mind*. London: Hutchinson.

Steward, J. (2005). 'How and where to go': The role of travel journalism in Britain and the evolution of foreign tourism 1840–1914. In J. K.Walton (Ed.), *Histories of tourism: representation, identity and conflict* (pp. 39–54). Clevedon: Channel View Publications.

Strachan, D. (2013, April 19). Real life: Guidebooks. *National Geographic Traveller*. Retrieved from www.natgeotraveller.co.uk

The Economist. (2013, April 3). Bookended: The guidebook industry. Retrieved from www.economist.com

Weaver, S. (2015). *Exploration: A very short introduction*. Oxford: Oxford University Press.

Wright, T. (Ed) (1899). *The travels of Marco Polo the Venetian: The translation of Marsden revised with a selection of his notes*. London: George Bell and Sons.

Youngs, T. (2013). *The Cambridge introduction to travel writing*. New York: Cambridge University Press.

2

TRAVEL JOURNALISTS AND PROFESSIONAL IDEOLOGY

Who is a travel journalist?

A PR company from the Italian region that includes Bologna contacted me through Facebook, inviting me to a wine tasting and dinner in London in early 2017. It was a press event, as I understood, where they would feature local products and information on their tourism industry. Ever the fan of pasta, I accepted, making it clear that I rarely wrote about Italy. Having just traveled to Genoa and Turin, I had published a blog post and numerous images on my social networks, no doubt attracting the PR agent's interest. I attended the event in East London, entering a tiny restaurant filled with Italian speakers and a smattering of international guests. I introduced myself, and an Italian woman flown in from Bologna with thick-rimmed glasses handed me my name tag, which read 'Bryan Pirolli: Instagrammer'. I laughed at the notion – with just a few hundred followers to my name on Instagram I hardly considered myself an Instagrammer. I was a journalist who used Instagram, and in my mind there was a difference. A significant difference.

Once inside, however, I realized that this press event wasn't as I had imagined it. I sat at a table with an Australian blogger who never wrote for a major publication, a young Instagram user who photographed and posted every step of the meal, and an older Englishman who wrote for a wine and spirits magazine. I had an identity crisis in that moment, when I neither identified with the younger online 'influencers', nor with the older 'journalist' who marveled as they uploaded filtered photos and snaps with ease. I struggled with trying to position my idea of a 'travel journalist' among these other individuals who were all, perhaps in their mind, producing travel journalism. What, if anything, made me different from these individuals?

While it is easy to assert that travel journalism is changing in a digital era, it is less clear who actually *is* a travel journalist. Moreover, it's even more debatable if such a distinction is really important to the tourism industry anymore in an age where anyone can become an influencer on Instagram or a prominent travel blogger. While professional accreditations like press cards are available through organizations like the National Union of Journalists in the UK, several online companies offer semi-recognized credentials to whoever is willing to pay for them. Travel journalism, it seems, is a professional activity with constantly shifting borders, but almost anyone can secure a passport in the form of a press accreditation to enter if they so desire.

Within the scope of this research, many of the journalists interviewed assert themselves as journalists because they write about travel for established publications. Most were unable to nuance their definitions much further, at least not easily. Upon closer examination, however, it became clearer what this group has in common and what sets them apart from the other content creators – bloggers, reviewers, Twitter users – who are contributing to the travel information flows available online. This exclusionary ideology is not new. Scott Gant describes how profit-driven news corporations 'hardened an artificial distinction between professional journalists and everyone else' (Gant, 2007, p. 34). Even in France, journalists throughout the twentieth century were defined by stating clearly who was not a journalist, so that professors or politicians couldn't claim professional status (Ruellan, 2007, p. 67). Many journalists still adhere to these artificial boundaries, preferring to describe what they aren't instead of what they are. Various authors tackle these questions, applying principles of boundary work to journalism (see Carlson and Lewis, 2015). The travel journalist identifies as a professional, which provides 'not just a shared identify, but a way of presenting oneself as a legitimate actor' (Carlson, 2017, p. 55). This legitimacy, however, is increasingly put into question with the enormous variety of travel information available online. How, then, can travel journalists remain relevant in the twenty-first-century ocean of destination-related media, and what do they contribute of value to tourists and news consumers?

A shared ideology – separate from, but similar to that of other journalists – does seem to exist among these individuals, to account for the unique demands and features of travel journalism that might not be present, for example, in political or current events reporting. This chapter breaks down this ideology, looking how travel journalists differ from 'hard news' journalists, and furthermore, how digital culture and new media are evolving their ideology. How do travel journalists remain relevant in the face of so much user-generated content, and is a shared ideology really important for this profession? This chapter will look at how an ideology is still a distinguishing trait of professional journalists, and how travel journalists are adapting their profession, and this ideology, to a digital age.

Journalistic ideology – what we know

Researchers have already laid out a foundation for travel journalism as a profession with a common ideology, but there is much to build upon. For example, Fürsich and Kavoori (2001) and McGaurr (2012; 2015) have addressed travel journalism as a specific field of study. Whereas early work by these authors signaled a lack of critical investigation into the genre, academics have increasingly paid attention to travel journalism as a serious research topic. A 2014 collective work by international scholars looks at the profession from a variety of viewpoints, contributing significantly to academic discourse on travel media. The editors propose a working definition of travel journalism that lays out a basic framework for professionals, describing it as:

> factual accounts that address audiences as consumers of travel or tourism experiences, by providing information and entertainment, but also critical perspectives. Travel journalism operates within the broader ethical framework of professional journalism but with specific constraints brought on by the economic environment of its production.
>
> *(Hanusch and Fürsich, 2014, p. 11)*

While such a definition accurately sums up the profession, I believe it's also necessary to zoom out and understand who a journalist actually is and what ideological principles guide his or her work.

Such an effort is difficult because, as discourse theory states, there is no meaning to journalistic practice, but instead such meanings are constructed through a 'process of articulation' (Bogaerts and Carpentier, 2013). As McNair states, journalism as a construction is 'an intellectual product embodying the technological, economic, political and cultural histories of the societies within which it is produced, inexplicable without knowledge of those histories, and impossible to interpret correctly without the context which they provide' (1998, p. 12). A framework set out by Mark Deuze opens up a deeper question as to the ideology behind its practitioners. In his definition, there are five main elements making up journalistic ideology: public service, objectivity, autonomy, immediacy, and ethics (Deuze, 2005). These are the building blocks to 'understanding journalism in terms of how journalists give meaning to their newswork' (2005, p. 444). Similar work by other authors identified additional elements, specifically a dedication to the truth, which combined form a fairly composite and accepted journalistic ideology over the past few decades (Kovach and Rosenstiel, 2007). This traditional view, however, is evolving. As Deuze states, there is no one-size-fits-all ideology for journalists. Today, the focus on journalism as a safeguard of democracy, as a civic watchdog, and as the Fourth Estate, is shifting. Researchers are asking if the changes wrought upon journalism are actually forcing a larger redefinition of its ideology. More recently, Deuze and Witschge question the very concept of journalism as a singular entity, stating, 'The amplification and acceleration of more or less new news genres, forms, products and services today point towards the fact that the occupational ideology of journalism allows for many different "journalisms" to flourish' (Deuze and Witschge, 2017, p. 121). As Waisbord posits, if we are rethinking collective nouns like 'media' and 'audiences', there is no reason that 'journalism' should be exempt from being questioned 'as a unified coherent institution and/or profession with shared norms, structures and dynamics' (Waisbord, 2017, p. 213). Such interrogations open up numerous possibilities to analyze and interpret different types of journalism, allowing travel journalism to stand alone as its own ideological unit.

This argument, therefore, allows us to rethink who a journalist is, especially when it comes to less traditional journalists in the lifestyle genre. For instance, what are the specific ethical issues that affect travel journalists that might not affect journalists in other domains? Who are its practitioners and what sort of ideology do they embrace? As researchers have shown, news values are not incompatible with change and journalists are able to adapt with the times (Wagemans et al., 2016). Travel journalists have demonstrated this clearly over the centuries, as their profession evolved from a long history of travel writing. In the twenty-first century, however, their professional identity is continuing to evolve with the industry and, notably, the web. This subsection of lifestyle journalism requires its own particular definition to help understand how travel journalists function, what values they embody, and how they might define their professional identities (Hanusch, 2012a). This chapter will look directly at how travel journalists describe their work in order to nuance Deuze's definition of journalistic ideology, to expand it, and to attempt to apply it to travel journalists who have their own particular profile due to the nature of their work.

Differing norms between news and travel

One way we can understand the travel journalist's ideology is to explore the differences between current affairs news – often referred to as hard news, if we look to authors like Boczkowski – and lifestyle news (Boczkowski, 2010). Hanusch has written extensively on lifestyle news, arriving at a definition that includes news about goods and services, mixing entertainment with advice and factual information, all while addressing the reader as a consumer (Hanusch, 2012a). Later, in their book about travel journalism, Hanusch and Fürsich (2014) explore the lifestyle dimensions of travel journalism, citing some of its unique features that set it apart from reporting on food or video games, for example. One important aspect, the representation of foreign cultures, has long been a focus of media scholarship. There is a cosmopolitan nature to travel journalism that distinguishes it from many other news genres. Likewise, travel journalism has a market and consumer orientation, according to the authors, that 'considers audiences unashamedly as consumers, rather than citizens, even though that does not mean some travel journalists do not also try to be critical in their reporting' (Hanusch and Fürsich, 2014, p. 10). These differences are important in contextualizing the work of its practitioners, but strict definitions and distinctions remain elusive. Lifestyle journalism, according to some researchers, has blurred with consumer and cultural journalism, rendering the three nearly indistinguishable (Kristensen and From, 2012).

Furthermore, the traditional news values associated with hard news journalism don't necessarily correspond to the demands of travel journalists – however they are defined. I'll cover this more in Chapter 3, but it's important to note it here. The different norms and demands of this style of reporting begin to reveal concretely how travel journalists distinguish themselves from their hard news counterparts. It may seem obvious at first glance how reporting on an election and reporting on a new hotel would be different, but a closer look can help pinpoint these differences. These changing traits and values have been evolving with social media and the web, as discussed in work by Harcup and O'Neil on news values in the twenty-first century (2017). Building upon their previous work and that of Galtung and Ruge's 1965 study on news values, the authors developed a non-exhaustive list of news values, some of which resonated with the journalists interviewed, including *good news, entertainment,* and *drama.* They write that news stories generally satisfy one or more of the criteria on their list, but caution that 'no theory of news values can explain everything, not least because arbitrary factors including luck, convenience and serendipity can come into play' (Harcup and O'Neil, 2017, p. 1472). While there are many interpretations of news values available to researchers, Cocking identified several that appeared often in travel pieces – including notions of *appeal, identification,* and *positivity* (2017). His analysis is a step towards understanding travel news values, which 'tell us something of the processes of interpellation through which the reader is appealed to – that is, how an article seeks to pique our interest, hold it, and encourage us to commit imaginatively, financially and culturally to particular travel experiences' (2017, p. 14).

Using their work along with Deuze's framework for journalistic ideology, the following sections aim to look more closely at how travel journalists delineate their professional identity and ideology in a digital age. I will look at the system of beliefs and traits that exemplify 'the general process of the production of meaning and ideas' among travel journalists (Deuze, 2005, p. 445).

Exclusivity vs contextualizing

When it comes to reporting the news, travel journalists do not uniformly share an urge to be the first on the scene. Exclusivity, described as 'stories generated by, or available first to the news organization as a result of interviews, letters, investigations, surveys, polls, and so on', is a hallmark of journalism generally (Harcup and O'Neil, 2017, p. 1482). Such a goal, however is not necessarily an important component of travel journalism. The very idea of a news scoop in travel is a rather nebulous one given the nature of audiences – what's new for one traveler may not be new for another. For example, one journalist declared that she has to consider who her readers are when writing about a Parisian experience. Are they first-time visitors? Have they been to Paris before? What are their expectations? All of these questions come into play when writing about a destination. One journalist said, 'It's not really that useful to be writing about the hottest, trendiest restaurants. Travelers haven't been to any restaurants yet, so why do they care what's new?' Whereas current affairs journalists can generally assume readers' ignorance of their topics, travel journalists cannot be so sure. For some people traveling to Paris, a visit to the Eiffel Tower will be a brand-new experience, but to veteran travelers seeking more offbeat experiences, it may seem passé. These audience considerations eventually impact how travel journalists consider their work.

How, then, do journalists embrace the idea of immediacy or exclusivity in their reporting? It's not as important to get a scoop and report on breaking news in travel journalism as much as it is essential to embrace the notion of *contextualizing*, akin to Cocking's idea of *identification*, whereby the 'accompanying text exhorts us to feel as though we are actually there' (2017, p. 10). Some seek a news peg in their stories to keep them fresh, even when discussing longstanding establishments and landmarks, but in general, news in travel journalism doesn't always have to be news in a traditional sense. Depending on their audiences and the publication, travel journalists are able to write about experiences and destinations without a dedicated news angle. Instead of focusing on immediacy, as one journalist described, if she is writing about an experience, she believes it's always important to justify her claims, to contextualize the experience for the reader so that they know what to expect, even if it's an establishment that's been around for years. For example, she writes about the many clichés that writers use when describing French dining. 'You can get French food anywhere; why do you need to get it here? Sometimes the place is scruffy, and that part is good and basic, and maybe they only have one kind of salad dressing, and when you write it's your job to make sure the traveler knows what to expect'. This role is increasingly important as 'best of' and 'top ten' lists become ever pervasive in travel media, with seemingly arbitrary rankings and evaluations devoid of any context, newsworthiness, or other justifications. As this journalist concluded, 'That's what makes you valuable, not that you know something is better but that you can tell someone *why*'. I will explore these ideas more in Chapter 3, to understand further what is news to these professionals and how they identify it.

Public service vs consumer service

When it comes to the traditional public service aspect of journalism as described by Deuze, there has been much research and writing on the watchdog or Fourth Estate role of journalists in western democracies. Travel journalists, however, reveal that they are not as beholden to this ideal in a democratic sense, and that they view their audiences more as consumers than citizens. Their reactions echo Deuze's re-evaluation of the public service model, which he argues 'maintains its primacy on storytelling while cautiously embracing the wants and needs of an audience' (Deuze, 2005, p. 456). Therefore, values described by Harcup and O'Neil, including *bad news* and *conflict* don't resonate enormously with travel journalists who are, instead, thinking about ways to appeal to their audiences more positively. 'Travel journalism cannot rely on capturing the reader's attention through shock, awe or the desire … to be politically informed' (Cocking, 2017, p. 5). Instead, Cocking proposes the value of *appeal*, where the journalist taps into the inviting and exciting aspect of a destination above all else. The very nature of travel journalism is to treat readers as patrons of travel experiences, and those interviewed consider that one of their main roles is to entice their readers. Journalists embrace this ideology, commenting that 'writing for their readers' is their main motivation. Hanusch clearly states the importance of consumerism in lifestyle journalism, and travel journalists confirm it (2012b). One journalist recounted that, during a radio travel broadcast covering French wine, her editor pushed her to be less technical and to reflect more on her listeners. 'They want to hear about wines that they can go get at the supermarket and that they can pair with a dinner that they can cook themselves', she said, clearly illustrating this focus on audiences as potential consumers of experiences covered in travel media.

Not only are journalists bound to their audiences, but they understand that they are an extension of their brand, perhaps more than a current affairs reporter may be. McGaurr explains that media brands to relate to the value derived from the publication, which may help explain why travel journalists are proud to work for brands like the *New York Times* or *Fodor's* (McGaurr, 2015). One journalist explained that she prefers writing for established brands because they empower both her and the audience, instilling more trust. She said, 'They validate something, and they are trusting you and it enforces what you feel about things'. Travel journalists are mindful of the layer of trust that their brands often give them, and position themselves against many online content creators who might not have the same instant credibility. One journalist explained his thoughts, saying, 'Clearly, the *Wall Street Journal* reporter or a *New York Times* reporter or [a reporter] from a similar well-known global news organization is going to have more access. You don't have any explaining to do.' This consumer-related aspect of their ideology helps set travel journalists apart from hard news reporters, and is a defining feature of their professional identity. Consumerism is a vital aspect of the ideology and, arguably, without a consumer angle, travel journalism might very well cease to exist.

Objectivity vs transparency

The notion of objectivity, long-debated in journalism studies, also seems not to apply stringently to travel journalists. While not a news value as much as a valued practice, objectivity is generally accepted as an unattainable ideal among practitioners (Kovach and Rosenstiel, 2007). In travel journalism, however, this practice doesn't figure quite as much in the ideology of those interviewed – on the contrary, it's often eschewed. Remaining balanced and unbiased in travel reporting conflicts with the critical aspect of a travel journalist's responsibility whereby they are often reviewing a hotel, restaurant, or other experience in order to give their audiences the information needed to make a spending decision. Journalists are very aware of this, underlining their first-person narratives and light-handed reporting that focuses more on their experiences than on some objective search for journalistic truth. As one journalist stated, '[Readers] want to know you've been there and you've experienced it and they can trust you, that you haven't just written from a press release'.

Instead of an objective approach, travel journalists espouse a related ideal of transparency. Friend and Singer described how this value functions as an alternative to objectivity (2015). In practice, transparency is a key feature of travel journalism, whereby practitioners are aware of the potential conflicts between, for example, a favorable article on an experience and the treatment that the journalist received. Greenman highlights transparency – in the form of disclosure – as one of the most important values of travel journalism and advocates on its behalf (Greenman, 2012). Because travel journalists so often work with marketing teams, much of their reporting could appear as nothing more than advertising for the free experiences they obtain. Hanusch's work on Australian travel journalists reveals that professionals understand simultaneously the need to work with marketers and the potential pitfalls of these public relations efforts (Hanusch, 2012b). This reality puts into question the autonomy component of a journalist's ideology. With so many sponsored trips, it becomes easy to critique travel journalists for being reliant and dependent on marketing agents. As one journalist said, 'The question is, did you write something favorable influenced by the freebie? I refuse. If there's something negative, I'll put it in the review. Anyone who doesn't do that is unethical and they are only then in it for the future freebies they can get.' Others echoed this attitude in their work, underscoring that it is one of the main features of their ideology that sets them apart, especially in the digital age. Moreover, it becomes a legal question when free services or products are not disclosed, as the US Federal Trade Commission attempted to reign in freebies parading as genuine content as far back as 2009, calling for mandatory disclosure for any blogger or social media users paid to endorse something. Unfortunately, there is no consistent practice among user-generated content, but journalists' credibility relies largely on remaining honest and transparent.

Objectivity and autonomy may take a back seat in travel reporting, but transparency acts as a substitute. In this way, journalists justify their position as professional critiques, providing a framework for their subjective observations or evaluations of travel experiences. I'll explore these economic considerations further in Chapter 4.

Changing landscapes for travel media

Their unique ideology, however incomplete, is not etched in stone. Much in the same way that innovations in the tourism industry allowed changes to travel writing over the centuries, shifting professional norms may uproot travel journalists' ideology even further. The tourism and media industries are in constant flux with the internet, as consumer habits respond to innovations like online bookings, smartphone applications, and anonymous review sites. The sharing economy alone – with Airbnb as a key example – has created a new online marketplace for commercial tourism. In the same way citizens can become newsmakers, consumers can become tourism industry agents by renting their apartments or spare rooms. An increasingly mobile society will change both producer and consumer habits, and journalists are not exempt. As bloggers and other user-generated content providers offer tourists useful and oftentimes highly valued information, journalists are forced to respond to these new actors, to understand how to work alongside and even with them to deliver information in a meaningful, relevant way. Considering blogging has only been a popular practice since the turn of the century, it has impacted journalistic practice in impressive, if arguably limited ways. Freelancing culture, new media outlets, and a more polyvalent approach to content creation shows how blogging practices are seeping into journalistic culture, at least in the travel genre.

Freelancing

Easy communication facilitated by the internet has allows individuals to produce travel information virtually anywhere, beyond the New York or London offices of glossy magazines and newsrooms. Travel bloggers, since the 1990s, have already embraced this potential, with countless travel blogs by both professional and amateurs covering destinations around the world. These innovations have led to an uptick in the number of journalists working as freelancers, with professionals increasingly working on contracts instead of careers, as researchers point out, resulting in precariousness as a common feature for practitioners (Deuze and Witschge, 2017, p. 126). In the UK alone, the number of freelancers has risen 67 per cent, from 15,000 to 25,000 according to the National Council for the Training of Journalists' 2017 report. Such changes are particularly salient in lifestyle journalism (Hanusch et al., 2017). In travel media, freelance life has become easier with smartphones, more widespread data coverage, and other mobile technology – though we must be cautious to remember that internet penetration worldwide only hovered around 50 per cent in 2017. Still, journalists living abroad can easily produce stories and photos that can be sent from Cambodia or Estonia to New York and London publishers – or simply uploaded to a website – challenging the need for destination marketers and PR teams that, for years, have provided travel to journalists. Such PR services are not yet obsolete, as one journalist suggested:

> Transparency is important, but I still believe in press trips. Country-sponsored trips that you wouldn't have access to, places like Jordan – I went to a few years ago and I think that even though you are invited there by the country I'm still objectively reporting while I was there. I was interviewing ministry officials about tourism. Increasingly with the business models magazines can't afford to send their writers all over the world.

Some areas remain inaccessible, but this is becoming less of an issue. Still, if local talent can provide similar or even more introspective stories easily, quickly, and cheaply, do journalists actually have to travel anymore?

It is unlikely that travel journalists and marketers will sever ties any time soon, as local writers in remote corners of the world are not universally available. Still, it is important to follow how professionals may return to a more autonomous approach as defined by Deuze. Will journalists free themselves from the need for sponsored travel as locals or expatriates established in far-off lands provide the travel journalism once provided by globe-trekking journalists? Until a commercially viable environment exists where travel journalists can actually travel and still earn a living, a reliance on these marketers may not fade any time soon. Ultimately it does pose other questions. If travel journalists are increasingly those who are expatriates or locals, how will they distance themselves from their 'homes?' How will they be able to know the needs of tourists when they themselves are not tourists in their destinations? An evolving career profile will lead to an emerging ideology in this vein, and travel journalists must be aware of how their work will reflect their realities. As a wandering journalist with pen and journal in hand becomes less normative, it is fair to ask if local perspectives are as nuanced, diverse, cosmopolitan, or distanced as travel journalism could be.

New media and gatekeeping

Travel journalists are embracing, albeit slowly, their diminishing role as gatekeepers of travel information. This historic role of the journalist as sole authority of the truth, acting in the public interest, has given way to new realities. As Broersma and Peters write, 'Public trust and reliance on the "expert" forms and institutions that modernity helped create is now continually being re-assessed as people turn to emerging alternatives' (2017, p. 2). The blossoming of Web 2.0 and the spread of social media has allowed audiences to become producers, creating videos on You-Tube, writing stories on blogs, and sharing photo essays on Flickr or Instagram. This shift from user to 'produser' challenges journalism, and travel journalists are not least among those who are learning to react to this influx of user-generated content (Bruns, 2008). I would even argue that the concept of produsage in travel media is particularly salient due to the number of user-generated websites dedicated to travel for large audiences. Axel Bruns describes the shift of gatekeeper to gate-watcher, whereby journalists should identify quality information instead of simply producing it (2005). Jane Singer takes it one step further describing user-generated visibility, wherein public shares and likes on social media promote articles that audiences deem worthy, ultimately deciding what will be most viewed or read (2014). Also called secondary gatekeeping, it is important to remember that such processes involve both technical aspects, such as algorithms, but also social elements, and that human participation is still very much part of the gatekeeping process, however it is defined (Nielsen, 2017, pp. 88–89).

What, then, are travel journalists bringing to the stage? How must their professional ideology account for their changing role in the media landscape online? One way that journalists are responding is by reasserting themselves as authorities, especially as expatriates who are living in a destination. As one travel journalist in Paris said, her experiences are what give her value, and she incorporates her status as a local into her professional identity. 'I underscore all the experience I have in Paris, the years here, that I am an authority, that I am steeped in this stuff all day long. My journalism degree might not matter as much', she said. Interviews with readers confirm that the status of the author is increasingly important, and a local contributor to a news site, blog, or review platform like TripAdvisor is considered more trustworthy than an outsider. It's almost paradoxical, then, that travel journalism is becoming less about the story of the destination and more about the journalist's status vis-à-vis the destination. Locals have more clout, and many tourists booking Airbnb accommodation and tours with 'insiders' are ravenous for this local insight. Combined with their aforementioned brand loyalty, which also gives them credibility in the eyes of their audience, travel journalists are shifting the way they see themselves situated among the endless online offers of travel content. Their professional ideology relies, in part, on their role as an authority on a location, arguably more than a journalist who writes about current events.

Multitasking in a digital age

Another reality facing travel journalists today is a certain expectation to multitask, a newly versatile profile made possible by the internet. Older journalists recalled the recent past whereby journalists provided stories, photographers supplied images, editors edited, and distributors distributed. The reality online, however, has led many journalists to embrace a more multifaceted approach to their work, if begrudgingly. In addition to writing stories, journalists need to publish them on online platforms, format them for search engine optimization, source photos without budgets, and promote their stories on social networks. As one journalist lamented,

> I believe photographers should be doing photography. I shouldn't have to do that. This is what blogging has created, where you have to do everything yourself. It has changed the journalist culture. People are getting paid less. People are expected to do everything.

These expectations have ruffled the feathers of some travel journalists, like one who said, 'So you have to tweet your stories and build up your own personal brand. Big name journalism was never about your personal brand. It was about the story.' But as bloggers rise in the ranks, achieving bylines in major publications alongside these self-identified journalists, the professionals are re-evaluating their work. While many interviewed oppose becoming multitaskers, some are slowly adopting a sink-or-swim attitude, migrating to Twitter and learning what many bloggers already know. A study on journalists in the US revealed that while journalists are reluctant to engage with readers online, they equate reciprocity with opportunities to build trust with their networks and communities (Lewis et al., 2017, p. 169). This industry reality, affecting journalists in all domains, is a distinguishing feature of journalists' professional ideology in the twenty-first century. This versatility may be an ideological feature of any journalist, but travel journalism especially embraces the need for strong visuals and audience engagement.

Redefining the travel journalist online

The travel journalist, at the beginning of the twenty-first century, is not someone with a clear-cut profile – and as technology continues to push tourism and the media in unexpected directions, such a profile may never materialize. Still, a professional ideology does emerge of a travel journalist working in a digital age. Building upon Hanusch and Fürsich's definition of travel journalism, in conversation with Deuze's concept of journalistic ideology, a more comprehensive portrait will begin to emerge, ideally becoming clearer after reading this book.

While focused on critique, consumerism, factual accounts, and entertainment, travel journalists also espouse ideals of transparency and contextualization, falling under the umbrella of journalistic ethics. The broad label of ethics in Hanusch and Fürsich's definition allows for extensive interpretation, but transparency and contextualization seem like two of the most relevant to travel journalists, and the most important to highlight. These are, arguably, qualities that characterize professional journalistic ideology regardless of their medium, whether they are producing reports for print or video.

As they continue to move in a more digital direction, however, there are new realities and special considerations to tease out gradually. First, travel journalists' increasingly mobile and freelance nature needs to be a key factor in how they identify themselves. The role of authority will play a larger role as travel journalists seek to situate themselves among local bloggers and globally-produced sites like TripAdvisor and travel wikis, where the status of the author counts more and more, according to many of the news consumers interviewed. I will address this in detail later. Locality, therefore, is an increasingly important part of professional ideology, referring to how a journalist identifies and expresses their role vis-à-vis a destination. Second, they need to embrace their role in the current media landscape, teetering between gatekeepers and gatewatchers, neither uniquely controlling the flow of travel information but still holding some authority under the banners of their brands. Third, travel journalists should be engaging with the multimedia and social media aspects of their profession, embracing a multitasking ideal. Versatility, while not welcomed by all travel journalists, seems to be becoming an ever more important value. How they develop this aspect of their ideology, acknowledging their relationship with user-generated content and the Web 2.0 realities, will ostensibly dictate how travel journalists will fare in the future.

While not a perfect ideology, and one very much in the making, the main issue here is that travel journalists are unconsciously or not defining themselves as something set apart from the user-generated content available online. They espouse general journalistic values – sourcing, researching, facts – and seem more concerned with how non-professionals are impacting their work. Much like journalists in the nineteenth century, who defined themselves in opposition to other professions – as not authors, not researchers, and not lawyers – travel journalists today seem only to identify themselves as 'not bloggers' or 'not content creators' (Ruellan, 2007, p. 63). A more complete and nuanced definition of their professional ideology may help travel journalists to situate themselves more clearly among the seemingly endless sources of information online.

Ultimately, these distinctions mean very little if readers do not acknowledge the fundamental difference between a work of journalism and user-generated content. Brands like *Travel+Leisure* and *Lonely Planet*, however, still maintain strong voices among other travel media. If their contributors, practitioners of travel journalism, embrace a common, well-defined ideology, they may be able to continue and promote journalism's core role while adapting it to an ever-changing market.

References

Boczkowski, P. (2010). *News at work: Imitation in an age of information abundance*. Chicago: University of Chicago Press.

Bogaerts, J., and Carpentier, N. (2013). The postmodern challenge to journalism: Strategies for constructing a trustworthy identity. In C. Peters and M. Broersma (Eds.), *Rethinking journalism: Trust and participation in a transformed news landscape* (pp. 60–71). Abingdon: Routledge.

Broersma, M., and Peters, C. (2017). Introduction: Towards a functional perspective on journalism's role and relevance. In C. Peters and M. Broersma (Eds.), *Rethinking journalism again: Societal role and public relevance in a digital age* (pp. 1–18). Abingdon: Routledge.

Bruns, A. (2005). *Gatewatching: Collaborative online news production*. New York: Peter Lang.

Bruns, A. (2008). *Blogs, Wikipedia, Second Life, and beyond: From production to produsage*. New York: Peter Lang.

Carlson, M. (2017). Establishing the borders of journalism's public mandate. In C. Peters and M. Broersma (Eds.), *Rethinking journalism again: Societal role and public relevance in a digital age* (pp. 49–63). Abingdon: Routledge.

Carlson, M., and Lewis, S. C. (Eds.). (2015). *Boundaries of journalism: Professionalism, practices and participation* (pp. 21–36). New York: Routledge.

Cocking, B. (2017). News values go on holiday: The ideological values of travel journalism. *Journalism Studies*, 1–17.

Deuze, M. (2005). What is journalism? Professional identity and ideology of journalists reconsidered. *Journalism*, 6(4), 442–464.

Deuze, M., and Witschge, T. (2017). What journalism becomes. In C. Peters and M. Broersma (Eds.), *Rethinking journalism again: Societal role and public relevance in a digital age* (pp. 115–130). Abingdon: Routledge.

Friend, C., and Singer, J. (2015). *Online journalism ethics: Traditions and translations*. Abingdon: Routledge.

Fürsich, E., and Kavoori, A. P. (2001). Mapping a critical framework for the study of travel journalism. *International Journal of Cultural Studies*, 4(2), 149–171.

Gant, S. (2007). *We're all journalists now: The transformation of the press and reshaping of the law in the internet age*. New York: Free Press.

Greenman, J. (2012). *Introduction to travel journalism: On the road with serious intent*. New York: Peter Lang.

Hanusch, F. (2012a). Broadening the focus: The case for lifestyle journalism as a field of scholarly inquiry. *Journalism Practice*, 6(1), 2–11.

Hanusch, F. (2012b). Travel journalists' attitudes toward public relations: findings from a representative survey. *Public Relations Review*, 38(1), 69–75.

Hanusch, F., and Fürsich, E. (Eds.). (2014). *Travel journalism: Exploring production, impact and culture*. Basingstoke: Palgrave Macmillan.

Hanusch, F., Hanitzsch, T., and Lauerer, C. (2017) 'How much love are you going to give this brand?' Lifestyle journalists on commercial influences in their work. *Journalism*, 18(2), 141–158.

Harcup, T., and O'Neill, D. (2017). What is news? News values revisited (again). *Journalism Studies*, 18(12), 1470–1488.

Kovach, B., and Rosenstiel, T. (2007). *The elements of journalism: What newspeople should know and the public should expect.* New York: Three Rivers Press.

Kristensen, N. N., and From, U. (2012). Lifestyle journalism: Blurring boundaries. *Journalism Practice*, 6(1), 26–41.

Lewis, S., Holton, A., Coddington, M. (2017). From participation to reciprocity in the journalist–audience relationship. In C. Peters and M. Broersma (Eds.), *Rethinking journalism again: Societal role and public relevance in a digital age* (pp. 161–174). Abingdon: Routledge.

McGaurr, L. (2012). The devil may care: Travel journalism, cosmopolitan concern, politics and the brand. *Journalism Practice*, 6(1), 42–58.

McGaurr, L. (2015). *Environmental communication and travel journalism: Consumerism, conflict and concern.* Abingdon: Routledge.

McNair, B. (1998). *The sociology of journalism.* London: Arnold.

Nielsen, R. K. (2017). News media, search engines and social networking sites as varieties of online gatekeepers. In C. Peters and M. Broersma (Eds.), *Rethinking journalism again: Societal role and public relevance in a digital age* (pp. 81–96). Abingdon: Routledge.

Ruellan, D. (2007). *Le journalisme ou le professionnalisme du flou.* Grenoble: Presses universitaires de Grenoble.

Singer, J. (2014). User-generated visibility: Secondary gatekeeping in a shared media space. *New Media and Society*, 16(1), 55–73.

Wagemans, A., Witschge, T., and Deuze, M. (2016). Ideology as resource in entrepreneurial journalism: The French online news startup Mediapart. *Journalism Practice*, 10(2), 160–177.

Waisbord, S. (2017). Afterword: Crisis? What crisis? In C. Peters and M. Broersma (Eds.), *Rethinking journalism again: Societal role and public relevance in a digital age* (pp. 205–215). Abingdon: Routledge.

3

REPORTING AND NEWSGATHERING IN A TRAVEL CONTEXT

Introduction

In 2014, two American expats were making news in Paris. Tourists in the city crossed the river daily using one of the most iconic bridges, the Pont des Arts, linking the historic Louvre museum to the Left Bank. Built in the early nineteenth century, it featured iron railings, reinforced later in the twentieth century with chain-link fence for safety reasons, and afforded sweeping views across the Seine river. In the early twenty-first century, a new tradition sprung up whereby tourists would stop and fix a padlock to the bridge, often with the names of two lovers written on it. They would then throw the key into the river as symbolic gesture of love. The Pont des Arts became known more commonly as the 'Love Lock Bridge' and morphed from a pedestrian passage where students would picnic in summer evenings to a tourist attraction, with pickpockets and illicit lock-sellers preying on unsuspecting visitors. Having known the bridge before the locks, I was aware of these changes, and others were beginning to notice. In early 2014, however, two American-born women took up a contentious petition on social media to ask the government to remove the heavy load of locks that were slowly pulling the bridge's fencing apart, dubbing their campaign 'No Love Locks'. My inner journalist lit up to get the scoop as fast as possible.

It all began on Twitter, where I picked up the story about the petition and contacted the organizers. While the No Love Locks campaign was adamant about preserving the bridge, many Twitter users lambasted them for attacking these gestures of love, and the conversations got heated. The story was a powerful one, with a strong social activist angle, and through Twitter I contacted the campaign, eventually getting the email address for one of its organizers who agreed to speak with me. From there, I pitched the idea to *CNN Travel*, where my editor was eager to publish a story about these locks. It had tension, it had underdogs, it had

Paris, but it also had information that was useful to tourists – mainly, how to be a 'good' tourist. It was an easy sell. Through Twitter, I found others who were rallying against the locks, such as a group of expats who invited people to come and cut off the locks using industrial bolt cutters. As I interviewed foreigners on the bridge that winter, it was surprising to them that anyone would want to remove the locks, but once I explained how the locks were undermining the structural integrity of the bridge, they began to see the other side. By 2015, I was publishing a second news article about how city officials were removing the locks for good, restoring the bridge to its earlier Napoleonic-era beauty. I felt like I had produced something truly journalistic – but was it travel journalism? Was it more journalistic or more useful or more respectable than some of my other stories about the best French restaurants in Paris or the weirdest medical museums around the world, also appearing in CNN's travel section? Why did I feel so invested in this story and not in others that I was producing weekly?

The relationship between news and tourism can be a complicated one. News is at the heart of journalism, and travel journalism is no exception. How we can interpret news in a travel context, however, is a different matter entirely. This chapter will discuss how travel journalists think about the news values of their stories and how they identify what topics should be published. Not all journalism is destined to create an informed citizenry, and Zelizer argues that scholars should rethink the journalism/democracy nexus, which 'has undermined the capacity of journalism scholars to speak reliably about the world of journalism practice' (2013, p. 469). The relationship between news and travel, I argue, is part of this underserved and poorly researched world of journalistic practice. Schudson writes that 'news media do not find and respond to an existing audience; they create one' (2011, p. 162). In most normative views of journalism as a safeguard of democracy, this may be true, but in travel media, audiences can exist independently of the media. Tourism existed well before mass media, after all. 'Travel news' is, in a way, responding to an existing audience – the traveler planning an excursion. We can begin to think then of the link between news and tourism as something separate from these normative views.

How, then, do professionals deal with this reality in their work? Instead of scanning social media or hanging out around the city hall to learn about daily news events, travel journalists need to do more than just wait for something to happen. They need to understand a place, understand its nuances, and connect with its local community, among other things. Without understanding the history and changes at the Pont des Arts, the No Love Locks campaign on Twitter may not have resonated with me or any other foreign journalist as easily and it may not have been newsworthy. In the context of their experiences and travels, they need to carve out stories by considering their publication and their audiences, keeping their ears to the ground to observe trends and events likely to interest potential tourists, like the love locks story. Sometimes they need to produce less ambitious articles about routine topics, always seeking out fresh angles on events like Bastille Day or the Christmas markets in the articles that circulate yearly in travel publications discussing Paris. When news events do happen – a hotel opening, a new restaurant, an art exhibition – journalists need to walk a fine line between sounding like a press release and presenting oneself as a reliable critic who has done actual research. While similar questions might arise for a political or current affairs journalist, this chapter will sketch out how travel journalists actually engage in their reporting, to highlight their unique concerns and practices.

Journalists and travel news

First, I should be clear that travel news is not the exclusive domain of travel journalists in a lifestyle context. Travel is a topic that transcends the hard news/soft news binary that often underscores much scholarship on the media. Boczkowski suggests that hard news and soft news, while exhibiting certain commonalities, require different means of production and are thus arguably two different types of journalism altogether, instead of different degrees of the same thing (Boczkowski, 2009). For example, political, business, cultural, and current events reporters might produce travel news at some point. News stories about the so-called US travel ban in 2017, terrorist attacks in Paris and Nice between 2015 and 2016, or a report about Airbnb banning racist and homophobic hosts, all relate to travel. These types of stories, however, don't typically fall under the working definition of travel journalism put forward by Hanusch and Fürsich, as they may lack a consumer or entertainment aspect, among other differences (2014). Again, this addresses the evolving notion of a 'singular journalism' that recent scholarship suggests rethinking (Broersma and Peters, 2017).

For the moment, I want to keep the focus on the more lifestyle-oriented category of travel reporting that is produced differently from a straight news story about travel. In other words, I mean travel stories that are written primarily with travelers in mind. How is this specific form of journalism reported and packaged as news? Recent scholarship in travel journalism reveals some distinguishing features of travel journalism with relation to newsgathering. For examples, I return to studies on news values introduced in Chapter 2 – discussed at length first by Galtung and Ruge (1965) and revisited by Harcup and O'Neil (2011; 2017). These studies begin to reveal certain values that may, together, be considered intrinsic to travel journalism. Cocking signaled ideas of *appeal, identification*, and *positivity* that he found recurrent in a sample of travel articles, calling for more research into news values specific to travel reporting. Hanusch explores how travel media follow similar trends in foreign news coverage, focusing more on elite regions like North America and Europe (2014). Little research, however, delves into the day-to-day practices of the journalists producing this content.

I'll break down how travel journalists work much like – but not identically to – more normative 'hard news' journalists as described in numerous texts (e.g. Kovach and Rosenstiel, 2007, Wahl-Jorgensen and Hanitzsch, 2009). Reporting, deadlines, editors, fact checking, and other basic issues are still routine for travel journalists, just like they are for most professionals, but they have their own unique characteristics that shape travel journalism if we delve more deeply.

I argue that what changes is the nature of their reporting, which, as most research has established, is largely focused on entertainment or consumerism. But what does that look like? Travel journalists, as lifestyle journalists, are not universally concerned with the most cutting-edge stories or with civic matters. Instead, I argue that today, travel journalism is continually focused on news you can use, and the web has not largely diversified the aims of travel journalism (Hanusch, 2012). While blogs and some websites – notably select sections of the *New York Times* online – offer more storytelling and diverse reports, much travel journalism online, it seems, is focused on the 'best of ...', the 'top 10 ...', or 'how to ...' guides for destinations. While glossy magazines may still publish long form features, the web presence of legacy media like *Travel+Leisure, Condé Nast Traveler,* or newcomers like *Afar* and *Matador* does not always push as far for this type of content, as demonstrated by my content analysis of the headlines of several publications. A closer look at how journalists actually approach their work reveals that their newsgathering processes don't facilitate the kind of in-depth stories and long-form narrative accounts that were once a hallmark of travel journalism.

While the demands for well-researched, long-form storytelling may be less prevalent online, travel journalists still have to engage in reporting, whether it's for a written piece or video package. I will outline the basic types of 'news' reported by travel journalists, based on my interviews with travel journalists in Paris, as well as a content analysis of their work. I'll discuss how newsgathering routines function for a travel journalist either stationed abroad or traveling to a new destination. How do they juggle between official sources – business owners, offices of tourism – and the flood of online material – from TripAdvisor to social media – available to them? How do they react to user-generated content in order to fulfil a gatewatching role as described by Bruns while reporting on destinations (2005)?

Rethinking news for tourists

Interviews with journalists and tourists reinforce the idea that travel news is a nebulous concept, without a clear, limited definition. Schudson asserts that 'news is related to, but is not the same as, ideology; it is related to, but is not the same as information; and it is potentially, but only indirectly, a social force' (1997, p. 3). In travel media, the social force is arguably a salient one, where news acts as both a commercial force and a consumer commodity. According to journalists interviewed, there are a few distinct ways that they frame how they think of news in travel journalism that relate to (1) traditional news stories, (2) revisiting non-newsworthy items, and (3) trendspotting.

Finding what's new

We can take a look at the kinds of approaches travel journalists take towards their news angles, or how they position their stories as newsworthy to editors.

First, there is a general consumer news angle that underpins much of what journalists produce. Keeping an eye on the market, discussing new services or establishments, and doing the sort of reporting that is generally associated with traditional hard news reporting is a part of what these journalists do. The love lock story, which addresses tourists as general consumers of travel experiences in Paris, demonstrates this approach, echoing Harcup and O'Neil's values of *exclusivity* and perhaps *surprise* (2017). I obtained the information from the source before any major media outlets picked it up, and readers were generally surprised that this was an issue at all. Especially with the demands for near-continuous content online, many assert the need to keep up with everything going on in Paris or whatever destination they are visiting, in order to maximize their output. As one journalist for the *New York Times* explained:

> That's inherent in journalism, especially because I am writing about what's topical or up and coming. The idea of breaking and being the first is super important. You're done if it's not up when it opens or the day after. Other people covered it and you're behind.

This statement reflects the nature of her publication, which focusses on new cultural openings in Paris. Not all publications, as we'll see, are so concerned with the newest of the new, as even the concept of *news* varies from a daily newspaper to an annual guide. Still, news stories about new restaurants or hotel openings, often working in tandem with PR companies, are a sort of bread and butter for travel journalists. These types of articles provide useful information and context for veteran travelers or first-time travelers alike who can all benefit from knowing what's going on in a potential holiday location. Above all, however, these journalists consider their audiences as consumers – even if in the love locks story, I was aiming to discourage travelers from becoming consumers of the locks in the first place.

Revisiting the old

Whereas much travel journalism focusses on up to date events, there is the possibility for travel journalists to revisit non-newsworthy topics and make them news items. This is especially important in the tourism industry because so much of what is interesting to visitors won't change drastically from year to year. Such values correspond to Galtung and Ruge's idea of *follow up*, with the caveat that tourist destinations or attractions do not have to have been in the news in the first place for a follow-up to make headlines. For example, the Eiffel Tower, a prominent attraction in Paris, changes in little ways quite often – whether it was the inclusion of glass floors on the bottom level or the addition of windmills to help power the tower's lights. These little changes are entry points to revisit the Eiffel Tower in a story for potential tourists, though for any other non-travel journalist, these changes might often hardly be newsworthy. Such an approach might go unnoticed by first-time travelers who have never been to Paris, but it is a way to keep the publication's content fresh for people who come back and who may not have considered returning to the Louvre or Notre Dame, and recent changes could at least justify media coverage.

One journalist, for example, worked in business journalism as well as doing travel pieces. She struggled with the idea of writing about something that has already been covered in the media, but realized gradually that travel journalism isn't universally scoop-driven. She explained her epiphany, saying, 'But now I am saying wait a minute, travel journalism, as it is, isn't something as strict as business journalism. Just because it's in one newspaper it can be in another.' She soon began to understand that she could always take a different angle on a city or destination, and that no one travel journalist ever really has the last say on a topic. This realization is especially important given the nature of the post-modern tourist, as described by Urry and Larsen (2011), who embraces the tourism industry, unlike the earlier, modern tourists described by MacCannell (1976). In a study on how travel journalists imagine their readers, Duffy and Mangharam describe one of the tropes found in their analysis, which focused on visiting well-known sites. As they write, 'Often the intention is to see a well-known sight so that they can share their experience with others or gain status by having seen something renowned' (2016, p. 9). Travel journalists, therefore, need to continue talking about subjects and places that may not have an inherent newsworthy angle, or at least not an obvious one, but that are still important to the fabric of a destination's tourism industry.

Beyond fulfilling the *follow-up* value, at least partially, this approach does not seem to correspond directly to any other news values detailed by scholars, though *surprise* arguably could apply (Harcup and O'Neill, 2017). In Galtung and Ruge's (1965) conception of events becoming news, issues like *cultural proximity, demand,* and *unpredictability* could potentially resonate with these sorts of news stories, but the point is that these types of stories are not news in the traditional sense, but are something unique to travel journalism. Understandably, these stories – like the glass floor at the Eiffel Tower installed in 2014 – might not be a newsworthy story outside of a tourism context. They are linked to the tourism industry, to refreshing and reinvigorating – or simply reintroducing – experiences to audiences. If another story about the Eiffel Tower never appeared online, people would still go, but travel journalists are often tasked with updating these topics year to year as changes occur. As journalists discussed, much of their work deals with cycles and fixtures in a destination, and finding ways to distinguish their work year to year requires finding these updates and fresh angles, however small they may be. We could, therefore, go so far as to propose *refreshing* as a news value for travel journalists.

Trendspotting

In the same vein, but slightly differently, travel journalists often find something new by discussing what is now trendy, or up and coming. Whether it's a gentrified district in Paris or a rarely-visited European city that's recently been put on the map, travel journalists strive to stay on the cutting edge of what is 'cool'. Trendspotting, as a marketing concept, involves multiple ways of surveying customer behavior to uncover consumer habits and tendencies, both through qualitative and quantitative means (see Du and Kamakura, 2012). Often these trendsetting pieces will be produced in conjunction with destination marketers or tourist boards trying to promote their cities or regions. At other times, journalists may organically cover gentrified or newly hip places simply by frequenting them – something that is much easier for expatriate travel journalists, who can act almost like foreign correspondents. Again, in a digital age, these stories are possible because of the rapid nature of publishing online – it would be hard, however, to imagine one of Murray's nineteenth-century guides covering what's trending in France, considering they took years to produce.

How, then, do journalists do this? As one journalist said, she makes it her mission to look at what other people aren't talking about.

> In Paris, it's hard to avoid the sort of snobbism in food, in boutiques, and I try to stay out of that, too. I try to stay out of 'Oh everyone is going here' but I try to find what is truly great about a place. Another thing I write about is the artisanal heritage of France, and what France has to offer that is unique and deeply, essentially French. It's a historical aspect. And it's what's disappearing quickly.

These trends are often short-lived, but with virtually no time lag between reporting and publishing them online, readers of major publications' websites like *Travel+Leisure* or *National Geographic* can get a more live, multi-faceted interpretation of a destination.

These sorts of attitudes varied greatly among journalists, but there is a general consensus that journalists still want to write about what's different or unique in a destination. But within this approach, they aren't looking for *one* new thing or *one* new event as discussed in the previous section. Perhaps there was a string of openings of new coffee shops and restaurants, as there once was around the trendy Canal Saint Martin in Paris. The Canal has been around for nearly two centuries, and fundamentally, little has changed. Individually, the openings of new establishments did not make headlines either, but the concentration of so much change in so little time led to the notion of a newsworthy topic for journalists in the early 2000s. Even the *New York Times* discussed the district in a 2009 piece about frugal travel in Paris. This sort of trendspotting is very much part of what journalists do, though social media users and bloggers play a similar role, and the piece in the *New York Times* cites websites and Twitter users who pointed the journalist to certain restaurants and hotels, illustrating Duffy's suggestion that journalists need to work with social media in a travel arena, especially in measuring trends (2016). This sort of trendspotting on a local level may not be as ubiquitous as this sample suggests. As one journalist reiterated, Paris – like other large, cosmopolitan cities – has a particular identity that caters to trends. She said,

> Paris in particular for a travel writer is extremely exciting to write about and discover while writing about it. There's always something that you find out. No matter how much of an expert you are, there's always more to the story.

Finding trends in remote regions of the developing world, for example, may be more difficult, or, contrarily, could be easier depending on the culture and society.

Clearly these three frameworks are similar, since all have to do with some notion of what is new or changing. What they illustrate is how the notion of 'news' in travel journalism depends on the topic, the perspective, and the audience. Rarely, however, has travel journalism been able to exhibit an instant reaction to some event, mostly due to lengthy periods of time for publications to print their stories. With the internet, however, travel journalists can now publish instantaneously, further confusing how travel journalists see the news in their work.

Sources of news

Much scholarship in the past decade has focussed on journalistic practice (Boczkowski, 2010; Kovach and Rosenstiel, 2010; Singer et al., 2011; Patterson, 2013, Brandtzaeg et al., 2016). Few studies, however, discuss these practices in a lifestyle or travel context. One study explores how lifestyle journalists face pressures involving advertisers, public relations, and free products in their work (Hanusch et al., 2017). Such concerns don't fit with the normative view of journalist as a watchdog of political power or a purveyor of democracy. How, then, do travel journalists actually operate in the field when they engage in reporting?

Travel journalists are fortunate to have the world's largest industry at their beck and call, and, combined with their position as commercial actors, sources are more often than not eager to speak to them. To that end, travel journalists report a wide array of sources at their disposal, beyond their own first-person accounts.

People and experiences

People who drive the tourism industry or work in some capacity related to it are key sources for journalists. Whether it's a head chef at a restaurant, a boutique owner, or the brainchild behind the No Love Locks campaign, individuals are primary sources for travel journalists. These people – and the experiences they provide – are all essential for good storytelling and information gathering for almost any travel piece. Journalists are aware of the importance of speaking to sources – a standard practice for journalists of all genres (see Berkowitz, 2009). As one journalist explained, it's a lack of such human contact that has degraded much of journalism and user-generated content in recent years. He shared:

> I am a shoe leather reporter, I do not pay attention to press releases. I do not trust according to a source close to Google. I am not a content provider. I am a foreign correspondent. I am a writer. I am a journalist. There is no news in a newsroom.

The problem is, today, news organizations with rare exception don't have the finance to keep foreign correspondents in the field. What was journalism, what was a craft, has now become for better or for worse, content providing, which from what I've seen is done mostly by people sitting in desks like factory workers, maybe making a phone call, but never going out or meeting anyone, never doing the kind of work we did in the old days. I am a dinosaur.

Dinosaurian or not, this mentality is still alive, even among younger journalists. Another journalist, writing freelance for multiple publications, described the importance for her work of actually talking to people:

I did an article on Air France and how they were changing their meals and they wanted me to contact these people to find out what they were doing. Even a restaurant review, sure you can talk about the food but that won't help anyone. You can also interview the chef, do research into their background, why did they pick certain dishes. You never read that.

These critical perspectives illustrate how travel journalism still relates to more normative views of the profession, between journalists and their sources who form a 'delicately negotiated relationship, with each party hoping to achieve their goals and maintain their organizational and societal status' (Berkowitz, 2009, p. 103). As one journalist explained, however, there is little imperative in lifestyle journalism to try and show two sides of a story. 'You never had to balance your sources. You'd just interview the person who ran the shop or did a trip and you wrote it up,' she said. Journalists, while interested in the presence of human voices in their work – as opposed to much of the author-focused writing of user-generated content – do not seem to think too deeply about the representation of their sources. While Berkowitz highlights the dangers of imbalanced source representation, more work is needed to look at travel journalism sources specifically. Yes, they rely on people, but who are the sources in question? Future research might ask if more local voices are heard or if there is strong diversity among travel journalists' sources – issues that I'll address in Chapter 11.

Offices of tourism and PR networks

Another obvious source for travel journalists are the outward facing tourism offices and PR representatives who offer them information and experiences, ultimately seeking coverage. Much research already exists on the relationship between destination marketers and information providers, including bloggers (Pan et al., 2007; Volo, 2010; Hays et al., 2013). These sorts of sources are commonplace among lifestyle journalists, and even more so among travel journalists who often rely on freebies to perform their duties. An extensive study of Australian and German lifestyle journalists reveals that advertisers, PR agents, and freebies are all major commercial influencers of their work, to varying degrees (Hanusch et al., 2017). As one journalist reported, she recognizes that press trips are essentially cheap, paid advertising, but she still believes in their utility. She said that when access to a location is restricted, a press trip is the best way to get the news. On one trip to the Middle East, she said, 'I was interviewing ministry officials about tourism. Increasingly with the business models, magazines can't afford to send their writers all over the world.' Gaining access to places that may not be otherwise accessible, or affordable, for journalists is a key reason why these marketing teams still function as important sources of information. What is changing, however, is the tradition of a press trip, which is morphing into the 'blogger trip' or 'Instagram trip'. The gatekeeping that journalists can apply to their own sources is now eroding as new actors are tapping in to the exclusivity that they once had.

Local language news sources

An increasingly mobile and expatriated body of travel journalists is also tapping in to resources that previously may have been less accessible to travel journalists crisscrossing the globe. The journalists sampled, all living in Paris, speak French to varying degrees. This allows them to consume local language news that may provide news that wouldn't otherwise make it into the Anglophone media. French media is something that journalists use often to help discover what's going on, allowing them to act as mediators between cultures. One freelancer was keenly aware of this, and described her strategy for engaging with French media:

> I'll follow the French press and some of the insider French journalists or the prefecture de la police. I'll find something that won't get picked up by the English press. You have to keep an eye on the local press and not just read blogs like yours.

Another journalist reinforced this sentiment, saying 'In terms of access to information, it's as simple as a language thing. I speak French, so Anglophones are not reading that, and I'll know about it before they do.' Her linguistic abilities allow her to access sources that other journalists outside of France, or those just parachuting in, may not necessarily be able to. In recent years, English-speaking websites like *The Local* and numerous blogs have begun to challenge this mediator role that some travel journalists have developed between the French press and Anglophone lifestyle media. Anglophones living in France are able to mediate between French sources and English-speaking audiences through various social media outlets, further eroding the gatekeeping position of travel journalists. Add these new sites to increasingly effective translation services online, and it becomes clear how local language media are effective sources.

News and editors

When it comes to deciding what's news, sometimes it's not up to the travel journalist. Working with editors, often those stationed in New York or London for

English-speaking publications, journalists sometimes struggle to push their own ideas of what was newsworthy in Paris. One way in which this occurs is when journalists pitch ideas. As one journalist recalled, her idea of what is 'new' often varies from that of her editors. She said,

> In Paris, I've given up pitching. *Time Out* asks for our ideas about what is new or what is unknown. Many of my original ideas don't catch their attention but they'll want ideas that have been done a million times before.

This disparity between what the local knows to be true and what the editor thinks to be true can lead to tension between both parties.

Editors, however, may propose ideas because they are what will work favorably with SEO or because they fit into a series that the publication runs. As one journalist explained, a stable relationship with editors is ideal and allows for a much easier approach to her work. She explained, 'When you kind of get in, you're tried tested and trusted, they send out subjects and they ask for propositions and they pick and choose.'

To that end, often editors will ask for ideas or articles that they know will reach readers easily, bypassing the traditional news values in favor of the newer ones proposed by Harcup and O'Neil, like *shareability*. Shareable content that spreads further is desirable for editors who need to justify their readership to advertisers and sponsors. To that end, while some of these stories may lack a real news value beyond shareability, they may also be spurred on by the need to satisfy advertisers by discussing a neighborhood where the journalist can include a mention of a sponsoring hotel or other advertiser. This sort of product placement is essential to travel media but treads a fine line between advertorial and journalism.

Rethinking the news for travel audiences

When considering news and work structures, the takeaway message is that travel journalists don't have a monopoly on their news sources, and press releases and freebies can find fertile ground in blogs and other websites that may not be connected to legacy media (more on that in Chapter 4). To that end, this final part details how travel journalists are beginning to – and arguably should – change their attitude to news gathering. Many journalists are already engaging with these practices, but to what end remains uncertain.

When it comes to social networks – like Instagram – these tools can help travel journalists navigate destinations and uncover previously untold stories or spot trends. By searching hashtags and keywords relating to a destination, users can take the temperature of a location, to find out what's happening there or what spots are of particular interest now. The immediacy of these social posts allows for real-time exploration of a destination, at least in theory. It's a form of ambient journalism described by Hermida, whereby 'the value does not lie in each individual fragment of news and information, but rather in the mental portrait created by a number of messages over a period of time' (2010, p. 6). While many journalists report not trusting user-generated content, they are beginning to acknowledge its potential to point them in new or unexpected directions, to steer their reporting towards topics that they would otherwise not observe. In the same way that journalists value local-language media, they could consider social media as a similar springboard for their research into a destination.

Emblematic of travel and social media, TripAdvisor is one example of how the voice of the masses can be useful. Journalists are inherently suspicious of TripAdvisor, describing an antagonistic relationship with it. One individual said, 'You don't know about that person on TripAdvisor who says it's wonderful, but their tastes could be totally different from yours.' However, taken collectively, these reviews can inspire journalists to ask questions or look further into a destination in new and unexpected ways. Duffy suggests that the travel journalist takes on a more curatorial role, 'who assess and judges UGC for inclusion' (2016, p. 179). I would argue that using TripAdvisor as a source should be almost instinctive for travel journalists covering any particular destination. How they can use it – in addition to other sources like Twitter, Instagram, and blogs – will be the topic of Chapter 7.

Furthermore, travel journalists should be rethinking the way they cover stories and frame the news. How do they respond to real-time events now that they can? How do they see their increasingly important role as local correspondents in destinations? Will travel journalists develop more strategic methods for taking into consideration not only the many voices on social media, but also the many voices indigenous to the destinations they are covering? These conversations about what is 'news' to a travel journalist and how they report on it are just beginning, as the internet has opened up countless new possibilities for how these professionals can approach their work.

References

Berkowitz, D. (2009). Reporters and their sources. In K. Wahl-Jorgensen and T. Hanitzsch (Eds.), *The handbook of journalism studies* (pp. 102–115). New York: Routledge.

Boczkowski, P. J. (2009). Rethinking hard and soft news production: From common ground to divergent paths. *Journal of Communication*, 59(1), 98–116.

Boczkowski, P. J. (2010). *News at work: Imitation in an age of information abundance.* Chicago: University of Chicago Press.

Brandtzaeg, P. B., Lüders, M., Spangenberg, J., Rath-Wiggins, L., and Følstad, A. (2016). Emerging journalistic verification practices concerning social media. *Journalism Practice*, 10 (3), 323–342.

Broersma, M., and Peters, C. (2017). Introduction: Towards a functional perspective on journalism's role and relevance. In C. Peters and M. Broersma (Eds.), *Rethinking journalism again: Societal role and public relevance in a digital age* (pp. 1–18). Abingdon: Routledge.

Bruns, A. (2005). *Gatewatching: Collaborative online news production.* New York: Peter Lang.

Cocking, B. (2017). News values go on holiday: The ideological values of travel journalism. *Journalism Studies*, 1–17.

Djerf-Pierre, M., Ghersetti, M., and Hedman, U. (2016). Appropriating social media: The changing uses of social media among journalists across time. *Digital Journalism*, 4(7), 849–860.

Du, R. Y., and Kamakura, W. A. (2012). Quantitative trendspotting. *Journal of Marketing Research*, 49(4), 514–536.

Duffy, A. (2016). How social media offers opportunities for growth in the traditional media industry: The case of travel journalism. In V. Beson, R. Tuninga, and G. Saridakis (Eds.), *Analyzing the strategic role of social networking in firm growth and productivity* (pp. 172–187). Hershey, PA: IGI Global.

Duffy, A., and Mangharam, S. (2016). Imaginary travellers: Identity conceptualisations of the audience among travel journalists. *Journalism*, 18(8), 1030–1048.

Galtung, J., and Ruge, M. (1965). The structure of foreign news. *Journal of Peace Research*, 2(1), 64–91.

Hanusch, F. (2012). Broadening the focus: The case for lifestyle journalism as a field of scholarly inquiry. *Journalism Practice*, 6(1), 2–11.

Hanusch, F. (2014). Along similar lines: Does travel content follow foreign news flows? In F. Hanusch and E. Fürsich (Eds.), *Travel journalism: Exploring production, impact and culture* (pp. 155–175). Basingstoke: Palgrave Macmillan.

Hanusch, F., and Fürsich, E. (2014). On the relevance of travel journalism: An introduction. In F. Hanusch and E. Fürsich (Eds.), *Travel journalism: Exploring production, impact and culture* (pp. 1–18). Basingstoke: Palgrave Macmillan.

Hanusch, F., Hanitzsch, T., and Lauerer, C. (2017). 'How much love are you going to give this brand?' Lifestyle journalists on commercial influences in their work. *Journalism*, 18(2), 141–158.

Harcup, T., and O'Neill, D. (2011). What is news? Galtung and Ruge revisited. *Journalism Studies*, 2(2), 261–280.

Hays, S., Page, S. J., and Buhalis, D. (2013). Social media as a destination marketing tool: Its use by national tourism organisations. *Current Issues in Tourism*, 16(3), 211–239.

Hermida, A. (2010) Twittering the news: The emergence of ambient journalism. *Journalism practice*, 4(3), 297–308.

Kovach, B., and Rosenstiel, T. (2007). *The elements of journalism: What newspeople should know and the public should expect.* New York: Three Rivers Press.

Kovach, B., and Rosenstiel, T. (2010). *Blur: How to know what's true in the age of information overload.* New York: Bloomsbury.

MacCannell, D. (1976). *The tourist: A new theory of the leisure class.* Berkeley: University of California Press.

McGaurr, L. (2015). *Environmental communication and travel journalism: Consumerism, conflict and concern.* Abingdon: Routledge.

Pan, B., MacLaurin, T., and Crotts, J. C. (2007). Travel blogs and the implications for destination marketing. *Journal of Travel Research*, 46(1), 35–45.

Patterson, T. (2013). *Informing the news.* New York: Vintage Books.

Phillips, A. (2010). Transparency and the new ethics of journalism. *Journalism Practice*, 4(3), 373–382.

Schudson, M. (2011). *The sociology of news.* New York: Norton.

Schudson, M. (1997). *The power of news.* Cambridge, MA: Harvard University Press.

Singer, J. B., Domingo, D., Heinonen, A., Hermida, A., Paulussen, S., Quandt, T., and Vujnovic, M. (2011). *Participatory journalism: Guarding open gates at online newspapers.* Chichester: Wiley-Blackwell.

Urry, J., and Larsen, J. (2011). *The tourist gaze 3.0.* London: Sage.

Wahl-Jorgensen, K., and Hanitzsch, T. (Eds.). (2009). *The handbook of journalism studies.* New York: Routledge.

Volo, S. (2010). Bloggers' reported tourist experiences: Their utility as a tourism data source and their effect on prospective tourists. *Journal of Vacation Marketing*, 16(4), 297–311.

Zelizer, B. (2013). On the shelf life of democracy in journalism scholarship. *Journalism*, 14(4), 459–473.

PART II

Travel journalism in practice: challenges and changes

4

ECONOMICS OF TRAVEL JOURNALISM PRODUCTION

My editor at *Time Out Paris* sent me an email out of the blue. She had set up a reservation at a newly redesigned Parisian hotel for a colleague in the London office. He would be taking the Eurostar the next day to test out the hotel, but suddenly he had to cancel, jeopardizing the coverage that my editor needed for a special insert in the magazine about traveling from London to Paris. She had a complimentary two-night stay in a luxury hotel, but now she had no one to take it. She asked if I'd be interested to fill in and, always excited for a staycation in my own city, I agreed. It was a boutique hotel, not far from the Champs-Elysées, so I was prepared for the opportunity to take advantage of the perks of travel writing – freebies. Free experiences are part of the draw to travel journalism, rendering it more glamorous than it often is. But I, in my mid-twenties and an impoverished journalist, rarely had the occasion to stay in a boutique hotel, so I packed an overnight bag and biked across town.

I checked in, not revealing that I lived in Paris. The concierge didn't need to know. The room overlooked the Eiffel Tower. It was small, but manageable, and markedly better decorated than my tiny flat. The décor was well-conceived, and the complimentary breakfast in the morning was many notches above my usual yogurt and granola. Everything about the experience, as far as I could tell, was what one would expect from a boutique hotel in this neighborhood. In the morning, I put on my journalist hat to ask a few questions and make sure I had all of the information I needed. Since I was training for a marathon, I went to the front desk to ask about going for a short run. A local, I knew where the best routes were, but I just wanted to make sure that the concierge was equally knowledge-able. Surprisingly, the woman at the front desk had to pull up a map to familiarize herself with the area, pointing to the nearest greenspace suggesting that it might be OK for a jog. A tiny detail, it was nonetheless a curious one, forcing me to question the service of the hotel if the front desk workers didn't know the neighborhood around them. How would they respond to casual tourists who wanted to know similar things about their surroundings? As I scribbled down a few notes later, I wondered, would I put that in the review? Did I want to point out any negative experiences even though this whole thing was for free?

Ultimately, the two nights that the hotel hosted me was probably significantly less expensive than buying advertising in the publication directly. Yes, it's an enviable perk as a travel journalist, but how do you balance honest coverage with keeping everyone happy? Do I need to keep the hotel owners happy? Would I even disclose in the article that the hotel invited me? How else would I have been able to write about the hotel in the first place without an invitation? All of these questions fluttered around as I began to write, unsure of what my end game was, and unsure of what my editor would expect of me.

Such are the realities for a travel journalist on the job. Whether it's dealing with free experiences or an aggressive PR person, professional writers are constantly juggling issues related to financing their work (Fürsich and Kavoori, 2001; Hanusch, 2012). The bottom line is that travel is expensive, and today, publications rarely pay enough to cover all of the expenses needed to do a story justice, especially for freelancers who generally travel more than their salaried counterparts in editorial offices.

This chapter will explore, if ever too briefly, the many economic considerations for travel journalism, especially those that have developed with the internet. Social media influencers, for example, were inconceivable before blogs and Instagram became popular, but today travel journalists find themselves reporting alongside individuals who are invited to hotels and restaurants simply because of how many followers they have on a social network. How do these developments provide both challenges and opportunities to travel journalists on meager salaries?

I'll start by outlining how legacy media – from local papers to national magazines – generally have a love–hate relationship with articles written from subsidized travel or invitations, while presenting a few of the submission guidelines of major publications. This will establish the traditional role of travel journalism as an independent – or at least honest – source of information. I argue here that the unique economic conditions under which travel journalism is produced do allow for free travel and other subsidies, but the opportunities are less of a given these days because of multiple actors clamoring for the same perks (see Hanusch and Fürsich, 2014). How did travel journalism traditionally fund itself, and what opportunities have developed thanks to the internet today?

After establishing these practices, I'll then ask if travel journalism can manage to fund itself if the invitations are fewer and fewer. I will look at how the web has forced travel booking and information sites to share the same platform. News sites like *The Telegraph* now offer travel deals, while dedicated travel sites like Eurocheapo.com offer news-like information funded by booking commissions through their site. This new relationship between online information and online travel agencies needs to be explained before moving on to how journalists deal with all of this. Ultimately, I'd like to instil in future practitioners some reflections on how travel journalism is and can be funded, and the issues that come along with these models.

Economic issues facing travel journalists

In 2008, an economic downturn highlighted to what extent the press was suffering, though this was just an acceleration of a process that had been eroding its value for years (Kaye and Quinn, 2010). Krumsvik's study on Norwegian media argues that new media outlets, via the internet, introduce competition for available advertising funds (2012). He argues, however, that digitalized news sources are not able to provide the funding that publications need (2012). New models, like crowd-sourcing, have attempted to tackle these changes by providing alternative forms of funding (Carvajal et al., 2012). Ample studies examine the effects of tourism advertising on destinations (Gretzel et al., 2000; Kim et al., 2005; Goodall and Ashworth, 2013). Few studies, however, look at the financial impacts inherent in travel journalism. One of the rare studies on this relationship focuses on PR more than direct funding of publications. Hanusch's study on Australian travel journalists and their attitudes towards PR reveals that practitioners believe they are immune to PR effects, but that these relationships are necessary or useful for their work, allowing plenty of room for more discussion in this area (2012).

In travel media, an editor's tightening purse strings can have an effect on how publications remunerate their journalists. Almost all of the writers interviewed reported disappointing earning potential, requiring them to patch together an existence that includes other activities besides travel journalism. Some teach, some lead guided tours, some subedit other publications. Few rely on their writing for subsistence. As Greenman states, when it comes to funding opportunities, 'traditional sources are both well understood and in decline' (2012, p. 147). Journalists should not expect to find a high-paying, full-time job at a travel publication, especially since advertising and subscription revenue are not what they used to be. In response, Greenman has mapped out ways that travel journalists can fund themselves, including self-funding, grant funding, user funding, and investor funding (2012, p. 148). Online, however, there are new ways that travel publications and journalists are replacing or reinventing how they operate, but they don't come without their challenges.

Travel journalists and PR: a longstanding relationship

Traditional advertising and subscriptions are no longer the only ways to fund journalism – especially not in the tourism industry. Back in the nineteenth century, when a fledgling travel press was developing, it was a new space for hotels and other tourism-related companies to advertise. The May 1866 edition of Thomas Cook's *Excursionist* features ads for businesses such as Lewis's Ornamental Repository and Photographic Album Depot, capitalizing on souvenir photos. There are ads for an Alpine boot company as well as for travel insurance, promising up to

£100 in case of death. An 1881 edition has ads selling Dr J. Collis Browne's chlorodyne to treat coughs, colds, asthma, and bronchitis, among other ailments. Travelers would have packed that along with Lamplough's Pyretic Saline, publicized in the same edition. While websites still use various forms of display ads – like like those of Louis Vuitton which figure prominently in the *New York Times* travel section – other forms of collaboration are evolving to fund the content appearing on both printed and web pages. It's not enough these days simply to buy space in a magazine or on a website to push a product or service. Companies are engaging with content marketing or with native advertising to get their messages across in different ways.

While the form of the content is changing, tourism marketers and PR, however, still maintain many of their standing relationships with journalists, especially when providing press trips and other freebies. As Hanusch reveals, travel journalists do not believe in relying on PR materials for their reporting, but they do value it as a starting point. Discussing his findings of a sample of Australian travel journalists, he writes:

> When delving into these results deeper, however, we saw three different types of travel journalists emerging, who have very different perceptions of PR, with views ranging from generally positive to highly critical. The analysis of the groups showed that gender, job status, time spent travelling, as well as a background in mainstream journalism play important roles in determining group membership.
>
> *(Hanusch, 2012, p. 74)*

While his study offers a rare glimpse into the relationship between PR and travel journalists, further research is needed to examine these relationships that are evolving online.

Publications and submission guidelines

One way that journalists deal with this issue of freebies – be it a meal, a night in a hotel, or a free guided tour – is by establishing industry-wide norms and ethics for their practice. Greenman (2012) discusses this at length in his book, writing, 'Conflict of interest is embedded in the way most travel writing is produced' (2012, p. 138). Today these conflicts stretch beyond writing to YouTube videos and Instagram posts, among other outlets. Readers will – or at least should – wonder how the author managed to get that particular shot or that exclusive interview. How were they able to travel to Singapore to do a budget travel piece? How did they equip themselves for that trek down the Amazon? If it's clear and apparent how the stories were produced, Greenman argues, then there is little issue for the journalist or the audiences, but disclosure and transparency are not standard fixtures in most publications, and are even less so on social networks. A quick look at one magazine, however, reveals how the internet is only making such transparent norms even more difficult.

Condé Nast Traveler, launched in the US in 1987, has been a bastion of good travel journalism practice since its inception – though even this brand faces challenges. The magazine's motto, 'Truth in travel', reflected a strict policy of not accepting preferential treatment for trips undertaken in the name of a story. As they write on their website, 'This ensures that we experience travel the way you do – with no special recognition, treatment, or obligations – and are free to report our findings honestly, with no conflict of interest or ulterior motives.' Moving online, *Condé Nast Traveler* maintained its guarantee of independent travel, with a 2011 post on the site declaring, 'Although some of the contributors to our Daily Traveler blog engage in work outside *Condé Nast Traveler* that does not always follow these rules, when writing for us they adhere to our standard and are transparent about any of their affiliations and sponsorships.' In 2013, however, a new editor-in-chief relaxed these rules, allowing writers to seek discounted press rates. While some professional norms have relaxed, much of the traditional travel press has maintained a high level of ethics. Many other newspaper travel sections and magazines adopt similar positions, maintaining their levels of transparency online – at least in theory. With ever-expanding networks of bloggers and content producers, and editors who are stretched thinner and thinner, we have to wonder if these rigorous policies are actually enforced or not.

A quick look at the submission guidelines for some current popular publications reveals a spectrum of tolerance for PR. Some publications, like *Wanderlust*, a popular English magazine printed since 1993, mention nothing about sponsored travel in their guidelines for writers online. Most legacy media, however, state something akin to how the BBC's travel section frames sponsored travel:

> BBC Travel does not allow press trips, sponsored travel, freebies, comps, funding assistance or media discounts, except in the rare case in which it is the only opportunity for press to be a part of something before the public launch, it is the only way to gain access to something or the story would be logistically unattainable otherwise.

Likewise, the *New York Times* follows suit, stating clearly in its guidelines online, 'The Travel Section will not publish articles that grow out of trips paid for or in any way subsidized by an airline, hotel, tourist board or other organization with an interest, direct or indirect, in the subject of an article.' The *Washington Post* and *LA Times* also refuse sponsored travel, but a slew of new media sites, from Buzzfeed Travel to Matador and HuffPost, do not have any steadfast rules against publishing about sponsored trips, at least none that they release publicly.

Publications are not alone. Travel writers' associations attempt to temper the influence of marketing and PR forces in their codes of ethics. The British Guild of Travel Writers offers a very short set of ethics, including one pertaining to freebies. The guild states that travel writers may

> accept facilities necessary for work offered to the press only on the understanding that they are in no way obliged to publicize any or all of the

operation concerned and that the provision of such facilities will not influence their judgement.

(2018)

Likewise, the North American Travel Journalists Association curbs conflicts of interest by stating, 'A member shall personally pay for all expenses incurred by that member that are personal or beyond the services voluntarily provided by the host' (North American Travel Journalists Association, 2017). These ethical codes, however, remain ambiguous and do not preclude freebies, nor do they promote transparency in the publication of stories produced with the aid of PR or marketing forces. Almost curiously, it's the Bloggers Travel Association that strives for a more transparent approach, writing in its charter, 'If writing about something or someone we are financially connected to, or something that is given to us or offered at a deep discount because we are travel bloggers, we disclose those facts' (Professional Travel Bloggers Association, 2018). Such disclosure would greatly reduce confusion and deception in a digital environment (Yaxley, 2012, p. 415). How such disclosures are policed, however, remains a challenge, and readers are largely left to judge on their own whether or not an article has been produced with financial help; this is something that travel journalists need to address. Disclosure remains a self-policing practice among professionals (Ikonen et al., 2016) and how future travel journalists engage with it, while being honest towards their audiences, remains a challenge in the developing digital media environment.

Evolving practice online

A closer look at these publications – which all have developed an online presence – reveals that sponsored travel may be low on the priority list of ways to keep travel writers writing. *Travel+Leisure* magazine has revamped its web approach, offering a variety of services to attract advertisers and sponsors. In their online media kit, they discuss offering sponsored posts, custom hashtags, Facebook chats, Twitter parties, custom Pinterest boards, and Instagram 'takeovers' as ways to connect with their audiences in new, more direct ways. Instead of PR companies approaching the press, the press is now offering its services directly to PR agents. Whether or not journalists perform any of these duties remains unclear, but the important message is that legacy media are trying hard to stay relevant online, and journalists may be called upon to participate in these marketing efforts.

Furthermore, it's not just the media outlets that are adapting. The tourism industry is taking strides to mesh more with the internet as well, beyond just bookings and online services. A growing emphasis on tourism bureaus and local businesses launching their own social networks pushes destination marketers and business owners to look for new ways to engage audiences online. Press trips are still an affordable way to transfer messages to audiences. As one journalist interviewed said,

Transparency is important, but I still believe in press trips. Country-sponsored trips that you wouldn't have access to, places like Jordan – I went to a few years ago and I think that even though you are invited there by the country I'm still objectively reporting while I was there.

These trips, however, are increasingly difficult to obtain, especially because bloggers and other social media content producers are now often a part of the mix. As one blogger explained, she can be discerning when it comes to accepting freebies and writing about them, and she doesn't feel bound by any agreement between her editors and a PR company to produce content. 'If I like it I'll do an Instagram or a tweet. If it fits with the blog, I'll do a post. I don't care how many presents they give me, it has to be good', she said.

Influencers

First blogs, then social networks, and now YouTube channels have led to new opportunities on social media that journalists have not yet fully exploited – but entrepreneurial travelers have. Bakker discusses the concept of advocacy in tourism marketing, explaining how social media has led to the rise of the online influencer. Influencers are social media users who write or produce content around a common theme – be it travel or a more specific focus like LGBT tourism or luxury travel:

This makes working with influencers extremely interesting since they can deliver a credible message to exactly the right audience, whereas broadcast media often delivers a generic message to a generic audience. Often, a message to thousands who are passionate, instead of to hundreds of thousands within a general audience can easily produce better results.

(Bakker, 2016, p. 293)

As discussed, many of the professional journalists interviewed do not actively engage with social media, allowing individuals who do to fill these new roles of influencers. The evolving relationship between media producers and public relations is also something that PR companies need to adapt to as well, to embrace the potential for real conversations through social media (Waters et al., 2010, p. 259). The new crop of influencers, however, with substantial audiences on Twitter or Instagram for example, will be invited by or paid by a tourism bureau or business to post content about their destination. Influencers will often take over a brand's Instagram or else post photos for a specific company. One travel blogger famously reported earning up to 9,000 USD for individual photos on his Instagram account (Fitzmaurice, 2017). While surely not the norm, these individuals illustrate to what extent advertisers and destination marketers are investing in social media, and travel journalists should take note. I do not suggest that these publications and posts are replacing true journalistic work, but they do arguably attract the PR and audience attention that once focused on journalists' stories. Some reports suggest that although travelers trust user-generated content, in general it is less trusted and less valued than professionally-produced information (Cox et al., 2009). While several studies address these issues, it is unclear whether or not audiences make the distinction between purely sponsored posts and more journalistic endeavors, or if they realize what influence these PR tactics have on them and their spending habits. What is clear, however, is that advertising and PR budgets are limited, but increasingly spread across more actors, from journalists and bloggers to traditional advertising and social media influencers.

Journalism as a marketplace

Interactions with PR, at the end of the day, are not reprehensible, and sometimes they are the only or most efficient way to get a story. Travel journalism has always been at the crossroads of promoting tourism experiences, writing about certain excursions or plugging certain destinations that offer readers discounts. Cook's *Excursionist* sold their tours in their magazine in the nineteenth century, and *National Geographic Traveler* still sells its own tours today, promoting experiences alongside its stories. Online, however, travel media is increasingly becoming a vector for booking and commissions as media sites double as third party booking sites. A look at a legacy brand like *The Telegraph*'s travel section or a web-only site like Eurocheapo.com reveals that users can book hotels and other elements directly through these sites. By skimming a commission off the top of these prices, media sites are able to generate revenue directly. While this intersection is not new, it is bringing commerce to what was originally a collection of information sources studded with advertising. Now, travel journalism sites are becoming one-stop shops for customers in ways that they were not previously, often implicating journalists. Vendors like Expedia and Airbnb have segued into providing more content in the form of blogs and print magazines, but they are built as commercial entities, pretending to be nothing else. In the other direction, news websites like *Telegraph Travel* are commercializing by adding package trip offers on their site, becoming marketplaces. It becomes more difficult a pill to swallow when a trustworthy information site starts selling things directly through its own website. As consumers, we are forced to ask where their priorities are. As journalists, we are forced to ask how our content reflects not just our advertisers' needs, but the products or packages that our websites are selling directly.

And through this convergence, obvious questions arise. If only companies or destinations able to provide a commission can afford to work with media brands, what happens to less affluent destinations? Is there an ethical problem related to diversity and representation that travel journalists need to reflect upon, and moreover, was this always the case? There will clearly be an interest for journalists working at these sites in pushing certain hotels, restaurants, or experiences that will generate bookings and, in turn, income for the website. Is travel journalism simply boiling down to advertising in a more obvious way than before, or can we accept that the consumer aspect is intimately intertwined with the web without sacrificing journalistic integrity? As we will see, travel journalism can often transcend its commercial nature, but understanding how to deal with some of these questions is pivotal for professionals in an online environment.

PR and transparency

As more websites and brands relax their stance on freebies, PR, and now online bookings will continue to be integral parts of tourism marketing for both journalists and other content providers, though attitudes towards these practices vary. Most writers only need to be concerned with freebies and PR, which affect their work directly. Rarely – so far – do booking considerations play a role for the writer, even if the content is crafted to encourage readers to book a specific experience through the site. Many of these considerations fall under the jurisdiction of editors and marketing teams behind publications.

Freebies, however, remain an ever-present and often contested component for both journalists and bloggers, who have multiple views on these issues, often occupying an ethical position on a practice that many deem contrary to the pursuit of journalistic objectivity. Whereas most journalists are aware of issues surrounding disclosure, there is no consensus that anything must be disclosed, or even how it should be done. Bloggers, on the other hand, are even less concerned about these questions, though some do take a moral stance.

Journalists generally recognize that there are potential conflicts of interest. One journalist said that freebies are typically not discussed openly, but they are essential, especially when she cannot justify paying for an experience that she is reporting on for a publication. When updating guidebooks or writing about an array of budget options, journalists will inevitably come across a luxury experience that is out of their means. 'Sometimes, like for guidebooks, you can't pay for places that you visit. And if you'll write about a place, you need to stay there. So, I've had press trips to places and stayed in places that we can't afford', she said. Another journalist, furthermore, stressed that transparency is key no matter what sorts of experiences she accepts, and she doesn't let freebies sway her critical approach. 'If there's something negative', she said, 'I'll put it in the review. Anyone who doesn't do that is unethical and they are only then in it for the future freebies they can get.' There is a general agreement, echoing Hanusch's findings, that PR should never affect coverage, though realistically such effects are difficult to measure (2012).

Over recent years, however, bloggers have stepped up to demand the same sort of treatment traditionally reserved for journalists. One journalist spoke of her surprise at a press event:

> I got invited to a journalist event, but it turned out that everyone at the event was a blogger. I guess bloggers are now journalists. That was an event specifically for the media, but when I think of media, I haven't fully integrated that bloggers are media, but of course they are a powerful force of people.

Journalists haven't fully recognized that bloggers are working alongside them and not necessarily against them. One journalist explained her view on bloggers, saying, 'Bloggers are not as closed off to PR companies as journalists. It should be an adversarial relationship, journalists and PR people. Bloggers are the opposite. It's a totally different way of looking at things.'

Bloggers, however, generally disagree that they are simply tools of PR companies. One blogger in particular is reticent to accept invitations in return for massive amounts of promotion. Instead, she is trying to give a value to her work, to work with brands more strategically. She explained:

> Journalists got invited to events or trips and they wanted you to write about it. In the blogging world, they are doing the same but under different circumstances. They think bloggers should do everything for free and that's not right. So, companies that offer a freebie doesn't mean that I will take photos, edit the photos, upload it, and then promote it across social media and the blog. It's worth money.

While this blogger is much more of an influencer than most, with a large social network following, her sentiments echoed many of the more amateur bloggers in the sample. Most are happy to write about things that resonate with their readers and their expectations, but they are more reflective than journalists make them out to be. They often look critically at the value of an object or experience and understand that it is often not worth their coverage. 'People want me to post their own content for marketing purposes. I have to believe in something if I am going to test it out,' said one blogger. Another blogger described how her mission is to help tourists plan their trip, and her choice of freebies or sponsored content reflects that:

> If it's something like a macaron class, I think that's cool because this is where they come from and the whole macaron culture is spreading around the world now. Also, things that can help, a lot of my readers come to Paris, and I'll link to things they can do. I help them plan their trip.

Value for their time and relevance to their audiences seem to be guiding factors for bloggers to accept and promote free experiences.

Brogan and Smith write, 'Being honest on the Web fosters empathy, creating a stronger understanding of people's feelings both online and offline (2010, p. 200). Bloggers, however, are not universally concerned with how their readers view their honesty as much as they are concerned with how they provide compelling content. Moreover, when it comes to disclosing these invitations, bloggers are split. Some don't think it's appropriate to disclose because, in their eyes, accepting invitations isn't well regarded in the media. They would sacrifice transparency in order to maintain an air of authenticity – something that runs contrary to what most journalism studies would suggest (Singer and Ashman, 2009; Greenman,

2012). Others, however, are happy to disclose because, as they say, it gives them some more credibility to work with a brand or company. One blogger summed up her experience with disclosing as follows: 'I say I was invited. It sounds chic.' For journalists, however, there should be a clear ethical obligation to disclose free or sponsored events. This code, part of their professional identity, is part of what separates the travel journalist from the social media influencers and bloggers who adhere less stringently to any ethical mandate.

Rethinking possibilities

Despite the US Federal Trade Commission's requirement to disclose sponsored content online, and avid discussion by the UK's Advertising Standards Authority and Committee of Advertising Practice, little enforcement is possible at the moment, especially in travel media. Researchers have suggested that current codes of ethics fail to meet the need for transparency, and that communications professionals need to ensure this value in order to preserve the quality of their content (Ikonen et al., 2016, p. 175). As the authors write:

> One cannot assume a media literate message receiver when using sponsored content, and thus the ethical burden is on the producer of the message. Effective codes of ethics should introduce moral norms to ensure that the rights of consumers are respected. Both brands and media companies do not want to lose credibility because of ethical pitfalls, and the ethical codes serve as a critical intermediate in guiding actions.
>
> *(p. 176)*

Such ethical implications apply to journalists, but not exclusively. While media companies are struggling to keep pace with the evolving nature of sponsored and native content, individuals including bloggers and other social media influencers are also without proper guidance. Rare are the personal Instagram accounts that feature clear hashtag like #ad or #sponsored in their posts. Moreover, there are just too many blogs, Instagrammers, and other users generating content to imagine policing all of it. With little or no regulation over these freebies, is much of the travel content available today any different from advertising? While both bloggers and journalists are aware of the ethical grey area surrounding freebies, only journalists have the mandate from above – notably from their editors – to either avoid it or disclose it fully. Their reputation and credibility are all they have, which can be whisked away with one careless, dishonest post or article.

The problem, however, is that consumers today do not unanimously condemn dishonest travel content providers. Such a phenomenon occurred in July 2017 when a popular Instagrammer was called out for allegedly editing herself into images of sites she was visiting – notably appearing in front of the Taj Mahal without any other tourists, nor with the scaffolding that featured prominently on one part of it at that time. Debates in the media condemned the practice, while others questioned if we should really be appalled by Insta-grammers selling an idealized version of a destination. The ploy was likened to fake news in that it is a 'worrying aspect of the erosion of authenticity online', according to the *New Statesman* (Tait, 2017). The problem is not just that the internet allows more people to produce wavering levels of quality content. Instead, the problem lies with the fact that many of these people are competing for brands and advertisers who will pay them substantial fees for their work which lacks any authenticity whatsoever. In turn, tourists, allowing their tourist gaze to be set by these individuals, will end up gazing at something that doesn't really exist (Urry and Larsen, 2011).

Perhaps travel journalists may regain much of their status by engaging in more of a watchdog role, or a curatorial role, whereby they help keep tabs on what is genuine information and what is not. By raising these questions – like publications from *Refinery29* and the *Daily Mail* to *The Times* and *Grazia* did during the doc-tored-Instagram affair – journalists can help counter the effects of the mass scramble for every sponsor dollar out there. Travel journalism is about place and people, but it is also about the industry, and publications like Skift.com are filling this watch-dog niche. By adding this curatorial role to their jobs, following the suggestions by Duffy, journalists need to integrate and collaborate more systematically with social media (2016). While the quest for clicks, advertisers, and freebies won't end any-time soon, travel journalists can still assert themselves as authorities in information flows if they endorse common practices of transparency and disclosure and take up more of an industry and media watchdog role. Perhaps financially their bread and butter is not in the trips to Bangkok or Budapest, but in helping to maintain an authoritative voice over content relative to these sites, whether that be scanning TripAdvisor or fact-checking blogs. Far from suggesting that travel journalists stop traveling, I suggest instead that their work may benefit from being as much about fact-checking what other people are saying about a location as well as finding their own unique stories to tell once there.

References

Bakker, W. (2016). Social media and the impact on travel and tourism. In H. J. Siller (Ed.), *Entrepreneurship und Tourismus: Unternehmerisches Denken und Erfolgskonzepte aus der Praxis* (pp. 287–298). Innsbruck, Austria: Linde International.

British Guild of Travel Writers. (2018). Introducing the British Guild of Travel Writers. Retrieved from http://bgtw.org

Brogan, C., and Smith, J. (2010). *Trust agents: Using the web to build influence, improve reputation, and earn trust.* Hoboken, NJ: John Wiley & Sons.

Campbell, M. C., Mohr, G. S., and Verlegh, P. W. (2013). Can disclosures lead consumers to resist covert persuasion? The important roles of disclosure timing and type of response. *Journal of Consumer Psychology*, 23(4), 483–495.

Carvajal, M., García-Avilés, J. A., and González, J. L. (2012). Crowdfunding and non-profit media: The emergence of new models for public interest journalism. *Journalism Practice*, 6(5–6), 638–647.

Cox, C., Burgess, S., Sellitto, C., and Buultjens, J. (2009). The role of user-generated content in tourists' travel planning behavior. *Journal of Hospitality Marketing and Management*, 18(8), 743–764.

Duffy, A. (2016). How social media offers opportunities for growth in the traditional media industry: The case of travel journalism. In V. Beson, R. Tuninga, and G. Saridakis (Eds.), *Analyzing the strategic role of social networking in firm growth and productivity* (pp. 172–187). Hershey, PA: IGI Global.

Greenman, J. (2012). *Introduction to travel journalism: On the road with serious intent*. New York: Peter Lang.

Fitzmaurice, R. (2017, April 4). Meet the Instagram-famous travel blogging couple who get paid up to £7,000 to post a single photo. *Business Insider UK*. Retrieved from http://uk. businessinsider.com

Fürsich, E., and Kavoori, A. P. (2001). Mapping a critical framework for the study of travel journalism. *International Journal of Cultural Studies*, 4(2), 149–171.

Goodall, B., and Ashworth, G. (Eds.). (2013). *Marketing in the tourism industry (RLE tourism): The promotion of destination regions*. Abingdon: Routledge.

Greenman, J. (2012). *Introduction to travel journalism: On the road with serious intent*. New York: Peter Lang.

Gretzel, U., Yuan, Y. L., and Fesenmaier, D. R. (2000). Preparing for the new economy: Advertising strategies and change in destination marketing organizations. *Journal of Travel Research*, 39(2), 146–156.

Hanusch, F. (2010). The dimensions of travel journalism: Exploring new fields for journalism research beyond the news. *Journalism Studies*, 11(1), 68–82.

Hanusch, F. (2012). Travel journalists' attitudes toward public relations: Findings from a representative survey. *Public Relations Review*, 38(1), 69–75.

Hanusch, F., and Fürsich, E. (2014). On the relevance of travel journalism: An introduction. In F. Hanusch and E. Fürsich (Eds.), *Travel journalism: Exploring production, impact and culture* (pp. 1–18). Hampshire: Palgrave Macmillan.

Hanusch, F., Hanitzsch, T., and Lauerer, C. (2017). 'How much love are you going to give this brand?' Lifestyle journalists on commercial influences in their work. *Journalism*, 18(2), 141–158.

Ikonen, P., Luoma-aho, V., and Bowen, S. A. (2016). Transparency for sponsored content: Analysing codes of ethics in public relations, marketing, advertising and journalism. *International Journal of Strategic Communication*, 11(2), 165–178.

Kaye, J., and Quinn, S. (2010). *Funding journalism in the digital age: Business models, strategies, issues and trends*. New York: Peter Lang.

Kim, D. Y., Hwang, Y. H., and Fesenmaier, D. R. (2005). Modeling tourism advertising effectiveness. *Journal of Travel Research*, 44(1), 42–49.

Krumsvik, A. H. (2012). Why old media will be funding journalism in the future. *Journalism Studies*, 13(5–6), 729–741.

McGaurr, L. (2015). *Environmental communication and travel journalism: Consumerism, conflict and concern*. Abingdon: Routledge.

North American Travel Journalists Association. (2017). *The North American Travel Journalists Association Code of Ethics*. Retrieved from www.natja.org

Phillips, A. (2010). Transparency and the new ethics of journalism. *Journalism Practice*, 4(3), 373–382.

Pirolli, B. (2014). Travel journalism in flux: New practices in the blogosphere. In F. Hanusch and E. Fürsich (Eds.), *Travel journalism: Exploring production, impact and culture* (pp. 83–98). Basingstoke: Palgrave Macmillan.

Professional Travel Bloggers Association. (2018). About the PTBA. Retrieved from http://travelbloggersassociation.com

Singer, J. B., and Ashman, I. (2009). 'Comment is free, but facts are sacred': User-generated content and ethical constructs at the Guardian. *Journal of Mass Media Ethics*, 24(1), 3–21.

Tait, A. (2017, July 12). The fake kids of Instagram? Behind the backlash against the internet famous. *New Statesman*. Retrieved from https://www.newstatesman.com

Urry, J., and Larsen, J. (2011). *The tourist gaze 3.0*. London: Sage.

Waters, R. D., Tindall, N. T., and Morton, T. S. (2010). Media catching and the journalist–public relations practitioner relationship: How social media are changing the practice of media relations. *Journal of Public Relations Research*, 22(3), 241–264.

Yaxley, H. (2012). Digital public relations: Revolution or evolution. In A. Theaker (Ed.), *The public relations handbook* (pp. 411–432). Abingdon: Routledge.

5

AUDIENCE EXPECTATIONS AND PRACTICES ONLINE

Introduction

To supplement my writing income, I often gave guided walking tours in Paris, using my knowledge of the city in a different setting beyond websites and books. One afternoon I met a client, let's call her Diane, at a posh little hotel in Paris. She hired me to take her on a tour of the city, to see the sights as well as a few offbeat places. It was her first time in Paris, and, suffering from a near-fatal brain issue, she wanted to see the city in case her impending surgery was not a success. The pressure was on, and we sat down to discuss what she wanted to experience. She wasn't my typical client in terms of her health issues, but in many other ways she was a normal tourist. She had done her research, created certain expectations, and prepared as best she could. As a tour guide, my job was to tell stories about Paris – essentially making my journalism a stage production in the streets. It was a natural extension for me as a storyteller who routinely wrote about the city. We sipped a coffee as I began to describe all of the places we could go over the next few hours – the Ritz Hotel, the opera house, the gardens. Diane lit up with each mention, and when we finished our coffee we set off from the hotel on foot to have what could very well have been her only experience of Paris.

There was only one problem. Diane was wearing six-inch stiletto heels. They were the kind of heels that you see in movies that you think must have been worn by a stunt double because they look too uncomfortable to be acceptable by any actors' guild or union. Diane was wearing them, however, and after about fifteen minutes of strolling down the block on this clearly-advertised walking tour, she could barely move. We sat down at a café again, this time for wine, to dull the pain. 'Everything I read and saw about Paris showed women wearing really fashionable clothes and shoes', she explained, 'so I thought I would try to fit in, to be a local.' A look around at the women in more sensible shoes strolling the cobblestones and dirt-covered paths of the Tuileries Gardens, however, revealed the truth. Diane had been duped by a media perception perpetrated by Hollywood, but also by travel writers. A few months later, when updating the *Fodor's* Paris guide, I came across a page that informed women on how to dress like Parisian women. Inspired by classic French actresses, all thin and white, the text told women that upon arriving in France, 'suddenly, virtually all the clothes you packed may feel outdated, frumpy, and wrong', and I instantly understood Diane's plight. The stereotyped descriptions were dated and, frankly, a bit sexist, but my editor did not respond when I suggested nixing the page. Instead, it remained the same in the upcoming issue. I shudder to think how many tourists like Diane continue to suffer because they think they need to look like someone's standard of a Parisian.

Journalism's first loyalty is to its citizens (Kovach and Rosenstiel, 2007). Travel journalism, therefore, has a similar duty to travelers. By suggesting erroneously that there was some sort of costume to adopt in Paris, I argue that travel journalism failed its audiences in this specific example. While a seemingly trivial incident, Diane's anecdote opens up the question of what travelers are actually expecting from their travel journalists. What are they looking for in their excursions and what are the difficulties in delivering what they need and want in a digital age?

In this chapter, I'll begin by addressing the increasingly active nature of audiences in a 'networked public sphere' where users become producers, or 'produsers' (Benkler, 2006; Bruns, 2008). I'll then highlight some of the dominant practices of tourists that help us understand why and how they inform themselves, focusing in part on the quest for the 'authentic experience' that has been discussed by numerous authors, especially in the current climate of 'experiential travel' (e.g. MacCannell, 1976). I'll introduce various notions of authenticity to understand how existential authenticity, as explored by Wang, should help travel journalists better understand their role in mediating or informing these experiences for tourists (1999). From notions of objective authenticity to more existential authenticity, travel media is rife with buzzwords catering to these perceived needs – *secret* tours, *local* housing, *off the beaten path* experiences – but there is no clear definition about what these terms mean to each individual.

So much has been written about authenticity and travel, so instead of rehashing all of it, I'll move to how writers from three different sources – journalists, bloggers, and travel forum contributors – all interpret this idea of authenticity in their work, and what we can learn from each. I'll also present results from interviews with tourists planning a trip to Paris in order to illustrate their desires and needs, and to understand what authenticity means to them. Do these 'authentic' experiences exist? Yes, but not independently of the person living them. I'll argue that it's not a matter of the experience existing, but more of a question of tourists feeling like they have achieved something specifically authentic to them, whether it corresponds to some mediated image of authenticity or not. I'll further argue that journalists, then, are not so much engaged with providing specific information towards defining what is or what isn't authentic, but in providing context and guidance that empowers tourists to achieve their own authentic experience, on their own terms, and preferably with the right footwear.

Towards an active audience

Travel journalism audiences are far from homogeneous. From package tour consumers who read a brochure to independent travelers who research every book and website available for a holiday, there is no single profile. Research into group travel shows that package tours still 'attract travelers who are price sensitive, less independent and look for social interaction' (Chang, 2007, p. 162). At the same time, independent travelers, especially with the rise in technology associated with their journeys, 'are now free to wander off and explore the destination with minimal planning and more spontaneity' (Huang et al., 2014, p. 170). This spectrum of tourists is complicated by Urry and Larsen's notion of the post-tourist, who, as I'll discuss, seeks both authenticity and kitsch while traveling. In short, there is a wide spectrum of information consumers who consult travel media, not to mention those armchair travelers who use the information mostly for entertainment. But even armchair travel, as Jørgensen posits, is changing as media changes, with new digital endeavors creating 'a communal experience that adds to the physical experience' (2014, p. 110).

Steward (2005) writes how travel media in the UK from the nineteenth century became specialized in order to attract specific consumers – be they culture seekers, women, health travelers, and so forth. This fractured consumer base is evident when one browses any newsstand or Google results for a particular destination. While there are many specific types of information to choose from, the internet has further introduced user-generated content in the form of blogs, wikis, social networks, and review sites like TripAdvisor and Yelp that each offer something unique and potentially useful to consumers. A look at how audiences use these sites reveals distinct practices among individuals, who may start with a magazine and move to TripAdvisor, or begin with a favorite blogger's recommendation and then research further via Google (Pirolli, 2016). These diverse practices make it difficult to know which tourists are visiting a site and for what purposes. Editors, however, can generally gauge the type of readers they attract, especially in an increasingly networked media landscape. As one travel website editor explained, 'Metrics are very useful in terms of sheer numbers, where users come from, the countries, etc., and how often they come back.' Editors and their journalists now know more about who is clicking on their sites, how much time they spend there, what pages they visit the most, how they land on these sites, and what keywords they may use to get there.

All of these possibilities are part of a larger shift in the relationship between journalists and their audiences. Over the past few years, journalism scholars have been exploring the evolving relationship between journalists and audiences (Anderson, 2011; Van Der Wurff and Schönbach, 2011; Domingo, 2011; Loosen and Schmidt, 2017). At the heart of these studies is the change from passive news consumers to more active media participants who can no longer be taken for granted. Audiences are making decisions, interacting with information providers, and continuing conversations on social media. As Loosen and Schmidt explain:

> So the relationship between journalism and audience is reflexive in a very practical sense: Journalism has to take information about its audiences into account in order to produce news that has a chance to be noticed and will be consumed.
>
> *(Loosen and Schmidt, 2017, p. 356)*

These changes have been amplified not just by the comments sections and data collection, but by pervasive social media use. Twitter, Facebook, and a host of other networks have given audiences a louder voice than before. Much recent research questions the impact of social media on journalism (Bruns, 2005; Hermida, 2010; Singer, 2014). One thing needs to be clear concerning social media and audiences. Since the popularization of outlets like Twitter and Facebook, researchers have turned to questioning how journalism researchers can conceptualize and study audiences' relationships with journalists (Loosen and Schmidt, 2012). Since the 2016 US presidential elections, however, it is no longer a question of taking social media as a serious news item, especially as public policy breaks on Twitter before anywhere else in Washington D.C. Whereas researchers assert that 'with social media, journalism and audiences met on "uncommon ground"', much of that ground has become incredibly familiar in the months following the US election (Loosen and Schmidt, 2017, p. 357). For lifestyle and travel journalists, there's even less of a divide, as travel is not perceived to be as serious as hard news topics. Further research, however, must interrogate how these sources are verified and integrated into news processes more specifically.

Beyond social media, journalists can know their audiences through all of the metrics discussed, ultimately able to cater their content accordingly. This possibility presents a danger, however, in limiting the scope of an online publication's subject matter. 'Journalists who only follow aggregated click data or who only follow the needs of those social groups that are articulating their demands and concerns online, might eventually neglect certain topics' (Loosen and Schmidt, 2017, p. 360). One editor explained how, on his site, articles about Paris attracted the most attention, often causing bumps in traffic that he would pursue. Ultimately, however, he found it futile to create content simply for shareability. 'Sometimes you see a spike in traffic and a lot of those readers don't stick around. So, trying to target our core audience is always the goal and then bring new ones into the fold', he explained.

All of these conversations about the emergence of more participatory audience for journalism leads me to examine travel audiences more closely. Several studies already look at how travel journalism frames foreign places for its audiences (Cocking, 2009; Fürsich, 2010). Few studies, however, have yet to look at how travel journalists meet the expectations of their readers or viewers, or what those expectations even are.

Understanding what travel audiences want: authenticity

Before understanding how audiences look to travel journalism, it's important to sketch out what is known about their expectations of tourists in general. Numerous studies explore the sociology of tourism and travel, examining why individuals push beyond the comfort of their home to see the world. What's important in these discussions is the notion of authenticity that, for the last century or so, has guided much of the tourism industry. Authenticity is the topic of numerous works, set in numerous contexts (see Taylor, 1991, or Trilling, 1974). As related to travel experiences, other researchers have built upon these theories (see Cohen, 1988; Cohen and Cohen, 2012). MacCannell explores this notion in his seminal work *The Tourist* (1976). Using Goffman's stage theory among other frameworks, MacCannell essentially describes tourism in the twentieth century as a quest for something simpler than what was found in modern society. Suddenly, factories, workshops, sewers, and other work displays behind-the-scenes experiences became popular:

> Modernity is transforming labor into cultural productions attended by tourists and sightseers who are moved by the universality of work relations – not as this is represented throughout their own work ... but as it is revealed to them at their leisure through the displayed work of others.
>
> *(1976, p. 36)*

This led to a quest among travelers to find experiences that conformed to a new notion of authenticity, but one that, according to MacCannell, was impossible. The tourism industry, he explains, engaged in 'staged authenticity' to capitalize on these desires. On tourists' search for authenticity, MacCannell states, 'Their hope of discovering something real is not non-existent, it is just doomed' (1976, p. 44). Still, guides like *Lonely Planet* and the *Rough Guides* have tried to tap into this ethos, while websites and blogs continue to promote 'insider' or 'secret' guides to famous destinations.

Post-modernity, however, has revamped the way tourists interpret their travels, leading us to the idea of a 'post-tourist' described by Urry and Larsen. They write, 'The post-tourist knows they are a tourist and tourism is a series of games with multiple texts and no single, authentic tourist experience' (2011, p. 114). This approach corresponds much more with how the tourists interviewed interpret their approach to travel. While most appreciate that there are certain tourist experiences to participate in, they are also eager to distinguish their travels from the masses. One tourist illustrates this idea clearly, saying,

> It's fun to do both. I like tourist trap things because often they are well known for a reason. In Paris, you go to the Eiffel Tower even if there is a ridiculously long line. I try to strike a balance between the two.

Others are keen to interact more with locals, to immerse themselves in local culture, like one tourist who said, 'So sometimes I like to find some of the touristy stuff first to see what the draws are and from there you can knock that off your list. You meet people and you see what they do.' Immersing oneself in a culture is important for many tourists, and engaging with the locals factors heavily into the tourist game. One traveler explained, 'I guess that sort of combination of doing some stuff that was tips from locals, walking and seeing what people were doing, and doing some tourist sites, that's kind of what I'm going for.'

Most tourists acknowledge the inability to have a clearly defined authentic experience, and few believed it was possible to plan for or research such an experience. One tourist said it's all about the context of her trip, explaining, 'I think authentic experiences, in summary, is really just being in that place in that moment and experiencing the culture and the surroundings with the people you are with.' Another admitted that there is no possible consensus on what is authentic, saying, 'We all have our own idea of authentic but it's a nebulous concept.' Still another tourist understands that perspective is important, saying, 'What's authentic to the inhabitant and authentic to the tourist do not often match. Honestly if I get right down to it, the authentic experience might be boring. It's just peoples' lives, but done in French or taking the metro – I don't know. It's a problematic concept.'

Authenticity, for most tourists interviewed, boils down to a personal question – one of taste, of preferences, of ability, of time. A common theme is that of getting lost or wandering, which is essential to achieving what researchers describe as existential authenticity. In her research, Wang explains that post-modern tourists 'are rather in search of their authentic selves with the aid of activities or toured objects' (Wang, 1999, p. 360). As MacCannell describes, much of these 'accidental irrelevancies' are what make tourism experiences the most memorable or authentic, and can never be planned (2011, p. 73). There is, therefore, no objective authentic experience that these consumers can seek out in the media, though it remains a buzzword in much of the industry.

Authenticity and the media

How then can travel journalism respond to these ideas, to help travelers achieve this existential authenticity, as personal as it may be? Some sites, like Airbnb – which has online guides and a print magazine – are facilitating these conversations. By offering lodging that is framed as more local than a normal hotel, the website has already appealed to the authentic sensibilities of the post-tourist. Their online travel guides, composed of reviews by local hosts, extend this quest for authentic experiences by offering 'insider' information, empowering tourists to push beyond their expectations. A closer look at the guides, however, reveals that most of the top suggestions are, simply, the main attractions that most tourists wouldn't consider local or insider – the top three picks on the lists for sightseeing in Paris, for example, are the Eiffel Tower, the Sacré Coeur Basilica, and the Champs Elysées. Any casual tourist in Paris would instantly recognize these as major tourist sights and not something requiring insider information.

Journalists on authenticity

Journalists, bloggers, and forum contributors, however, attempt to address and demystify these post-modern expectations by speaking about authenticity – but there doesn't seem to be a consensus. One journalist said, 'If I'm writing a destination piece I would try to provide those insider details so that someone can have that local experience. Everybody has to address that now because it's a big trend.' The trend, however, seems to amount to little more than finding the right synonym for the idea as one journalist explained, saying, 'We like to do secret, underground, alternative. Alternative and insider are big buzz words for us.' The problem, I argue, with trying to provide information that will help post-tourists is that there is no standard by which to measure authenticity. Aware of this difficulty, a journalist described her process for trying to provide information that would be truly useful for those seeking to experience a city as a post-tourist:

> I choose [experiences] because you remember what it's like visiting a city for the first time. Yes, you want to see the Coliseum in Rome, but at the same time you want to find that little pizzeria where they only speak the local dialect and really immerse yourself. When you're choosing places, you do half and half.

This strategy allows travel journalism to act in a post-modern context, to provide a larger scope of information instead of trying to adhere to some modern notion of 'authentic' that doesn't exist. More importantly, however, journalists are aware of their position as local experts who understand a destination intimately. As one journalist said,

> To me authenticity is knowing the scene and being able to say, OK, among all the things happening in a big city, these are the interesting ones. It's a sense of scope and being able to pick out what's the most intriguing.

Likewise, another journalist addressed the importance of not just knowing the location, but also the audience. 'I guess it depends on who is giving you the direction or the assignment and look at who the audience is. Sometimes you know what is best for the audience, and you'll know what they are ready for,' she said. By putting themselves in their audience's shoes, journalists can attempt to gauge the relevance of an experience to the specific tourists they are targeting. Whether or not all travel journalists actually sympathize with their audiences in such a way is a question that might run contrary to Bourdieu's idea of taste, and the taste-makers who impose their values. He proposes that the new bourgeoisie – be it tourism executives or journalists – have an agenda. He writes, 'Through their slyly imperative advice and the example of their consciously "model" life-style, the new taste-makers propose a morality which boils down to an art of consuming, spending and enjoying' (Bourdieu, 1984, p. 311). It becomes relevant, then, to ask whether most journalists are simply pushing the idea of 'authentic travel' as a model, or whether it's something tourists are universally – or actively – aware of seeking anymore, or if it's achieved the cultural value of an Eiffel Tower keychain or snow globe.

Bloggers on authenticity

Matters of taste aside, it's on this idea of delivering a certain kind of information to post-tourists that journalists collide with bloggers, who are essentially aiming to provide a version of insider experiences. One blogger explains that she is aware of the variety of readers who may come to her blog:

> You have the tourists that want to tick off the boxes. Then you have the tourists who want to know the Paris that most people don't know. Then you have the layer of people who have been to Paris so many times that they couldn't care less about the hot spots and just want to find the little oddities.

In the same spirit, another blogger emphasizes her role in mediating a local version of Paris for her readers:

> In that sense, that's exactly what the blog and I do – bring a local perspective and give advice on where to go, where to spend your money, what to eat and drink, how to act. Travelers come here and they want to see and experience Paris like they live here.

But bloggers, even more than journalists, eschew the touristy components of their destination, often vehemently.

> It frustrates me because if you want to follow the cliché path of Paris and eat at the big names, then go. But that's not what I am about. I don't succumb to the highest rated restaurant. I like to find the little gems.

This idea that the touristy is somehow repugnant surfaces more often among some bloggers, who position themselves against a classic, touristy view of the city. One blogger explained her approach, saying, 'Perhaps some of these American websites may be more interested in what they call authentic Paris, an *Amélie*-esque vision of Montmartre, the Moulin Rouge – and I don't think that's authentic. It's am embalmed vision of Paris. A Disneyland.' What these blogs illustrate is not an ignorance of the realities of the post-tourist, but arguably the continued diversification of travel information made possible by the web (Pirolli, 2016). Tourists – post-modern or not – are not beholden to a limited pool of resources, but can and do cast a wide net through various search engines and social media research, and no single media source has to provide them all that they need or seek.

Forum contributors on authenticity

Part of that net will usually cover travel forums, notably those on TripAdvisor, which often appear at the top of search engine results for a specific experience. These forums, as opposed to journalists and bloggers, do not always sell a dream image of a destination. They offer practical insight into travel experiences that, as many commentators reveal, often runs counter to the rosy images painted elsewhere in the media. Many of these individuals paint a more realistic – often downbeat – image for their readers. The advantage of these sites, however, is that commentators can respond to individual comments by responding to a thread that a user might post. Information is not necessarily solicited, and forums allow many different voices to express their views more democratically. As one TripAdvisor contributor explained, 'There isn't a one size fits all solution', which is why these forums are attractive to tourists. This extremely personal interaction between a self-described expert and a consumer is an impressive departure from traditional travel media.

The interactions can often be contentious. One contributor described how she sometimes suggests experiences contrary to what tourists think they want:

> I'm kind of known as the bubble buster. What I tell them is that what you want is the postcard picture. What you think you want, well I can tell you where to get it. If you want to live in a less touristy area, around République or Bastille, OK fine, but they're not going to like it.

And still another contributor expressed his realistic approach to TripAdvisor, downplaying requests for information leading to 'authentic' experiences, which he equates with request for 'non-touristy' experiences. For him anything that appears on a travel website is, by nature, touristy, rendering these demands inherently impossible. He said: 'If you don't want to go where the tourists are, don't take any of the restaurant recommendations [on TripAdvisor]. If you are getting a rec for something non-touristy, then by definition it's already touristy because it's written by tourists.' But like bloggers and journalists, these commentators do reflect on their audiences, trying to cater to their needs. In the forum it is easier, because users can share their specific situation. One contributor said that this is always a consideration, saying, 'It depends what kind of person is asking and what kind of visit it is for them.' This allows contributors to provide tailored information that other users can then read, to understand more transparently why a certain experience was suggested to a certain person, featuring a thread of comments from other users as well. This sort of information, if consumers are willing to sift through it, helps empower them to experiment and push further afield than they normally might.

While information providers give tourists a variety of information, it's impossible to say that any one source leads to a more 'authentic' experience than another. Travel journalism gets caught up in shades of 'authenticity', 'local', and 'traditional' among other jargon that journalists often employ carelessly without context. Travelers will find their own experience, usually without any planning whatsoever, often by allowing themselves to be guided by local knowledge – a hotel concierge, an Airbnb host, a local tour guide. I argue, however, that mediating some concept of authenticity is ultimately an impossible task, but that writers can help orient readers in a general direction or inspire them somehow, to nuance their travels in true post-tourist fashion, to look critically at, but well beyond, the touristy experiences that will inevitably occupy them.

Steps towards interacting with audiences

In trying to achieve these experiences and providing what consumers need and want, how can travel journalists move forward with their readers? I argue that two main practices are developing that journalists need to integrate into their routines.

Interact with audiences

First, there should be some level of two-way interaction between journalists and their public. Journalists need to embrace these conversations, to help understand what readers want and to help provide pertinent information while also identifying knowledge gaps among their readers that they as journalists can fill. Second, journalists need to take a cue from other types of journalism that are already integrating social media with their articles – be it a tweet from a US president or a TripAdvisor comment from an everyday citizen. Using social media as sources, featuring it in story packages, and curating users' content is maybe not *the* solution, but is certainly *a* solution to the combativeness expressed by many travel journalists interviewed. A more critical approach to this content is also needed, to avoid the homogeneity created by the increasing prevalence of online sources used by journalists, as suggested by Duffy (2016).

Journalists' role as gatekeepers of the tourism industry and tourist experiences has been eroded in many ways by social media. The rise of blogs and review sites like TripAdvisor, as well as user-generated sites like Wikivoyage and the unrelated Wikitravel, has given a greater say to individuals directly who want to create or edit travel content. Audiences are informing audiences, and journalists have expressed a lack of desire to engage in these conversations. Professionals, however, are beginning to exhibit some practices that put them in contact with their audiences directly, opening up new possibilities for their work (Broersma and Graham, 2012; Groshek and Tandoc, 2017).

One of the more popular ways that some journalists are doing this is by live Twitter events. Already discussed as effective tools for educating students by allowing openness and feedback with peers, these lessons about live Twitter chats can easily apply to a travel context (Hitchcock and Young, 2016). One journalist participates actively in them, illustrating a willingness to converse with not just tourists, but also industry actors. Live Twitter events are usually scheduled by a host – often by tourism industry actors – but can logically be led directly by a journalist or media brand as well, after advertising the event, and often with a designated hashtag (#TravelTuesday, #HolidayChat, #TravelChat). Formats vary, but typically an organizer begins the chat with a question and then the public responds, using the designated hashtag to keep connected to the conversation. Through these types of events, unexpected voices can appear, and unheard-of experiences can come to light as Twitter users from around the world weigh in on the topics.

While not a yet a pervasive practice in the tourism industry, and restricted to Twitter, it is a clear example of how journalists can engage with their audiences. As the participating journalist said, she began joining in live Twitter events originally to build her Twitter following. Now, however, she uses it as an outlet to interact with and find other experts both in her field and beyond:

> Audience members who participate, in a lot of them, it's just the same travel bloggers talking to each other, which doesn't seem particularly useful. I like to go on non-travel chats like #BrandChat or #adweekchat and add my expertise to the conversation as a travel expert.

For her and other experts, this networking possibility opened up new points of view beyond their own social media bubbles, which could have positive consequences for her travel journalism overall.

Verify and curate user content

The second way that travel journalists could engage with social media is through verifying and then curating user-generated content, following Duffy's suggestion. He writes that while journalism provides professional standards, and Web 2.0 provides social standards, 'a hybrid will be recognizable neither as professional newsroom nor as amateur social media, but a new species with features of both' (Duffy, 2016, p. 173). American travel guide *Fodor's* attempted something in this vein when they posted TripAdvisor comments from the web in their printed guides. Such an example, however, is less a hybrid and more a failed graft, where the comments did not fit the content of the guide. Instead, journalists can use social media in more proactive ways, to find scoops from blogs, to take the temperature of an experience using TripAdvisor, and to identify misinformation or misrepresentation when necessary. As watchdogs, journalists need to be able to spot fake content as well as good content. The example in the previous chapter of the Instagrammer who used Photoshop on her images is just one example of how travel journalists can engage with social media as watchdogs. They can verify certain anecdotes or information provided by users, helping steer audiences clear of inaccurate reports or suggestions. Such a position is increasingly important now as fake news plagues journalism, and travel journalists should not consider their profession exempt from these alarming trends.

Moving forward

This chapter, rather ambitiously, sketches out how relationships between travel journalists and their audiences could evolve. Consumers, tourists, users – however we label them – are becoming more active in their pursuit of information and in their own content creation. Professional media needs to embrace these changes in order to continue to provide relevant information to their audiences. While post-tourists are still seeking some degree of authenticity in their travels, the definition is fluid, and they are still looking for the typical tourist experience traditionally on offer in a destination. Journalists can orient them in these quests, but bloggers and other social media users can as well.

What journalists provide is some level of consistency and trust that social media lacks – the professional standards described by Duffy (2016). In the future, travel journalists should, I argue, apply these professional standards to social media, extending conversations through Twitter, for example. They can talk with audiences to understand what authentic means to them. They should also accept a watchdog role, helping consumers identify erroneous information on social media, in order to demonstrate that they are experts, engaged with the tourism industry and the destinations that they are covering. While such assertions are ambitious, they are hardly prescriptive or all-encompassing – nor set in stone. As the sharing economy evolves, for example, the tourism industry will shift in new directions, and travel journalists may find themselves writing about specific Airbnb properties instead of specific hotels, as some writers are already doing. Preparing to be flexible for these changes and learning to use social media as a credible source are major challenges for travel journalism in a digital age.

References

Anderson, C. W. (2011). Deliberative, agonistic, and algorithmic audiences: Journalism's vision of its public in an age of audience transparency. *International Journal of Communication*, 5, 529–547.

Benkler, Y. (2006). *The wealth of networks*. New Haven, CT: Yale University Press.

Bourdieu, P. (1984). *Distinction: A social critique of the judgement of taste*. Cambridge, MA: Harvard University Press.

Broersma, M. and Graham, T. (2012). Social media as beat. *Journalism Practice*, 6(3), 403–419.

Bruns, A. (2005). *Gatewatching: Collaborative online news production*. New York: Peter Lang.

Bruns, A. (2008). *Blogs, Wikipedia, Second Life, and beyond: From production to produsage*. New York: Peter Lang.

Chang, J.-C. (2007). Travel motivations of package tour travellers. *Tourism*, 55(2), 157–176.

Cocking, B. (2009). Travel journalism: Europe imagining the Middle East. *Journalism Studies*, 10(1), 54–68.

Cohen, E. (1988). Authenticity and commoditization in tourism. *Annals of Tourism Research*, 15, 371–386.

Cohen, E., and Cohen, S. A. (2012). Authentication: Hot and cool. *Annals of Tourism Research*, 39(3), 1–27.

Domingo, D., Quandt, T., Heinonen, A., Paulussen, S., Singer, J. B., and Vujnovic, M. (2008). Participatory journalism practices in the media and beyond: An international comparative study of initiatives in online newspapers. *Journalism Practice*, 2(3), 326–342.

Domingo, D. (2011). Managing audience participation. In J. B. Singer, A. Hermida, D. Domingo, T. Quandt, A. Heinonen, S. Paulussen, and M. Vujnovic (Eds.), *Participatory journalism: Guarding open gates at online newspapers* (pp. 76–95). Chichester: Wiley-Blackwell.

Duffy, A. (2015). The road more travelled: How user-generated content can lead to homogenized travel journalism. *Continuum*, 29(6), 821–832.

Duffy, A. (2016). How social media offers opportunities for growth in the traditional media industry: The case of travel journalism. In V. Beson, R. Tuninga, and G. Saridakis (Eds.), *Analyzing the strategic role of social networking in firm growth and productivity* (pp. 172–187). Hershey, PA: IGI Global.

Fürsich, E. (2010). Media and the representation of others. *International Social Science Journal*, 61(199), 113–130.

Groshek, J. and Tandoc, E. (2017). The affordance effect: Gatekeeping and (non)reciprocal journalism on Twitter. *Computers in Human Behavior*, 66, 201–210.

Hermida, A. (2010) Twittering the news: The emergence of ambient journalism. *Journalism Practice*, 4(3), 297–308.

Hitchcock, L. I., and Young, J. A. (2016). Tweet, tweet!: Using live Twitter chats in social work education. *Social Work Education*, 35(4), 457–468.

Huang, W. J., Norman, W. C., Hallo, J. C., Mcgehee, N. G., McGee, J., and Goetcheus, C. L. (2014). Serendipity and independent travel. *Tourism Recreation Research*, 39(2), 169–183.

Jørgensen, F. A. (2014). The armchair traveler's guide to digital environmental humanities. *Environmental Humanities*, 4(1), 95–112.

Kovach, B., and Rosenstiel, T. (2007). *The elements of journalism: What newspeople should know and the public should expect*. New York: Three Rivers Press.

Loosen, W., and Schmidt, J. H. (2012). (Re-) discovering the audience: The relationship between journalism and audience in networked digital media. *Information, Communication and Society*, 15(6), 867–887.

Loosen, W., and Schmidt, J. H. (2017). Including the audience in journalism. In B. Franklin and S. Eldridge (Eds.), *The Routledge companion to digital journalism studies* (pp. 354–363). Abingdon: Routledge.

MacCannell, D. (1976). *The tourist: A new theory of the leisure class*. Berkeley: University of California Press.

MacCannell, D. (2011). *The ethics of sightseeing*. Berkeley: University of California Press.

Pirolli, B. (2016). Travel information online: Navigating correspondents, consensus, and conversation. *Current Issues in Tourism*, doi:10.1080/13683500.2016.1273883

Singer, J. (2014). User-generated visibility: Secondary gatekeeping in a shared media space. *New Media and Society*, 16(1), 55–73.

Steward, J. (2005). 'How and where to go': The role of travel journalism in Britain and the evolution of foreign tourism, 1840–1914. In John Walton (Ed.), *Histories of tourism: Representation, identity and context* (pp. 39–54). Clevedon: Channel View Publications.

Taylor, C. (1991). *The ethics of authenticity*. Cambridge, MA: Harvard University Press.

Trilling, L. (1974). *Sincerity and authenticity*. Cambridge, MA: Harvard University Press.

Urry, J., and Larsen, J. (2011). *The tourist gaze 3.0*. London: Sage.

Van der Wurff, R., and Schönbach, K. (2011). Between profession and audience: Ccodes of conduct and transparency as quality instruments for off-and online journalism. *Journalism Studies*, 12(4), 407–422.

Wang, N. (1999). Rethinking authenticity in tourism experience. *Annals of Tourism Research*, 26(2), 349–370.

6

WRITING ONLINE

Suggestions and considerations

Travel writing and journalism as craft

I had just finished revising a travel guide when the editor wrote me an email asking about a list of cafés in the book. The list purported to name the top cafés in Paris, and I made a few changes to keep it fresh. She wanted to know if these were really the best cafés in Paris. If not, could I provide some new suggestions. In a foggy haze of having worked on this guide for weeks, I responded with a long-winded email, proclaiming that trying to name the ten best cafés was a fruitless task because most cafés are inherently unremarkable. They are simply neighborhood hangouts that sell mediocre coffee and food. The places on the list were a mix of old and new, touristy and less-touristy, frilly and simple. I personally didn't go to most of them, but many were popular among tourists, our main audience. But what made the best café anyway?

After another email exchange, we established that ultimately there would be no criteria for the list other than they be places worth visiting. In my estimate, any establishment that will serve you coffee was worth a visit, so it became harder to narrow down the 7,000 or so Parisian cafés to just ten. The very notion of 'top' or 'best' became an ornament devoid of any meaning whatsoever as we simply slotted cafés into the list to show a healthy geographic spread around the city, ultimately making a more attractive map to run with the list on the guide's pages.

This is the way of much travel journalism in the twenty-first century. Buzzwords, keywords, and taglines often replace meaningful descriptions and explanations. Storytelling takes a back seat to top ten lists and bite-sized chunks of information. The internet is only amplifying these changes. Those buzzwords have now become ways to optimize content in order to reach audiences through search engines like Google. Lists and round-ups are increasingly shareable items on Facebook and Twitter, facilitating an easy read for hurried audiences on tiny screens. The point is that travel journalism is not just changing in terms of audiences and financing, but also on a lexicological level. We need to think how our words, their positioning, and their overall structure into articles – or lists – manage to reach audiences.

As discussed in Chapter 1, travel journalism stems from a long history of writing, inspired by ships' logs, diaries, personal correspondence, and scientific discovery. Journalistic elements discussed in the previous two chapters underscore how travel journalism differs from travel writing, with elements like news values, objectivity, and other ethical implications. Travel journalism, as I explain to my students, is still *journalism*, with sources, research, and news hooks featuring in stories. These and other journalistic elements separate the travel journalist from the travel writer (Greenman, 2012, p. 8). Despite its best efforts, however, professional travel journalism will always face challenges. Carl Thompson suggests that 'even forms of travel writing that strive for accuracy and objectivity offer only a partial depiction of the world, and an incomplete picture of a far more complex reality' (2011, p. 62). In this chapter, I want to focus on the styles and formats that travel journalists need to be aware of when producing their stories on a more practical level. Understanding how to craft writing for digital publications has added new layers and complexities for professionals. Thinking about how stories will be shared online, how they will perform with search engines, and how they can reach global audiences are just a few of the ways that digital travel journalists need to adapt to an online environment.

When it comes to writing, non-fiction narrative writing guides abound, as any quick online search will confirm. Blundell's *The Art and Craft of Feature Writing*, based on the *Wall Street Journal*'s style guide, has been a solid reference since the 1980s. Zinsser's *On Writing Well* tackles different genres, with a chapter dedicated to travel writing. There is arguably little excuse today for travel journalists to have substandard style and storytelling skills. Writing is an art, but as Zinsser argues, 'Anybody who can think clearly can write clearly, about any subject at all' (2001, p. x). Perhaps his view is a bit optimistic, but this chapter goes beyond sentence structure and narrative, which journalism students and practitioners arguably should have mastered if reading this book.

Journalism manuals also instruct aspiring professionals how to choose their words. The problem is that these handbooks so often focus on the structural elements of the profession, like leads and sources. When it comes to discussing the minutiae of travel journalism, however, there is little guidance on just how to choose the right words or what is considered good writing. Greenman's *Introduction to Travel Journalism* doesn't go much further beyond stressing the importance of basic structure, following subjects with verbs, and revising drafts thoroughly (2012, p. 81). Any adherent to Strunk and White's *Elements of Style* could probably identify common issues in a travel publication, but most critiques are subjective at best. Instead of trying to dictate a style for travel journalists in a digital age, this chapter seeks to suggest ways to be mindful when composing travel stories for professional media online. Magazines and websites should provide their own style guides for what they accept and refuse. Instead, I want to look at practices highlighted by journalists in interviews that could apply to a travel journalist working for any publication, in order to raise their writing to the highest possible level while also being versatile. Some indications are timeless recommendations that continue to resurface as more and more writers across a spectrum of ability publish online. Others are specific to changes brought on by the internet, which will help digital travel journalists think about the environment that their work will inhabit.

SEO

First, several journalists interviewed lament having to engage with meeting the demands of search engine optimization, or SEO. In short, SEO involves catering to the algorithms of search engines to make an article seem 'friendly' and thus to be placed higher up in the search results. Understandably a website on page 15 of a search results list has less chance of being viewed than a website on the first page, and research illustrates how websites benefit from both building links and social media to improve their traffic (Zhang, 2017). Thus editors, and by extension journalists, need to be proactive in ensuring that their content is as SEO-friendly as possible so that it manages to appear higher up in search results, ultimately reaching larger audiences. The bottom line is to increase the advertising and sponsorship revenue that keeps online publications afloat. Dan Gillmor, in discussing the changing face of journalism education, argues that business practices – including marketing, social media, and search engine optimization – need to be a part of degree programs (2016, p. 816). Such an argument easily includes study programs targeting travel journalists who, due to their commercial interests, would benefit from a stronger business background. Search engine optimization is just one example of such an extended education.

While many travelers report using search engines as their primary method of research, journalists have to consider how their articles will reach their audiences (Pirolli, 2016). To that end, specific keywords, phrases, or formats become necessary to include in their articles, and many journalists resent these new rules, viewing them more as limitations. Their responses echo authors who suggest that some print journalists initially thought that SEO 'renders copy dry and formulaic', despite ultimately being necessary to maintain relevancy in an online world (Richmond, 2008, p. 52).

As far as journalists are concerned, this does not yet mean having to understand SEO and algorithms beyond acknowledging the basics. These considerations often fall to the editors or marketing teams to help identify the terms, keywords, and tags best used on a journalist's story. For example, one online magazine's content management system that I wrote for simply notifies writers that their articles are not suitable in terms of SEO, administering a grade, as if in school. In order to get top marks, and to be able to publish the story in question, the system recommends changes that could be as simple as including a keyword ('Paris', 'spa', 'budget') in the first sentence instead of the third. This level of automation allows journalists to work more organically – for the moment – and to tweak their writing later in the process.

Some SEO, however, guides journalists more directly. Editors may ask a journalist, for example, to write a certain story because a topic or a story format happens to be popular at the moment. As audiences start increasingly searching on certain terms, research teams and third-party applications purchased by a publication will translate this data to the editorial teams and trickle it down to journalists. Journalists may often not even be aware that they are writing a certain article on the basis of catering to search engines, but editors report actively taking these things into consideration. As one editor at *Time Out* explained,

> We need the audience and the stats to get the ads to pay our staff to be able to exist. The type of content and the way in which we present it online – there are formats known for getting bigger amounts of traffic.

Journalists, therefore, need to question and understand what these formats are – maybe top ten lists, neighborhood round-ups, seasonal pieces – in order to understand how individual publications can benefit from them. Not all SEO-friendly formats will produce the same results for every publication. Still, it became obvious that SEO was a guiding factor when several publications asked me for a list of day trips from Paris in the same year, reflecting an uptick in audience searches for this particular theme.

These new considerations are irksome to numerous travel journalists who see it as another form of control on their profession. One journalist likened SEO to a factory, where journalists are pushed only to achieve a maximum number of clicks. While SEO often depends on a period of trial and error, different publications have their own ways of implementing SEO rules, and not all publications require massive edits – like the aforementioned content management system that grades its journalists. While hardly restrictive in what kind of content can be published, it may hamper creativity, as one journalist explained, saying, 'You can't have play on words in titles anymore. And part of the pleasure for me is play on words and trying to be clever with sentences. And all of that is being gradually evened out.' Many journalists feel restricted by these new considerations that seem more limiting than simply adhering to a publication's style or voice. The bottom line is gaining readers, but as one journalist lamented, 'I'm writing for Google at the moment.'

Whether it hinders creativity or enhances relevance, or both, SEO is a vital component for travel journalists publishing online. A basic understanding of how it will impact their writing, however, will evolve through conversations with editors of specific publications.

Narrative and first-person writing

Another change that many travel journalists report is a trend towards more personal writing, to get more intimate, to share more of themselves. Journalism, historically, lost its authorial anonymity in the late nineteenth century as magazine writing introduced more of the writer into the writing. A focus on first-person subjectivity, however, has been a growing feature of travel writing for centuries. Thompson writes that 'its starting point was a growing desire, and requirement, to emphasise the traveler's eyewitness status, and so give greater credibility to their report' (2011, p. 98). With social media innovations over the past ten years, the role of eyewitnesses has only become more commonplace in society, allowing citizens and travelers to share their first-person narratives online as easily as only a journalist could once do in print.

While much of travel writing historically is rooted in personal experiences, journalists feel that this style of writing is at odds with standard journalistic practice that has developed over the last two centuries, which typically strives for a more objectively-produced piece of writing. Despite this, Greenman argues that travel writing needs a personal voice, a point of view, and humor, among other elements (2012, pp. 86–87). While bloggers foreground themselves in their writing, journalists still prefer to maintain their distance, despite many editors asking for the opposite. One journalist stressed that she is not writing for herself, saying, 'I'm writing for a publication that has their own thing going on. It's not objective and dry, but it's not about me ultimately.' Her statement echoes those of other journalists who put their publication before themselves, avoiding the first-person narratives that fuel blogs, review sites, and other social media.

Bloggers, on the other hand, don't tiptoe around presenting their views and opinions in their posts. As one blogger said,

> I try to put myself in the text. That's one thing actually that people say, they want more of me. They want to see me. Personal stuff. I can relate because when I read blogs I want to know more about the person and you become a bit obsessed, find out more, learn more.

Journalists, on the other hand, remain much more reserved when it comes to foregrounding themselves in their articles. In travel journalism there is more room for the journalist to participate and share their own perspectives, and they arguably should.

Trends towards more personal writing, however, are challenging the journalistic adhesion to more objective, distanced writing. One journalist, working for a major guidebook company, revealed that her editors urged her to write more personally. She said, 'You can use "I" and "we recommend" this or that – they wanted us to be opinionated and outspoken in our reviews.' Another journalist, in the minority, justified the strides towards more personal writing. 'I adapt totally,' she said. 'They want to know you've been there and you've experienced it and they can trust you, that you haven't just written from a press release.' As Duffy points out, travel journalists should learn how to incorporate their own voices with the voices of others, to show that they have been there but that others live there, too. In discussing how to educate travel journalism students, he writes:

> One answer might be to teach students how to report on personal experiences but with a view to others – the reader on behalf of whom they travel, and the

host nation to whom they are indebted for hospitality and the story itself – in order to give the reported experience a depth that takes it beyond solipsism.

(2014, p. 107)

While there is no clear-cut rule, travel journalists are struggling to find a balance between the personality-driven nature of online content and the journalistic tradition of objectivity. More and more, it seems that their writing might be returning to historic forms of travel writing, to essays and journals that foreground the authors and their experiences.

If already grounded in a firm understanding of journalistic norms and theories of objectivity, a travel journalist should be able to include him or herself into their stories without sacrificing professionalism. For one particular piece, an editor asked me to write an article from my perspective as a runner, hitting the pavement in Paris. At first such an approach seemed at odds with my journalistic integrity. The story wasn't about me. It was about the city. Little by little, however, I learned to use my experience as a vehicle to transport the reader through the story. I was a character in the story, but I wasn't the whole story. Travel journalists should increasingly be embracing this sort of narrative storytelling. Such writing, however, usually entails a longer form of journalism, one at odds with another format, the top ten list, that travel media embraces wholeheartedly, especially online.

Top ten lists

While not related directly to words, but more to structure, the top ten list has become a mainstay of travel media and journalism both on and offline. Online, however, it is much easier to publish a list without much justification or context. Websites like Buzzfeed and Thrillist package such lists, highlighting the best restaurants in a destination or the must-see attractions. Buzzfeed has been a catalyst for online lists, and has switched from mostly 'listicles' to actual news coverage since its launch in 2006 (Tandoc and Jenkins, 2017). Dorling Kindersley have even devoted an entire guidebook series to the top ten of selected destinations. Such guides, while compact and easily digestible, don't always provide much in the way of a rationale for their rankings, leaving readers to trust them implicitly or take them with an enormous grain of salt. The format, however, is extremely friendly to the internet where it can be adapted effortlessly to video or audio content, making it an attractive option for any publication to produce easy, shareable content.

Some journalists, however, have engaged in ranking responsibly, such as those in France's *Figaro* newspaper. They often run stories about the best food items in Paris, like the top eclairs or madeleines. While ultimately subjective, journalists go to certain lengths to package their rankings along with clear criteria, explaining the methodology to audiences. Such journalists – like those of the popular *US News and World Report* university rankings in the United States – practice the transparency that is required of journalists. While these formats can make an impact (see

Meredith, 2004), many journalists are critical of them, underscoring their often-arbitrary nature.

To that end, travel journalists who embrace the list format, useful as it may be, should consider how they can best be transparent with their readers about how such a list was produced. What criteria did they use? Was it just a question of taste? Of access? Of geographic significance? Of course, the level of transparency will ultimately depend on the publication's editors, but the ubiquitous nature of lists – or listicles, as they are often called in the industry – lowers their value. Longer lists, like the 50 foods to eat in Budapest or the 100 things to do in Paris, push the bounds of typical top ten lists, and could risk seeming trite and forced simply in order to attract readers. At the same time they could provide useful information. As long as they are updated and maintained regularly, such lists can become successful perennial content for travel websites. Ultimately, the more detailed the list's title and accompanying text are, the more likely it is to seem credible to audiences.

The bottom line, I'd argue, is that lists need context. Journalists should be forthcoming about why a certain restaurant or hotel is the best or in a top ten list. Too often, publications will alter a list to include sponsor properties alongside others chosen by journalists. This sort of reporting blurs the lines between journalism and advertising, upending the legitimacy that lifestyle journalists struggle to maintain.

Clichés and stereotypes

Zinsser wrote, 'The race in writing is not to the swift but to the original' (2001, p. 35). Travel journalism, whether written or spoken, is often victim to the 'trite, overused, hackneyed' expressions, like those listed in a 2015 round-up of clichés (Perlman, 2015). Existing research on cliché in tourism uncovers how the industry employs certain phrases or images (see Voase, 2000 or Daan, 2001). Travel journalists, however, need to think critically about whether they need to engage with clichés or if they can do without. Clichés come in many forms, but are 'merely reductions of a formulaic expression' (Beller and Leerssen, 2007, p. 297). In travel journalism, faced with the complexities of making the unfamiliar familiar, it is all too easy to rely on well-known phrases to avoid having to spend a few extra words describing exactly why something really is the way we perceive it to be.

Journalists often use certain words or phrases while unaware that they are clichés. Some of the most common include 'hidden gem' to describe something allegedly unknown to most people, or 'Mecca' in reference to something that's a huge draw for a certain group of people, as in 'a Mecca for foodies'. Both sound perfectly acceptable to the untrained ear, but reading enough travel journalism will reveal how often such clichés sneak into even the most mainstream, professional outlets:

Travel to a hidden gem, the Banteay Chhmar temple.

(CNN, 26 October 2017)

it's a hidden gem of exceptional scale and beauty.

(Daily Mail, *24 October 2017*)

Despite the top-notch facilities, this remains a hidden gem.

(Guardian, *13 June 2016*)

The Japanese city being hailed as hidden vegan gem.

(Independent, *9 May 2017*)

The idea of a hidden gem fails to describe what the journalist is actually trying to say, and readers understand the absurdity of the cliché. One comment at the end of the *Independent*'s article mentions, rather sarcastically, 'Don't tell people this, it's a hidden gem!' Audiences might swallow clichés if not given a chance, but they are equally prepared to mock journalists who have no qualms about taking the easy road in their stories. They are a hallmark of what professionals would label bad writing. Some of it, unfortunately, may stem from SEO, though it is unlikely that people would search 'hidden gem London' or 'shopping mecca Kyoto.' Thanks to SEO, words like 'secret', 'hidden', or 'unusual' might lead to more concrete results, instead of a website on some little-known English sapphire located at Trafalgar Square.

While clichés may often be harmless, outside of damaging a writer's credibility, stereotypes carry weight, creating beliefs about groups of people. Such beliefs may lead to negative attitudes, or prejudice (Stroebe and Insko, 1989). Walter Lippmann rationalized stereotypes, stating bluntly, 'For the attempt to see all things freshly and in detail, rather than as types and generalities, is exhausting, and among busy affairs practically out of the question' (1922, p. 88). I'll explore these ideas in more detail in Chapter 11 when I discuss how some online tools may actually help fight stereotyping. When producing content, however, journalists should be mindful that the clichés they might write could be reinforcing stereotypes. 'Rude French waiters' and 'ugly American tourists' are clichés that perpetuate unfair stereotypes that could have real-life implications for the interactions between travelers and their host countries. Steering away from clichés in the first place is way to act more responsibly as a travel journalist.

Professionals need to think critically about their words and descriptions to make sure that creative license doesn't accidentally lead to reinforcing a cultural stereotype for their readers. Good travel writing, according to Holland and Huggan, 'becomes available as an instrument with which we can begin to refine, revise, and deconstruct the clichés that have reduced zones of great historical range and cultural complexity to a clutch of "instant" images and one-dimensional stereotypes' (2003, p. 110). Moreover, as a brand of consumer journalism, travel journalists should, ideally, be describing the product as clearly as possible. Therefore, using a cliché or stereotype is a sort of false advertising that, in distorting a destination or its people, misrepresents the very product – idea, experience, destination, whatever it may be – that we are trying to convince consumers is worthwhile. Anyone can drone on about how 'awful British food is' and that the Sagrada Família is a 'true gem', but a real travel journalist will be able to go beyond these stereotypes and clichés to share a concrete truth. Travel journalism needs to address audiences as consumers, and a consumer can't really make an informed decision when the language is vague and repetitive (Hanusch and Fürsich, 2014).

Cultural relatability

Having written about Paris for publications based in the US, UK, Hong Kong, and France, I have learned the pitfalls of not switching my keyboard to British English or writing 'flat' when 'apartment' would be better suited for readers. While always writing in English, I had to remember constantly that my readers were not all American-born, and that my cultural upbringing did not translate across the globe, no matter how far Hollywood and Starbucks reached.

Through my interviews with other writers, something that they all reflect on – from journalists to review site contributors – is their audience. Online media has globalized the information market place, which, as will be discussed in Chapter 11, presents challenges for anyone publishing on the web. That is, content providers cannot be sure who will click on their websites, and thus need to be accessible to readers from around the world. A brand like US-based *Travel+Leisure* can no longer operate on the assumption that readers are predominantly American because readers anywhere in the world can access their website. While many studies look at globalization's effects on journalism (e.g. Thurman, 2007; Cottle, 2009), the effects on travel journalism more specifically remain poorly understood. What is clear, for the moment, however, is that English-speaking travel journalists need to be careful to write or speak in a more global English, to ensure comprehension wherever audiences live.

Whereas local journalists writing about regional or even national affairs may not have to worry so much about foreigners reading their stories, travel journalists' topics can easily appeal to global audiences. An article about Paris written by an American will appeal to anyone worldwide seeking to travel to France, and the author's nationality likely has little bearing on that. The words used, however – whether written or spoken – can quickly cause confusion as not all tourism con-sumers speak the same language, even though they might appear to. A seemingly clever cultural reference to can leave readers scratching their heads. A common word could resonate poorly with some cultures. Imagine how a statement about 'stubbing out fags in Paris' might raise American eyebrows, while British audiences wouldn't think twice about it. Keeping the audience in mind is paramount for a travel journalist, and in a digital world, the audience we cater to is as diverse as ever.

Furthermore, beyond cultural references and word choice, travel journalists need to be aware that different cultures have different expectations and tastes. As such, writing needs to be more precise than ever. A 'small hotel room' for a North American may seem palatial to a Londoner. When discussing travel writing and travelogues, Thompson states, 'All travel writing must be to some degree ethnocentric' (2011, p. 149). The degree of superiority one culture feels over another, however, often manifests itself in negative criticisms that are not valid for everyone. Through the inevitable process of othering, travel journalists addressing a global audience – at least in English – can potentially turn away readers who share a language but not a cultural framework. Travel journalism, therefore, needs to engage constantly with expressing clearly how its practitioners evaluate and critique experiences.

TripAdvisor users interviewed in this study are keenly tuned into these factors, in part because TripAdvisor profiles clearly indicate the person's nationality. These indicators help guide their posts, as the reviewer explained. 'For reviews, you just read them and you can tell right away where they are from, if they are European than North American – my tastes are more European. I don't want to be in an international chain – that's comforting for an American', she said. On TripAdvisor, it's easy to skip to the next reviewer who may share a cultural framework, but if a travel story in a major publication alienates a reader somehow, it's not certain that they will stay on the site instead of clicking away to another brand's publication.

Such challenges force travel journalists to adhere to the old adage of show, don't tell. Clear, descriptive writing understandable to a wider audience is preferable to language that requires certain cultural filters to decipher. Like the limitations imposed by SEO, such considerations may stamp out a certain creativity that travel journalists formerly appreciated, but it's a practical consideration that professionals must make. There is no advantage to alienating readers, so taking a more international approach to their language is a way for travel journalists to maintain a voice of authority in the media landscape.

Suggestions, not restrictions

Travel writing is an increasingly personal endeavor, with expectations of authenticity justifying a more author-led approach in articles (Pirolli, 2014). Unlike bloggers, however, travel journalists can't just write their stories without the research and reporting that defines much of what journalism is. Moreover, if they want their stories to be read – or viewed, or heard – they need to understand that reaching audiences is not an immediately organic affair. Tailoring stories to meet the requirements of search engine optimization and an increasingly globalized audience are just a few of the new challenges that weigh on digital journalists of all genres.

Travel journalists, given the universal appeal of their topics, are arguably some of the most exposed journalists to global audiences. Thinking critically about their word choice, their cultural references, and their audiences are steps towards contributing more effectively to conversations about a destination in English. Of course, Bulgarian travel writers may not need to be so universal in their approach, but English-speaking content providers face these realities. Maintaining a healthy dialogue with editors will help ensure content is tailored to the publication's needs, allowing journalists to stay up to date with factors affecting search engine optimization. By all of this, I don't suggest that journalists should avoid being creative and original, that they should simply follow data provided by editors and marketing teams. There is still an inherent value in telling a story about a little-known destination that may not be a highly-searched term. Still, there are usually ways to work with editors to make sure that stories are relevant, so that they reach the widest possible online audiences.

Above all, travel journalists need to avoid cliché and stereotypes in an era when there is already an excessive amount of information available about most destinations. If travel journalists are to maintain their relevance in an online world, they need to keep the bar raised by providing stories and writing – either in text form or in video scripts – that goes beyond the bland and the clichéd. This requires reading travel writing by expert and upcoming authors. It requires reading blogs and review sites to parse through both good and bad examples of user-generated content. It requires opening oneself up to criticism by editors and audiences to understand what kind of writing works and what doesn't. Not every travel article will be a brilliant example of prose or Pulitzer-prize winning story, but I suggest that travel journalists need to make that their goal, however unattainable, if they are to remain authorities in an already-saturated information environment.

References

Beller, M., and Leerssen, J. T. (2007). *Imagology: The cultural construction and literary representation of national characters: A critical survey.* Amsterdam: Rodopi.

Cottle, S. (2009). Journalism and globalization. In K. Wahl-Jorgensen and T. Hanitzsch (Eds.), *The handbook of journalism studies* (pp. 341–356). New York: Routledge.

Dann, G. M. (2001). The self-admitted use of cliché, in the language of tourism. *Tourism Culture and Communication*, 3(1), 1–14.

Duffy, A. M. (2014) First-person singular: Teaching travel journalism in the time of TripAdvisor. In E. Fürsich and F. Hanusch (Eds.), *Travel journalism: Exploring production, impact and culture.* Basingstoke: Palgrave Macmillan.

Gillmor, D. (2016). Towards a new model for journalism education. *Journalism Practice*, 10(7), 815–819.

Greenman, J. (2012). *Introduction to travel journalism: On the road with serious intent.* New York: Peter Lang.

Hanusch, F., and Fürsich, E. (Eds.). (2014). *Travel journalism: Exploring production, impact and culture.* Basingstoke: Palgrave Macmillan. Holland, P., and Huggan, G. (2003). *Tourists with typewriters.* Ann Arbor: University of Michigan Press.

Isaac, M. S., and Schindler, R. M. (2013). The top-ten effect: Consumers' subjective categorization of ranked lists. *Journal of Consumer Research*, 40(6), 1181–1202.

Lippmann, W. (1922). *Public opinion.* New York: Harcourt, Brace.

Meredith, M. (2004). Why do universities compete in the ratings game? An empirical analysis of the effects of the US News and World Report college rankings. *Research in Higher Education*, 45(5), 443–461.

Perlman, M. (2015, February 2). Journalism and clichés. *Columbia Journalism Review.* Retrieved from https://archives.cjr.org

Pirolli, B. (2014). Travel journalism in flux: New practices in the blogosphere. In F. Hanusch and E. Fürsich (Eds.), *Travel journalism: Exploring production, impact and culture* (pp. 83–98). Basingstoke: Palgrave Macmillan.

Pirolli, B. (2016). Travel information online: Navigating correspondents, consensus, and conversation. *Current Issues in Tourism*, doi:10.1080/13683500.2016.1273883

Richmond, S. (2008). How SEO is changing journalism. *British Journalism Review*, 19(4), 51–55.

Stroebe, W., and Insko, C. (1989). Stereotype, prejudice, and discrimination: Changing conceptions in theory and research. In D. Bar-Tal, C. F. Graumann, A. W. Kruglanski, and W. Stroebe (Eds.), *Stereotyping and prejudice: Changing conceptions* (pp. 3–34). New York: Springer.

TandocJr, E. C., and Jenkins, J. (2017). The Buzzfeedication of journalism? How traditional news organizations are talking about a new entrant to the journalistic field will surprise you! *Journalism*, 18(4), 482–500.

Thompson, C. (2011). *Travel writing: The new critical idiom*. Abingdon: Routledge.

Thurman, N. (2007). The globalization of journalism online: A transatlantic study of news websites and their international readers. *Journalism*, 8(3), 285–307.

Voase, R. (2000). Explaining the blandness of popular travel journalism: Narrative, cliché and the structure of meaning. In M. Robinson (Ed.), *Expressions of culture, identity and meaning in tourism: Reflections on International Tourism* (pp. 413–424). Sunderland: Centre for Travel and Tourism/Business Education Publishers.

Zhang, S., and Cabage, N. (2017). Search engine optimization: Comparison of link building and social sharing. *Journal of Computer Information Systems*, 57(2), 148–159.

Zinsser, W. (2001). *On writing well: An informal guide to writing nonfiction*. New York: Harper and Row.

7

ENGAGING WITH USER-GENERATED CONTENT FROM TWITTER TO TRIPADVISOR

I pitched an article to my editor about a marathon in France called the Marathon du Médoc. It was a destination piece, describing how this little southwestern corner of the country attracted runners from all over the world each year for a unique event. Far from the most competitive marathon, it was one where participants hydrate on more than just water during the race. Chateaux along the route open their doors to runners, serving up robust red wine, making it a popular race that was becoming even more in-demand as competitive running teetered from a niche sport to a nationwide obsession in France. As I researched my piece, I realized there was a notable lack of runners' voices in it. Sure, I had run it before and could share my perspectives, but my sources shouldn't be limited to my own views if I could help it. The organizers were not willing to hand out names and contact numbers of other races to me, and my running friends knew no one who had raced this particular marathon before. I was running out of options.

It didn't take long for me to remember that it was 2014 and Twitter existed, and a quick search for the 'Marathon du Médoc' revealed numerous discussions among those who had, and who would, run the marathon. I jumped into the conversations, introducing myself, and asking if I could speak briefly with any of these runners who would be in the upcoming race. After following each other's accounts we were able to message each other directly, exchanging contact information, and continuing with a short interview like any traditional journalistic source. By connecting through social media, I was able to source quotes from people who would be traveling from Poland, the US, and India to take part in the event, offering their comments on why they were participating and what they thought about the wine-soaked run.

It's a simple example, but this method of sourcing illustrates how social media can provide pragmatic solutions and unexpected information for journalists. For travel journalists, this method of reaching people in faraway places is especially poignant. Had Twitter not existed, how would I have managed to contact participants who were coming from beyond France for the event? Social networks like Twitter make it both faster and easier, allowing me to apply traditional newsgathering practices to the digital world, as discussed by many authors (e.g. Swasy, 2016). In previous chapters I discussed how many travel journalists resist changes brought on by social media, but in this chapter I argue strongly for an increased awareness of the possibilities of social media for their work. It's not just about connecting with audiences, as discussed in previous chapters, but about opening up the newsgathering process to a larger scope of conversations occurring beyond journalists' usual pool of research.

Wikitravel, Yelp, Hotels.com, online forums – the list of websites publishing travel content and information continues to grow. The number of tools and websites available to travelers online has expanded impressively in the past decade. While most research focuses on how consumers use these tools, few studies look at how they influence lifestyle media, specifically travel journalism (Xiang and Gretzel, 2010; Sigala et al., 2012; Munar and Jacobsen, 2014). How can journalists use these sites to their benefit, and what problems do they pose? I demonstrate that, while user-generated content is often criticized for its lack of veracity, many travelers interviewed claim to be comfortable with it and voice only minor reservations. The argument, therefore, is that journalists should learn to engage more with UGC to go beyond official sources and their own experiences and tap into the potential of social media and other sites. Building on existing research, I'll suggest ways that journalists can work with UGC to produce meaningful content.

I'll start by identifying a few key ways that UGC can help travel journalists in their reporting, speaking first and foremost with journalists. Authors like Duffy have proposed a more hybrid cooperation between professionals and amateurs in order to push travel journalism forward, embracing UGC instead of fighting against it (2016). I have already briefly discussed how *Fodor's*, an American guidebook, collaborated with TripAdvisor a few years ago by publishing selected TripAdvisor comments in its paper guide, indicating a step towards cooperating with the brand that ultimately did not endure. What, then, are the ways travel journalists can benefit from social media?

Journalist need to go farther, albeit cautiously, in engaging UGC. As Hayes et al. (2007) propose, there are three guiding principles that influence journalistic credibility in today's media landscape: authenticity, accountability, and autonomy. Using these concepts as a touchstone, this chapter will explore the relationship between travel journalists and the networks nourished by user-generated content. I'll identify some of the critiques I heard during my interviews on various UGC, including cultural bias, anonymous reviews, and undisclosed motivations that travel journalists need to be aware of when using UGC in their reporting. Pushing further, I will introduce voices from interviews with non-professionals themselves who contribute to blog and review sites, to understand how they add to these conversations. Despite journalists' skepticism of social media, however, the lifestyle and consumer nature of travel journalism needs to embrace the voices of consumers, which are now more accessible than ever.

When user-generated content knocks

Journalism and its relationship with social media has been a near-constant conversation among researchers over the past decade, with multiple studies highlighting the challenges (Bruns, 2005; Robinson, 2011; Singer, 2014). Though I do stress, as Steensen explains more thoroughly than I will here, that the blurring of private and public conversations thanks to social media, and all of the challenges that this presents, is not new to journalism (2016). The intersection of subjectivity and journalism has existed in the form of reportage as far back as Herodotus and more recently in the 'new journalism' of the 1960s (p. 121). Zooming out from these studies, I want to stress why the convergence of journalism and tourism is essential. Henry Jenkins sketched out much of this framework conceptually. Convergence 'represents a cultural shift as consumers are encouraged to seek out new information and make connections among dispersed media content' (Jenkins, 2006, p. 3). This dispersed media, from magazines to review sites, from YouTube to blogs, is slowly finding itself connected as media brands plant themselves across the spectrum of platforms available online. Jenkins further claims that consumption has become a collective process, and the travel industry is a clear example of how convergence culture manifests itself in a specific domain (2006, p. 4). The process of organizing a trip is a multifaceted process that relies on word of mouth as much as various media outlets at different stages of the planning (Pirolli, 2016).

Social media, user-generated content, participatory media – whatever we call it – is playing an ever-greater part in these processes. 'Audiences are making their presence felt by actively shaping media flows, and producers, brand managers, customer service professionals and corporate communicators are waking up to the commercial need to actively listen and respond to them' (Jenkins et al., 2013, p. 2). The authors talk about the idea of 'spreadable media,' which blurs the distinctions between producers, marketers, and audiences (2013, p. 7). This user content, however, has intrinsic value, even if audiences don't consciously create content with such a value in mind. But enterprises have developed ways to build value 'as a side effect of ordinary use of the application' (Naughton, 2012, p. 222). Travel journalism, I would argue, is perhaps waking up slowly to this value. While editors are harvesting metrics and data behind the scenes, journalists on the ground have expressed less interest in engaging with social media content. As my experience with Twitter sources during the Marathon du Médoc reveals, however, the results can be promising.

Looking favorably to UGC

Concretely, UGC offers travel journalists benefits that they may not be aware of or that they may not have standard practices to exploit. For those who do not have extensive social network experience, using the tools for research can seem daunting. For those who do, using them professionally instead of socially may be a hurdle.

Much work has been done on this changing culture. At first glance, social media has been regarded as problematic. 'A networked public sphere, where individuals share, discuss, and contribute to the news, subverts media flows based on the idea of a mass media audience' (Hermida, 2012, p. 311). This subversion, however, has not led to the demise of journalism. Domingo and Heikkilä suggest that social media and networks may be a way towards reinforcing the media's credibility, establishing three normative principles central to media accountability (2012). They describe actor transparency, where journalists need to be clear about who they are and who they work for. Second, they describe production transparency, referring more to how news organizations on a larger scale function. Finally, they stress the importance of responsiveness, including how publications deal with feedback and discussion regarding their content (2012, p. 272).

Pushing further, early research into how journalists operate with networks like Twitter reveal diverse practices. One study of Swedish journalists revealed four distinct profiles of journalists with regard to how they use social media – the social journalist, the skeptic shunners, the pragmatic conformists, and the enthusiastic activists (Hedman and Djerf-Pierre, 2013). These divides fall largely across generational divides, with younger journalists embracing social media more enthusiastically. As the authors write, this activist group 'shares most of the fundamental professional ideals of other journalists, but differs in its approach to audience adaptation and personal branding. It holds the view that the profession must undergo profound changes because of social media' (p. 383). In Chapter 2, I described how travel journalists fall, more or less, into these same categories. Now I want to explore the benefits of social media for journalists' work concretely, to understand why Duffy and others might be calling for more collaboration between travel journalists and audiences in more structured ways. Most of the research on journalism and social media looks at it through a democratic or civil lens, seeing its potential for maintaining values key to an open democracy. These basic tenets, however, can, and arguably should adapt to lifestyle media, including travel journalism. Through the framework of three values described by Hayes et al. (2007) – authenticity, accountability, and autonomy – the rest of this chapter will explore how travel journalists can engage with social media to achieve these values that help grant them credibility in a digital media landscape.

Authenticity: public persona and identity

While in Chapter 5 I discussed authentic experiences, it is also prudent to discuss the notion of authenticity within travel media as it relates to journalism. Authenticity, especially linked to the credibility of an established brand, leads to instant credibility for a journalist, offering them 'a ready-made reputation rather than one that has to be built up word by word, story by story' (Hayes et al., 2007, p. 269). These brands are now, however, being challenged by user-generated content. In their study on *Guardian* journalists, Singer and Ashman observed that 'Journalists felt confident that they took adequate steps to ensure what they wrote was credible, but they felt helpless to either assess or improve the credibility of what users provided' (2009, p. 13). Travel journalists interviewed reveal the same sort of relationship with social media, where it is a challenge that pushes them to create better overall output in light of user-generated content. One journalist said that having a blog and Twitter – in short, a robust social media presence – is indispensable today to give her an air of authenticity.

> Having your blog and Twitter lets people know that you are there, and you are that authority. I can't imagine not having that. When I Googled the other writers in the *Moon* [guidebook] series, I couldn't find some of them. That seems weird in this day and age. You need to be out there.

Several authors, in discussing sensory representations in travel journalism, suggest that knowing the journalist was there gives more value to their experiences, as well as more information to help future travelers make decisions (Pan and Ryan, 2009).

Not all journalists, however, embrace the authenticity-enhancing potential of social media. One individual said that digital writers spend too much time fashioning themselves as brands, focusing less on the writing. He said, 'I believe, or at least claim to believe, that travel writing – or any sort of non-fiction feature writing – needs to have some mystery surrounding it and the author.' This idea of maintaining mystery is a curious one, but it is a practice rooted very much in journalistic traditions of maintaining distance and objectivity. Social media, however, does not necessarily provide a solution to questions of identity and experiences, but may actually drive journalists to be less open. One travel writer explained that she is adamant about privacy and she keeps her personal life to herself because of painful prior experiences where other online commentators made disparaging remarks about her. 'When I was trolled, it really drove it home to me. Having personal attacks … it really made me want to protect that even more.'

While many bloggers are generally upfront about their identities and sharing their lives online, many forum contributors – TripAdvisor and Reddit in this case – are hesitant to share their identities. In the same way as the journalist above removed herself from her writing because of personal attacks, forums and review sites can also create contentious environments. According to one TripAdvisor user,

> There is a huge mob mentality. People are intimidated to say what they think or sometimes they don't say it because everyone else says A and I must be wrong that I think B. You know it, it's not freedom of speech. What is really interesting is that it's controlled by the mob. If people disagree they get your post removed.

Another TripAdvisor user echoed these ideas, explaining that she has learned from past errors how to behave in the forums. She explained, 'I feel like I am opening myself up to attack. I am really careful. Really protective. I don't want to be wrong. I don't want to say the wrong thing. If I'm not 100% sure, I won't post it.'

Therefore, it is fair to ask whether social media enhances content providers' authenticity if there are so many questions of what can and cannot be said. One study of newspaper comment sections – forums in their own right – revealed that anonymous comments tended to be overwhelmingly less civil than non-anonymous ones, demonstrating a certain restraint inherent in individuals who make their identities public (Santana, 2014). The author also reported, however, that anonymous comments led some users to avoid engaging in these forums, which often degenerated into insults. Ultimately, despite its limits, social media does provide a public outlet that can bolster a journalist's perceived credibility by rendering them more authentic. We have to be careful, however, not to conclude that social media represents a true and total vehicle for authenticity.

Accountability: personal disclosure and evidentiary support

With so much user-generated content available online, the question of how that content was produced is arguably more important than ever. How, then, does social media hinder or enhance the value of accountability specifically for travel journalists? As Hayes et al. explain, 'The unbounded and interconnected nature of the medium gives journalists an unprecedented opportunity to build credibility through a form of information transparency that has never before been feasible' (2007, p. 271). With so much travel content sponsored by various PR or marketing forces, these questions are especially salient to travel journalism.

As far as evidentiary support, one of the main components of accountability, is concerned, travel journalists use social media lightly in their research, rarely depending on it as a source. One journalist explained how editors encourage social media use mainly for promoting her work to audiences, but she is adapting to using it for basic research as well. She said, 'For research, yeah, I need to see what's been written, who is writing about it, what are the names. A quick fact-check with the spelling of a name, for example.' Another journalist explained that certain networks are useful for finding timely, fresh ideas for stories. 'In terms of other sources for news,' she said, 'Twitter is excellent, I use it a lot. You can get scoops from the tourist office or from someone who sees something.' Again, however, the use of social media as evidentiary support is not yet systematic among journalists, who might use it as a starting point, like one journalist who said, 'I am starting to use social networks for ideas or to inspire me to do something related.' Beyond that, few travel professionals actually source from social media, but one travel journalist does consider Twitter fair game for crowdsourcing, even if only among a select few individuals, saying, 'I do reach out to some of the most educated people on Twitter to ask for quotes on topics I am writing about.'

Generally, however, travel journalists are not sourcing information from the masses. Though she uses social media, one professional said that she uses the network to source from her professional network instead of citizens. She said, 'With

Facebook, a lot of my friends are journalists and I like what they post. They direct me towards interesting stories. It's a community of journalists who pick the best of the press and documentaries.' Others, however, are less adapted to the web, preferring to adhere to more traditional, pre-web ways of reporting and newsgathering. As one travel reporter explained,

> The research came from the mass of information that I had acquired from on the ground working for *Time Out*. It was me doing the research. And I think what's expected now is that you do internet research and I feel it's wrong.

Furthermore, the idea of contacting people – professional, citizen, or otherwise – on social networks is not something that all travel journalists embrace. One professional said, 'I usually don't contact people. I follow people for information, but I've never tweeted at someone to contact them yet. It seems a little easy or really a last resort. I want to email or call them directly.' There remains a resistance to using social media as a source of news, but as younger journalists illustrate, the trend is shifting towards greater acceptance of such practices. These practices become especially important on a practical level as restaurants and other companies switch from traditional websites to Facebook pages, as my work on Parisian travel guides has illustrated. Often a bar or boutique won't have an office phone number, but will instead rely on Facebook Messenger to communicate, maybe leading to a conversation on the owner's personal mobile.

The idea of personal disclosure, however, in the form of transparency, leads to humanizing the news, and I'd argue that such an effect is especially true in travel media (Hayes et al., 2007, p. 273). Ultimately, accountability and authenticity go hand in hand. While travel journalists have made it clear that they do not want to share much of their identity online, they are equally dubious of user-generated content where the author is not necessarily identifiable. One journalists asks, 'You can know about people through Twitter and social media, but do you really know them?' Those creating UGC, like journalists, are hesitant to share too much of themselves online. One contributor to travel forums on Reddit said, 'I think people know my first name, but aside from that I don't post revealing info. In college, we learned about being careful what you post on the internet.' Likewise, a forum poster on TripAdvisor said, 'All of the regulars know who I am. I Googled my ID name and you'd be amazed at what a famous person my pseudo is. Whereas my real name is nowhere.' This general environment of anonymity leads to problems when we consider the effects that sites like TripAdvisor can have on local businesses (Scott and Orlikowski, 2012). By not being authentic online, both audiences and information providers are making it difficult to demonstrate that they are truly accountable for what they publish.

Autonomy: staying up to date and free expression

A third value, autonomy, 'is prized as a means of safeguarding the credibility of what journalists produce, ostensibly free from outside pressures that might shape information toward ends that serve vested interests rather than those of the general public' (Hayes et al., 2007, p. 275). The authors discuss showing both sides of a story, as well as correcting errors in a timely fashion, as ways to safeguard journalists against attacks on their autonomy. Neither interpretation is entirely important to travel journalism, where balanced reporting gives way to more subjective reporting, but we can consider how travel journalists deal with autonomy in their own unique ways. Errors, on the other hand, are a natural occurrence as information becomes outdated quickly, which is why much travel journalism with a strong service focus is cyclic, with annual guides and 'best of' lists updated clearly year to year. What once was true may become incorrect, but the internet does not simply suppress yesterday's news, and a search engine could easily lead tourists to outdated material. The web, however, has made it easier to update outdated information, though such a task can be difficult to execute. As one journalist said, he dedicates part of his job to keeping old articles relevant year to year. 'Sometimes for seasonal content we try to refresh it. Why write a whole new article on Oktoberfest when we already have an excellent one?' he said.

Even for non-professionals, however, these considerations are a concern. One blogger said she is aware of the need to fact check every statement she makes, but it becomes impossible to go back and update old materials. This is an interesting shortcoming of social media that traditional printed press didn't have to compete with in the same way. For example, a magazine from 1997 would clearly not be a reliable source of timely information for a reader in 2018, but websites aren't as clear on when they were published or updated, with some posts lacking time stamps altogether. One journalist discussed a post on her website that attracts lots of clicks despite being out of date:

> One of my most frequently searched posts is about the ice rink that was on the Eiffel Tower. If someone goes back to my old post, they'll read about it and be disappointed if they go to the Eiffel Tower. But I hope they'll see the date of the post is 2011. I can't go back and correct every single post because Paris changes so rapidly.

There are more obvious ways that maintaining autonomy in travel journalism is problematic. One of the greatest challenges to practitioners is the interaction with PR and marketing forces that is often essential to producing their work (see Chapter 4). Professionals accepting help from these external forces walk a thin line between honest reporting and shameless promotion, and this is an issue that has plagued travel journalism. While these situations have not changed with the web, social media sites are equally aware of providing autonomous content, which could be useful to journalists. For example, TripAdvisor, for all of its faults, has strict rules against content that is paid-for or commercial in some way. One TripAdvisor contributor experienced the policing of content with commercial aims. He said:

> So when I give people my reports, I make sure that there is no link to my website, so it is not violating any TripAdvisor guidelines. You can't link to

your blog. People do link to their blogs but there was a period where regular users had stopped using TripAdvisor who would start a topic to promote their blog and eventually it started getting reported. Even if there was nothing commercial, it didn't matter.

Other TripAdvisor users told similar stories, illustrating how far the community can go on the website to police content. While more research into this phenomenon is needed, it is a starting point for demonstrating how social media can coincide with journalistic values and ultimately be of use to travel journalists looking to enrich their stories.

Using social media constructively

While social media has not universally bolstered travel journalists' authenticity, accountability, and autonomy, there are clear benefits to using social networks beyond simply researching story ideas. Sharing photos and video from their travelers allows writers to reveal certain aspects of a story's production, for example. Instagram stories and posts, if done honestly, can reveal who journalists traveled with, how they got there, and where they stayed. Such posts can be seen as a backstage glimpse into the production of an actual piece of journalism, giving a more complete and realistic view of the journalist's work. What journalists need is training in the nuts and bolts of social media use – using hashtags, taking the perfect Instagram shot, hosting a live Twitter event – but understanding why they are engaging with thee practices in the first place is indispensable.

By engaging to produce a more authentic view of their work on social networks, journalists are also solidifying their role as an accountable source of information. By revealing other aspects of their trips, journalists are immediately more accountable for what they write. On a basic level, if a travel journalist shares photos – or is shared in photos – with other journalists a press trip, but fails to disclose the trip in a publication, such a professional can more easily be held accountable for his or her lack of honesty. Whereas previously these backstage operations were hidden from view, there is now no reason to hide the conditions of production from audiences. In fact, attempting to hide them could actually cause more problems for a travel journalist with audiences or editors if the latter are left with questions concerning a story's production.

In the same vein, travel journalists should also steer clear of having to disclose sponsorships in every single social media post or article. In other words, if all social media posts by a travel journalist have the hashtag #sponsored in them, readers might start to wonder how independent these actors are in the first place. By requiring a level of authenticity and accountability, travel journalists can actively fight against the sponsorships to avoid seeming like constant advertisements. In print journalism there are fewer occasions for travel journalists to express themselves, so a sponsored article would not seem out of the ordinary. If every Instagram post and blog entry, however, clearly reveals some PR link, audiences might start to lose confidence in the professional's authenticity and ultimately in their credibility. Research also suggests that readers hold negative views of content that is clearly advertorial in nature (Cole and Greer, 2013). While not all sponsored content is necessarily advertorial, it's clear that travel journalists who are constantly posting disclosures could potentially appear less credible to audiences. News sources that try to create informed consumers by disclosing advertorials may ultimately be damaging their own credibility (Wojdynski and Evans, 2016). If such effects occur in publications with native advertising, the same effects might be seen in journalists' social media profiles.

What travel journalists must also avoid doing is using social media as a crutch. When scouring blog posts and review sites replaces original reporting, travel journalism suffers. In 2017, a *Vice* writer created a fake restaurant in London that ended up being the most popular dining establishment in the city on TripAdvisor, despite not existing (Wiseman, 2017). Such stories, while anecdotal, illustrate the potential of misinformation with social media. Desk reporting is understandable for some situations, but any practitioner needs to question the value of writing about a travel experience that they did not, in fact, experience.

Moreover, websites and blogs seem like attractive sources, but journalists do not always use them responsibly. One website owner interviewed in this study shared an email from another journalist seeking information. It should be clear why the email frustrated the website's owner. It read:

> I'm a UK journalist, writing a travel tips series for [name of publication deleted] I'm looking for an expert who can provide some tips on 'The best ways to enjoy/experience the Eiffel Tower', and I wondered if someone at [website] might be interested in being that expert?
>
> All we need is 5 short tips, approx. 120 words each. Tips could include the best time(s) to go, how to buy tickets to avoid queuing, where to get the best photo angles, must-buys or must-sees, etiquette rules to be mindful of etc.
>
> We will fully credit the expert and [website]. The deadline is 24 January.

There is a noticeable difference between asking people online for help and asking them to provide actual copy. This would be akin to stepping into an interview with someone and telling them simply that you needed five 120-word quotes about the topic in question. That's not the way journalism – travel or other – operates. The website owner, herself a journalist, responded to this email, making clear her position. She wrote, 'Sounds great! How about you send me your editor's email and I'll just send the completed story and my invoice directly to her?' In the end, as might be expected, they did not collaborate on the story.

In the end, travel journalists need to engage with social media as sources and outlets, but also as windows into their own life to help bolster their credibility. Such efforts require balance and constant recalibration with the networks and tools used at the time, which is why I make no attempt to give specific suggestions here. They would likely be outdated by the time of this book's publication. The general ideas presented here, however, should help guide travel journalists towards under-standing whatever tools are at their disposal, whether it's a nearly-defunct Google Plus or some new application or concept that has yet to be developed.

References

Ayeh, J. K., Au, N., and Law, R. (2013). 'Do we believe in TripAdvisor?' Examining credibility perceptions and online travelers' attitude toward using user-generated content. *Journal of Travel Research*, 52(4), 437–452.

Bruns, A. (2005). *Gatewatching: Collaborative online news production*. New York: Peter Lang.

Cole, J. T., and Greer, J. D. (2013). Audience response to brand journalism: The effect of frame, source, and involvement. *Journalism and Mass Communication Quarterly*, 90(4), 673–690.

Domingo, D., and Heikkilä, H. (2012). Media accountability practices in online news media. In E. Siapera and A. Veglis (Eds.), *The handbook of global online journalism* (pp. 272–289). Chichester: Wiley-Blackwell.

Duffy, A. (2016). How social media offers opportunities for growth in the traditional media industry: The case of travel journalism. In V. Beson, R. Tuninga, and G. Saridakis (Eds.), *Analyzing the strategic role of social networking in firm growth and productivity* (pp. 172–187). Hershey, PA: IGI Global.

Gretzel, U. (2017). #travelselfie. *Performing cultural tourism: Communities, tourists and creative practices*, 115.

Hayes, A. S., Singer, J. B., and Ceppos, J. (2007). Shifting roles, enduring values: The credible journalist in a digital age. *Journal of Mass Media Ethics*, 22(4), 262–279.

Hedman, U., and Djerf-Pierre, M. (2013). The social journalist: Embracing the social media life or creating a new digital divide? *Digital Journalism*, 1(3), 368–385.

Hermida, A. (2012). Social journalism: Exploring how social media is shaping journalism. In E. Siapera and A. Veglis (Eds.), *The handbook of global online journalism* (pp. 309–328). Chichester: Wiley-Blackwell. Jenkins, H. (2006). *Convergence culture: Where old and new media collide*. New York: NYU Press.

Jenkins, H., Ford, S., and Green, J. (2013) *Spreadable media: Creating value and meaning in a networked culture*. New York: NYU Press.

Munar, A. M., and Jacobsen, J. K. S. (2014). Motivations for sharing tourism experiences through social media. *Tourism Management*, 43, 46–54.

Naughton, J. (2012). *From Gutenberg to Zuckerberg: What you really need to know about the internet*. London: Quercus.

Orlikowski, W. J., and Scott, S. V. (2013). What happens when evaluation goes online? Exploring apparatuses of valuation in the travel sector. *Organization Science*, 25(3), 868–891.

Pan, S., and Ryan, S. (2009). Tourism sense-making: The role of the senses and travel journalism. *Journal of Travel and Tourism Marketing*, 26(7), 625–639, doi:10.1080/10548400903276897

Peters, C., and Broersma, M. J. (Eds.). (2013). *Rethinking journalism: Trust and participation in a transformed news landscape*. Abingdon: Routledge.

Pirolli, B. (2016). Travel information online: Navigating correspondents, consensus, and conversation. *Current Issues in Tourism*, doi:10.1080/13683500.2016.1273883

Robinson, S. (2011). Journalism as process: The organization implications of participatory online news. *Journalism and Communication Monographs*, 13(3), 137–210.

Santana, A. D. (2014). Virtuous or vitriolic: The effect of anonymity on civility in online newspaper reader comment boards. *Journalism Practice*, 8(1), 18–33.

Scott, S. V., and Orlikowski, W. J. (2012). Reconfiguring relations of accountability: Materialization of social media in the travel sector. *Accounting, Organizations and Society*, 37(1), 26–40.

Sigala, M., Christou, E., and Gretzel, U. (Eds.). (2012). *Social media in travel, tourism and hospitality: Theory, practice and cases*. Farnham: Ashgate.

Sigala, M., and Gretzel, U. (Eds.). (2017). *Advances in social media for travel, tourism and hospitality: New perspectives, practice and cases*. Abingdon: Routledge.

Singer, J. B. (2014). User-generated visibility: Secondary gatekeeping in a shared media space. *New Media and Society*, 16(1), 55–73.

Singer, J. B. (2015). Out of bounds: Professional norms as boundary markers. In M. Carlson and S. C. Lewis (Eds.), *Boundaries of journalism: Professionalism, practices and participation* (pp. 21–36). New York: Routledge.

Singer, J. B., and Ashman, I. (2009). 'Comment is free, but facts are sacred': user-generated content and ethical constructs at the Guardian. *Journal of Mass Media Ethics*, 24(1), 3–21.

Singer, J. B., Domingo, D., Heinonen, A., Hermida, A., Paulussen, S., Quandt, T., Reich, Z. and Vujnovic, M. (2011). *Participatory journalism: Guarding open gates at online newspapers*. Chichester: Wiley-Blackwell. Steensen, S. (2016). The intimization of journalism. In T. Witschge, C. W. Anderson, D. Domingo, and A. Hermida (Eds.), *The handbook of digital journalism* (pp. 113–127). London: Sage.

Swasy, A. (2016). *How journalists use Twitter: The changing landscape of U.S. newsrooms*. Lanham, MD: Lexington Books.

Wiseman, E. (2017, Dec. 17). The best restaurant in London? You literally can't get a table. *Guardian*. Retrieved from https://www.theguardian.com

Wojdynski, B. W., and Evans, N. J. (2016). Going native: Effects of disclosure position and language on the recognition and evaluation of online native advertising. *Journal of Advertising*, 45(2), 157–168.

Xiang, Z., and Gretzel, U. (2010). Role of social media in online travel information search. *Tourism Management*, 31(2), 179–188.

8

REPORTING FROM FOREIGN LANDS

When travel journalists stumble

It was a concept that few often associated with Paris, but in 2016 the English-speaking press was pushing a story about 'doggy bags' that would not relent. The story, according to most of the outlets, was that France would pass a new law requiring restaurants to provide doggy bags for customers, essentially encouraging people to take leftovers home with them. A benign act in and of itself, it sparked a certain amount of outrage among a cultural elite who saw this as an affront to French culture. A dining experience is meant to occur in the restaurant, and the idea of forcing doggy bags on Parisian diners was inconceivable. Publications in Ireland, the US, and beyond were running this story, discussing the merits of not wasting food with the attack on cultural norms.

There was only one problem in all of this reporting – there was no doggy bag law at all. The rumor, as it ended up being, stemmed from an erroneous report in a French paper, which was retracted, but had already spread to the English-speaking world unchecked and unverified. Newspapers and websites propagated the same misinformation that they saw on an English-speaking French news channel, and the story took hold. When an editor at *Travel+Leisure* asked me to write a response to it for the website, I stressed in my short article that this was a non-issue, and no one was forcing Parisian diners to walk home with their leftovers in tow. Travelers wouldn't have to worry about stinking up their hotels with last night's duck confit, and portions weren't going to become so hefty that normal humans couldn't finish a meal. It was all false, and an unfortunate misunderstanding exacerbated by poor journalism.

Such are the realities of reporting from abroad, when cultural and linguistic barriers can become insurmountable for journalists who simply do not know any better and do not have the time or resources to verify a story correctly. Cultural difference is no excuse for lazy journalism, but it's almost more forgivable than most bad journalism produced by practitioners within their own language and culture. The internet offered the perceived possibility to shatter cultural boundaries, perhaps too optimistically. In 1995, Nicholas Negroponte wrote that the internet will have clear decentralizing and harmonizing effects, though companies like Google and Facebook illustrate how these ideals have not been upheld (1995). In a 2000 study on international news sites, one researcher posits, 'One could say that the Internet as a symbol of globalism is more or less an Anglo-American invention, blinded by cultural naivety' (Aldísardóttir, 2000, p. 242). The research, however, found that English was not as widely embraced on the web as previously thought, emphasizing the local focus of news which preserves many of the cultural boundaries already in place. Nearly two decades later, I'd argue that local online media is still important, but travel, by its very nature, transcends the local/foreign divide. Reading a travel article, both local and foreign notions appear, juggling interpreting natives with living like them, visiting a destination 'like a local' while seeing the sights that most locals do not engage with on a daily basis. Only about half of the visitors to Disneyland Paris are actually French, for example, illustrating, however obvious it may seem, that the theme park may not be on the local radar, but is still important to many people (Le Média Institutionnel de Disneyland Paris, 2016). Travel has become, in the early twenty-first century, a post-modern mashup of being an unabashed tourist while also seeking to play the role of local. In all of this, however, the internet offers increasingly effective automated translation services that erase questions of linguistic monopoly, liberating travel media.

Where the internet cannot immediately help travel journalists is in actually understanding foreign places. Numerous factors lead Williams to describe the shift to foreign correspondents who are no longer defined by national or regional boundaries, challenging the very notion of what is local or foreign (2011, p. 2). There is no automation available for such an endeavor, not yet at least. From language and cultural practices to stereotypes and clichés, there are hurdles that journalists need to anticipate. There are also practical steps that can be taken to help overcome them, including downloading free translator apps, relying on tourism offices, and connecting with locals via social media. In this chapter, I argue that the internet in many respects has made the travel journalist's job easier than ever, almost to a fault, where he or she does not even need to leave their home to report on foreign lands. It's even possible to visit many of the world's most iconic destinations simply using Google Maps. I'll explore the challenges faced by travel journalists and the tools made available online to bypass them: language, cultural differences, and access, to name a few. The net result, however, is a positive one, as more stories and points of view are ultimately possible online.

More importantly, I argue, the internet has allowed editors to cull local talent – including but not limited to expats – to work as travel journalists. Looking at the interviews with journalists in Paris, I can identify how this group has been able to rise up as a new set of foreign correspondents and overcome many of the issues faced by travel journalists who have to go abroad to cover a certain destination. I argue that, ultimately, it is not surprising and in fact sometimes preferable that expats become travel correspondents for publications in their home countries, which allows them to mediate cultural differences and manage tourists' expectations more efficiently. I will explain, however, that their points of view alone do not act as a substitute for sending journalists abroad to cover travel topics, as expats do not typically engage with all of the same aspects of travel as somebody who does not live in the destination. The web, however, has allowed their unique points of view to become a part of mainstream travel journalism, bringing in more local views.

In the end I hope to illustrate, albeit cautiously, that reporting from abroad is logistically easier because of instantaneous communication with editors, access to online research, and increased wi-fi connectivity. Still, challenges remain for travel journalists in accurately representing a destination and in catering to consumers' needs. Future travel journalists, therefore, need not apply for a visa and pack up their lives immediately to engage with their profession, but it is important to understand what these challenges are and how to respond to them.

Challenges reporting abroad

Through interviews with travel journalists, one understands that there are a few key – if not obvious – challenges to their type of reporting. Such issues are not necessarily unique to their craft, as war reporters and other foreign correspondents deal with many similar issues on a daily basis. An understanding of the complexities of international journalism, as introduced by Williams, is a good place to begin. For example, foreign correspondents have created distinctions between the long stay reporter and the parachute journalist who drops into a story for a short time. 'The struggles between the two types of reporters and their different *modi vivendi* have always had a bearing on the nature of international news' (Williams, 2011, p. 25). Technology doesn't ultimately make the life of the foreign correspondent easier, but rather complicates it in other ways, requiring them to be always on, always connected (p. 106). Travel journalists, however, are less bound by the 24-hour news cycle that foreign correspondents generally need to work within. While further research can delve into how these issues might affect reporting, I simply want to introduce them here, to acknowledge that there are unique hurdles for travel journalists today that, thanks to the internet, are largely surmountable, at least more so than ever before.

In Chapter 4, I already discussed the economic considerations that challenge travel journalists in a digital age. Such challenges are felt more by lifestyle journalists than by other foreign correspondents. For any journalist traveling abroad, however, the following key issues still present themselves, though tools exist to overcome them.

Language

First, evidently, any journalist abroad confronts issues related to language. Traditionally, local fixers would act as intermediaries for foreign correspondents.

Williams writes about the important of fixers, or local translators and guides, who provide services for foreign correspondents (Williams, 2011, pp. 120–121). In lifestyle media, press trips would act as a sort of fixer and alleviate much of this burden for travel journalists in a similar way, albeit with more commercial goals. Speaking the local language could be problematic and impair objectivity, according to Williams (2011, p. 100). For travel journalists, though, speaking the local language gives them access to the people living in a destination as well as to local press. Digital tools, however, have largely lightened the linguistic burden for journalists abroad who can automatically translate web content – though the quality of such translations still leaves room for some ambiguity. An array of smartphone applications allows individuals to translate real-time while in the field, but realistically, these tools are not lifelines for travel journalists.

Cultural comprehension

Second, and especially for a parachuting journalist, understanding cultural norms and practices can be a major hurdle. I'll go into more depth in a later chapter, but essentially, travel journalists are working to mediate cultures. As one researcher explains, 'cultural efflorescence has usually been based on intercultural mingling' (Pieterse, 2015, p. 32). How can such efflorescence occur, however, if the mediator does not inherently understand the culture that he or she is mediating in the first place? This returns us to questions of the 'mediatised gaze' discussed by Urry and Larsen, who write, 'Gazing is a performance that orders, shapes and classifies, rather than reflects the world' (2011, p. 2). Gazing can lead to larger ethical questions, as Fürsich and Kavoori suggest, relating to cultural imperialism and identity formation (2014). Simply put, how does a travel journalist mediate cultures? A big question with even bigger answers, it is clear how the internet can offer research into foreign cultures that is arguably much richer than ever before. Far from suggesting that the internet provides a solution to cultural misrepresentations in travel media, I merely propose that it offers a broader window on the world, with more voices and conversations available to the journalist through local news sites, blogs, and other social media. Journalists are taking advantage of these new tools, which can lead to greater understanding of places and people.

Story ideas

Third, finding story ideas about a destination remains a pivotal challenge. Again, fixers and press trips might be a way to find what's happening in a destination. Such structures, however, are often limited. When I was planning to attend a press trip to the south of France, the office of tourism organizing the trip wanted to know in advance the topics for the stories I would write, without having actually participated yet in the trip. In this case, the PR was not facilitating the task at hand. I was left to scour the internet to find out what was going on in the destinations proposed in the press trip, but I couldn't be sure that the stories I found would be part of the trip, forcing me to abandon my participation altogether. Social media (see Chapter 7) is clearly an entry into the inner workings of a destination, alongside local press outlets that might be automatically translated, but having access to people and places, facilitated by press trips, is still an important practice, I'd argue.

Many of these issues though – language, cultural comprehension, and access to news ideas – are difficult for travel journalists because they don't always live in their destinations. Furthermore, there is a slew of other considerations that they need to consider when parachuting in – from transport and lodging to money exchange and security (Marthoz, 2008). When travel journalists *do* live in a destination, however, many of these issues are not actually issues at all. By virtue of living abroad, an English-speaker is likely to engage with local language and culture more than a professional who parachutes in. As David Morley writes, '[P]lace comes to act as a generator of cultural belongingness, so that the geographical boundaries round a community also come to carry a symbolic charge in separating out those who belong from those who don't' (2000, p. 212). The stories and contacts available to someone belonging to a society will arguably differ from someone who is perceived as other, rendering two different interpretations of a place.

Furthermore, in today's digital age, a growing number of global immigrants are more connected than ever before, creating opportunities for many to produce journalism in their native language while abroad. There is a lack of research into the idea of expat journalists, but it's worth noting that the number of migrants is constantly on the rise. There were 244 million international immigrants in 2015 compared to 173 million in 2000, and most were professional, lifestyle, or economic migrants (United Nations, 2016). It is therefore worthwhile to introduce this notion of expat travel journalists – as separate from foreign correspondents – to understand how they might contribute to travel media in unique ways, and what challenges they still present to travel journalism as a profession.

Expats as new travel journalists

As stated above, all of these tools and technological advancements have led to another development in travel journalism that needs to be explored in more detail. The immediacy of information exchange thanks to email has allowed for travel journalism to become an act performed not by roving wanderers, but by expatriates living abroad. I by no means suggest that expats have never before acted as travel journalists, but the internet has made it significantly easier and more routine for publications. Immersed in the culture, these expats offer a unique perspective, a more local view while still outsiders, and the internet has allowed them to flourish in the mainstream press thanks to its connective power. Little research exists on the role of expatriates in media production, but it is clear that living abroad and writing for publications in other countries with a common language is easier than ever. Websites like Twitter are allowing a greater voice to these expats, as was the case during the Arab Spring uprisings (Bruns et al., 2013).

Clearly such a phenomenon is not pervasive worldwide – certain languages may not be as well represented in the expatriate community as English, Spanish, French, Portuguese, or Chinese. There are also countless socio-economic considerations to take into account. For example, one researcher suggests that expats should be examined carefully as journalists, because they often come from privileged backgrounds (Marthoz, 2008 p. 243). For the moment, however, I want to open up a conversation about the challenges faced by travel journalism as stories about a destination are increasingly able to be produced by those living there, and not merely visiting.

For the purposes of this chapter, the terms expatriates and expats refer to individuals living in a foreign country voluntarily. Some research attempts to differentiate more stringently certain types of expat, for example business expatriates, from others including students and volunteers (McNulty and Brewster, 2017). Because of the wide variety of persons who can become journalists, however, there is little advantage to distinguish among the various types of expatriate. What does need to be clear is that not all information providers – especially among those interviewed in my study – moved to Paris with the express hope of becoming a travel journalist. A deeper analysis of the demographics of these expats will certainly be worthwhile at some point, but for the moment it is interesting to note that most expat journalists interviewed are female and come from fairly educated though not always affluent backgrounds. They are diverse English speakers from the US, Canada, and Britain, but clearly not representative of all expat journalists living in Paris. With so little research into the notion of expat travel journalists, the aim here is to introduce the questions that could guide future research by exploring this initial sample. These expats shared their thoughts on the advantages and challenges of being expats who engage in travel media. It is important to note that most are freelancers, though some work consistently for the same publications. This phenomenon coincides with the general trend towards freelance work among foreign correspondents. As Williams explains:

> The ability and capacity to operate as a freelance correspondent has been facilitated by technology as well as the expansion of media outlets to which freelancers can sell their product. The relationship between journalists and their news outlets has changed; for some it has enabled the reporter to free him or herself from the editorial restrictions of single organisations.
>
> *(2011, p. 15)*

As freelancers, these journalists focus on France and tourism as their major beats, rarely branching out to more generalist topics. For most journalists, it was unanimously viewed positively that they live in Paris. It gives them an advantage over travel journalists who merely visit, or parachute into the country. As one journalist said, editors selected her for a job because of the fact that she was an expat journalist and could engage with Paris – the topic of her pieces – more than the average traveler. She said:

I know a lot of expats and I got the job because I lived through the experience and I am an expat. I think that's one of the differences between good writing and not so good travel writing. It's hard to write about a place you don't really know.

Another journalist underscores her unique experiences beyond journalism, working in the tourism industry, that further nuances her profile. A contributor to *Condé Nast Traveler*, she attributes her professional success to her expat status. She said:

Condé Nast uses us because we are in the destination. Because I also work in tourism that changes things. I know what the tourism experience is more than people who travel themselves or have friends who come to visit because I live it every day. I know how to make the perfect travel experience for anybody.

In some particular cases, the status of being an expat is indispensable to the publication. One journalist, writing for a series of travel guides aimed at future expatriates in France, obtained the contract to write the book because she herself was an expat. 'I was selected to write these books because I have the experience as the target audience. I am and was that person who moved here', she said.

More specifically, however, expats can engage with local culture in ways that perhaps traveling journalists cannot. When it comes to dealing with local languages, for example, expats may be more likely to speak it than someone who flew in for the week. This means that expat journalists have access to people and events that other writers might not, especially through their own personal and professional networks. One expat described how she accessed the local French press as a way to provide content for a publication in English. She shared:

[Editors would] want 6 stories a week about French news, and they didn't care what the content was. Usually the *Riviera Times* would give me an idea. We'd go through the French newspapers and find out what's going on and rewrite it for the expats.

More than simply rewriting content, however, this same journalist explained how she follows the French press – even on Twitter – in order to stay ahead of the curve and to know what's going on in France outside of the English-speaking bubble. The spread of English as a global language has created power imbalances relating back to ideas of imperialism that Pennycook identifies (2017). On a simpler level, however, language can understandably form a sort of filter bubble or echo chamber for news consumers, and such effects are particularly liable to occur when discussing travel in a destination where audiences don't speak the language – leading to mishaps regarding fears of doggy bags in Parisian restaurants, for example. Expats can – at least in some cases – transcend these linguistic divides by virtue of living abroad and engaging with local languages.

To that end, expat travel journalists are aware of their role as foreign correspondents of sorts, keeping a finger on the pulse of local culture. In a way, they are their own fixers. One journalist recognized that things like dining and the arts are part of her beat, and that she should be maintaining them. She said, 'I don't eat out much but part of our job as being a local correspondent is to be watching all the time.' They have access that visiting journalists might not, as one expat confirmed, saying, 'The advantage of being in Paris is that you see first-hand what's going on now.' Another journalist embraces her role writing for the *New York Times*, maintaining a local perspective that she can deliver easily as an expat. She said, 'This is my local life and I have access to interesting things and so people who want access to that point of view, that's what is asked of me, for a local sensibility.'

Assuming a sort of authority as a local, having access to media and sources, and being steeped in local culture daily, these expats seem well positioned to create articles and content for travel publications. Their ability to create and publish such content easily has also created a tension among those who live in Paris and those who don't, as one journalist explained. She said, 'Especially as residents here, it irks me when folks are hired to write about Paris or France and they don't live here, and they don't know, and it's rife with errors.' This movement towards expat journalists has created a kind of elitism among those living abroad who see themselves as authorities, as opposed to the parachuting travel journalist who offers a less experienced view of a destination. While all local journalists do not provide quality content, and while all visiting journalists do not provide incorrect content, there is clearly a deeper question here between these two different types of travel journalists – if they can be categorized under the same umbrella in the first place.

All expats, however, are not as confident in their ability to serve audiences completely, as one journalist for the *New York Times* explained. From her point of view, she offers something unique and important, but her vision is by no means complete or sufficient for tourists. She had this to say:

> The person who has the sense of living in a place for a while, you see how things shift and change and trends and new developments and all of that. That point of view will always be more informed than someone who just comes to town. To be able to talk about 'now' you have to know how 'now' has evolved. So, someone who knows a place well can do that with more nuances. But coming with a clean slate, or someone who comes with a more impromptu sense of the city might yield other things.

This argument leads to the final discussion of this chapter. While the internet and increased connectivity allows expats to contribute easily and efficiently to travel publications, we need to zoom out to understand how their contributions fit into the greater goals of travel journalism. While entertaining, with critical perspectives, and with factual information, as Hanusch and Fürsich (2014) define it, travel journalism produced by those who are not technically traveling could present some issues. Are locals' critiques universally useful to a casual tourist? How can a local provide the factual information needed for someone coming to Paris for the first time if such a journalist is not immersed in those types of experiences? Urry and Larsen discuss how post-tourists are engaged in a 'multitude of games' when they travel (2011, p. 114). They are seeking local experiences as well as touristy experiences, aware of the impossibility of any truly authentic experience. I want to open up a larger debate about the value of expat travel journalism to understand how more traditional visiting journalists are still ultimately essential to travel journalism.

Travel journalists still need to travel – right?

While some researchers like Duffy propose a new ecosystem where travelers provide information and stories and journalists curate and package it, there is still an argument for a travel journalist to parachute into a destination (2016). First, critiques of expatriates as hedonists and 'artistic types' serve to undermine them in more serious professions (McCarthy, 1996). Other authors suggest that expats do not engage with local cultures, but take a more passive approach. 'More and more like voyeurs of the decadent and exotic, the expatriates see 'others' or 'otherness' but do not yet divine their own role as actors in the production of the world they believe they are simply observing' (Kaplan, 1996, p. 47). It can be argued, therefore, that while expats are performing many of the duties of a travel journalist, they may be limited by their position in several ways. Both journalists and bloggers attest to their own shortcomings when providing travel information, illustrating an argument for more traditional roving or parachuting journalists to continue writing about travel alongside the local views of these expats.

First and foremost, expats, by virtue of living abroad, have effectively cut out the 'travel' portion of the consumer experience. While they do know about public transportation and other important elements like airports and train stations, it's fair to question how keyed in they are to the actual trek. Few expat journalists in Paris are necessarily making frequent trips between the US and France, for example, so understanding the airports, how they change, and how travel is evolving is one way that traditional travel journalists are still relevant. They must make the trip and therefore can comment, in a timelier and more routine manner, on the quality of services and presentations available to travelers. I by no means suggest that expats cannot perform these duties, but it is not built into their work the way it would be with a traditional travel professional, parachuting into a destination.

Second, expats may shy away from mainstream topics in favor of the local topics, angling towards more authentic or local experiences as described in Chapter 5. Expats are steeped in their destination and offer a more discerning opinion or perspective, yes, but often to the detriment of the touristy experiences that most post-tourists still seek, in addition to other more local or potentially authentic experiences (Urry and Larsen, 2011). As one journalist explained, she appreciates tourist sites as a traveler herself, but when it comes to recommending or writing about them, she is often severely tempted to bypass them. 'There are these things you have to see', she said. But then in a second breath, she admitted that she would omit certain touristy destinations in Paris reporting because of the crowds. She said, 'The one thing I will say, like the Catacombs. I wouldn't tell someone to go there, because the line is so long.' The post-tourist, however, knows and even embraces that he or she will be waiting in line as part of their experiences, thus it is questionable if the expat travel journalist is responding adequately to the audience's needs and expectations.

Journalists also prefer to distinguish their work from the more basic topics that seem obvious to them. The problem, I argue, is that basic tourist elements of a city or region are not necessarily obvious to tourists, especially first-time travelers. A growing and changing population of tourists requires constant informing, and not just of the off-the-beaten-path experiences that locals – perhaps jaded by their time abroad – don't pay as much attention to anymore. While review sites like TripAdvisor may be able to address these topics through anonymous reviews, there is still something to be said for professionals who can discuss major tourist attractions under the banner of a trusted brand.

Third – though perhaps not finally – there is an argument in general for fresh perspectives in travel journalism, to hear the voices of people with varying experiences and expectations. An expatriate will arguably have a different world-view than an American, Australian, or Canadian traveling to France for the first time. Such experiences and points of view, in a professional context, are indispensable to consumers who themselves may be first-time visitors. For one journalist, she accepts the difficulty of writing for tourists when she herself is not one. 'You have to pretend to be a tourist lost in the city you live in', she said. This sort of artificiality could lead to ethical dilemmas that MacCannell may not have foreseen (2011). It remains unclear how we can research this phenomenon, especially since the residential status of each travel journalist is not immediately evident when reading an article or viewing a video report. Bylines don't always include denominations like 'Parisian expat' or 'London native' next to them. What's clear, however, is that audiences are thinking about these things more and more as their expectations are changing. One tourist interviewed explained that in researching her trips she wants to find local blogs or expat writers, because, she said, 'I want to experience the city and what it would be like to live in the city rather than what travelers or tourists do in the city.' While such attitudes appear in much of the tourists' discourse on the topic, most tourists also feel the need to participate in basic sightseeing. 'It's unpleasant but the lines of the Eiffel Tower, it's part of Paris. It is what it is and maybe you'll hate it but you gotta see whether you like it or not', one tourist said. If expat journalists – and as I also discovered, local bloggers – aren't writing about these experiences, is anyone producing accurate, updated information about them or are they being neglected? Or will traditional travel journalists, parachuting into Paris, continue to provide updated, fresh looks at these institutions, from the Eiffel Tower to the Taj Mahal?

Moving forward

With little research on the practices employed by travel journalists, or on the relationship between expatriates and travel media, there are plenty of questions that this chapter raises. How has the internet made travel journalism easier to produce? How has it empowered a conceptually new population of expatriate content producers to produce travel journalism more systematically? What issues arise due to this changing nature of information production? I don't pretend to have all of the answers here, but this chapter strives to present these questions for future research, and to prepare travel journalists for the realities ahead of them.

What's clear is that the internet has made things easier, but not without complicating the lives of travel journalists who are faced with the challenges of social media as discussed in Chapter 7, and further with the concept of self-branding, to be tackled in Chapter 9. Journalists have not systematically embraced the possibilities provided by the internet, but abundant research capabilities and online translation services are obvious examples of a growing toolbox. Whether they are parachuting into a destination for the first time or are long-time expatriates who are fully integrated, travel journalists need to be thinking about their audiences more than ever. The internet, for better or worse, has closed the gap between professionals and audiences, creating a new dynamic whereby audiences can evaluate a travel journalist not just by his or her publications, but by their personality, interests, and experiences as made public on social media. If readers – and journalists for that matter – had more thoroughly scrutinized the media coverage of the Paris doggy bag incident, that false report may not have spread so pervasively. The internet has given us the tools to do our own background checks into those who are creating content, therefore cultivating this public image will be just as important as creating verified and engaging stories for readers through any medium.

References

Aldísardóttir, L. (2000). Research note: global medium – local tool? How readers and media companies use the web. *European Journal of Communication*, 15(2), 241–251.

Bruns, A., Highfield, T., and Burgess, J. (2013). The Arab Spring and social media audiences: English and Arabic Twitter users and their networks. *American Behavioral Scientist*, 57(7), 871–898.

Cappelli, G. (2008). 'Expat's talk:' Humour and irony in an expatriate's travel blog. *Textus: Special Issue on Humour*, edited by Delia Chiaro and Neal Norrick, 1–21.

Cocking, B. (2009). Travel journalism: Europe imagining the Middle East. *Journalism Studies*, 10(1), 54–68.

Duffy, A. (2016). How social media offers opportunities for growth in the traditional media industry: The case of travel journalism. In V. Beson, R. Tuninga, and G. Saridakis (Eds.), *Analyzing the strategic role of social networking in firm growth and productivity* (pp. 172–187). Hershey, PA: IGI Global.

Fürsich, E. and Kavoori, A. P. (2014). People on the move: Travel journalism, globalization and mobility. In F. Hanusch and E. Fürsich (Eds.), *Travel journalism: Exploring production, impact and culture* (pp. 21–38). Basingstoke: Palgrave Macmillan.

Hanusch, F., and Fürsich, E. (2014). On the relevance of travel journalism: An introduction. In F. Hanusch and E. Fürsich (Eds.), *Travel journalism: Exploring production, impact and culture* (pp. 1–18). Hampshire: Palgrave Macmillan.

Kaplan, C. (1996). *Questions of travel: Postmodern discourses of displacement.* Durham, NC: Duke University Press.

Le Média Institutionnel de Disneyland Paris. (2016). La 1ère destination touristique d'Europe fête ses 25 ans. Retrieved from http://disneylandparis-news.com

Lewis, S. C., and Usher, N. (2013). Open source and journalism: Toward new frameworks for imagining news innovation. *Media, Culture and Society*, 35(5), 602–619.

MacCannell, D. (2011). *The ethics of sightseeing.* Berkeley: University of California Press.

Marthoz, J. (2008). *Journalisme international.* Paris: De Boeck Supérieur.

McCarthy, M. (1996). A guide to exiles, expatriates, and internal emigrés. In M. Robinson (Ed.), *Altogether elsewhere: Writers on exile* (pp. 49–58). New York: Harcourt Brace.

McGaurr, L. (2012). The devil may care: Travel journalism, cosmopolitan concern, politics and the brand. *Journalism Practice*, 6(1), 42–58.

McNulty, Y., and Brewster, C. (2017). Theorizing the meaning(s) of 'expatriate': Establishing boundary conditions for business expatriates. *International Journal of Human Resource Management*, 28(1), 27–61.

Moon, S. J., and Hadley, P. (2014). Routinizing a new technology in the newsroom: Twitter as a news source in mainstream media. *Journal of Broadcasting and Electronic Media*, 58(2), 289–305.

Morley, D. (2000). *Home territories: Media, mobility and identity.* London: Routledge.

Negroponte, N. (1995). The digital revolution: Reasons for optimism. *The Futurist*, 29(6), 68.

Pennycook, A. (2017). *The cultural politics of English as an international language.* Abingdon: Routledge.

Pieterse, J. N. (2015). *Globalization and culture: Global mélange.* Lanham, MD: Rowman and Littlefield.

United Nations, Department of Economic and SocialAffairs, PopulationDivision. (2016). *International migration report 2015: Highlights* (ST/ESA/SER.A/375). Retrieved from www.un.org/

Urbain, J.-D. (1991). *L'idiot du voyage: Histoires de touristes.* Paris: Petit Bibliothèque Payot.

Urry, J., and Larsen, J. (2011). *The tourist gaze 3.0.* London: Sage.

Williams, K. (2011). *International journalism.* London: Sage.

9

SELF-BRANDING THE TRAVEL JOURNALIST

Paris attracts many expats from all over the world. In the early days of Twitter, however, it seemed like there were only a few English-speakers tweeting in the French capital, writing and sharing stories about life in the city. I routinely saw the same names pop up on social media and in the press when articles were discussing Paris. I only joined in 2011 after living there for nearly three years, but it quickly became a lifeline to parts of local communities that I didn't interact with otherwise. I became a part of the expat scene, sharing my own views and blog posts on the network. I never really thought about it as a calling card, but I did reflect before tweeting anything, always aware that an editor might stumble upon my account. Still, I tweeted about things that interested me, things that I was participating in, and topics that I wrote about. Fortunately, my cautiously-curated Twitter feed did pay off when a fellow writer contacted me about working for *Time Out Paris*. We weren't extremely close, but we knew each other and followed the other's social accounts. We were colleagues of sort on the freelance scene, despite rarely meeting, and she knew I'd be the right fit for this job immediately, not least because of my conversations on Twitter. My accidental online calling card had earned me a gig.

By 2012, *Time Out Paris* was just a website, having ceased printing a magazine, but it was still a respected brand that I had been keen to write for since beginning my journalism career. The editor was looking for contributors for very specific sections, notably family travel and LGBT nightlife in Paris – not your typical travel beats. As a tour guide who worked extensively with families and as someone who could name all of Paris's LGBT venues, the role was a perfect fit for me. I had already written about these topics for smaller blogs and had clips and research to show for it. The editor was quickly convinced of my qualifications and I began my tenure as correspondent for *Time Out Paris*, cultivating my family and LGBT travel expertise.

It wasn't just Twitter or a personal connection that helped me get the job – it was the brand that I had built up around myself, as someone who was competent in these areas. Surely, had the job called for a beauty, shopping, or art expert, my name would not have even been a blip on the radar. Having a 'beat' is not something new to the journalistic profession, but I would argue that just being a *travel* journalist isn't enough today, that the beat needs to be even more specialized in order to remain relevant among all of the content available online. Travel journalists need to think about how to brand themselves, not just as travel journalists, but as specialists within travel media.

Travel branding: an online renaissance?

By having an outward profile and persona, I opened myself up to an opportunity that I may have otherwise overlooked, or that may have overlooked me. This idea of having a personal brand, while contentious among many journalists, is something that travel journalism almost requires – after all, it was Murray's expertise, experiences, and unique personality that people sought when buying his eponymous guides. Travel brands, especially those tied to individuals, began to take shape as consumer branding became commonplace in the late nineteenth century (Olins, 2000). Today, brands like Expedia, Airbnb, Lonely Planet, and easyJet are commonplace, as are the names of individuals who have carved out their niche in the industry. The tradition of personality-led travel brands has continued today, with names like Anthony Bourdain and Rick Steves appearing on a professional level, and Nomadic Matt and Adventurous Kate finding success online in the blogosphere. Travel information is guided so much by word of mouth, and knowing the source is often a critical component of trusting those suggestions, especially online (Litvin et al., 2008). Research suggests that knowing the identity of a reviewer online leads to greater overall trust than with an unidentified reviewer (Kusumasondjaja et al., 2012). We can consider journalists in the same light, and arguably, knowing more about them will lead to a stronger relationship between professionals and their audiences.

A travel journalist is not just someone who simply travels and writes about it for a magazine – there are already countless people writing about their voyages online. A travel journalist can also no longer depend on their publication's reputation alone to attract readers. While *Travel+Leisure* and *Lonely Planet* develop their websites, readers are equally attracted to blogs, review sites, and sites like Matador that exist only online, offering content tailored to a specific traveler. With so many voices online, I argue that travel journalists need to be branding themselves on many levels – including blogging and adopting sound social media practices – in order to create their own niche as well as to cultivate a rapport with their audiences. It's not enough just to be a travel journalist anymore because travel has fragmented in so many directions, and consumers need specialists to help navigate the many options and offers available to them. I argue that professionals need to take on a more entrepreneurial role, to embrace the change and disruption that has bred opportunity for newsmakers (Briggs, 2012, p. xxiii). Much of this potential relies on opening themselves up from the increasingly stale objective/subjective divide that dominates much journalistic discourse. Even before the internet, modern travel writers went 'to much greater lengths than was ever previously the case to situate their journeys in a larger personal history of the self', and much of this literary practice has carried over into journalism (Thompson, 2011, p. 113). Perhaps professionals have strayed too far from these literary authors who shared themselves in their work, and they need to recalibrate for audiences online.

Whereas I have already discussed how journalists can use social media in their reporting, this chapter will identify how travel journalists should be using the web to advance themselves, to create their own brands online, to contribute to Goffman's idea of performance. He writes about the importance of a 'front', the part of a performance that is stable and gives meaning to those who observe it. If we consider travel journalism as a performance, there are already norms and expectations associated with their front of professional journalism about destinations. As Goffman says, even when changing the nature of the performance – in this case, adapting to a digital environment – the performer relies on the fronts which have already been established (1959, p. 27). Should travel journalists change, adopting a front akin to that of a narrative travel writer? Or that of a blogger? Or is there a way to bring these fronts together, to integrate parts of the social front of one routine to other routines?

I will explore how most journalists interviewed report feeling left behind in face of bloggers and younger writers who are mastering online tools. Furthermore, many of these non-professionals are rising in the ranks, publishing for travel media brands themselves. I'll compare interviews between bloggers and journalists to explore what bloggers do that journalists could be doing as well in order to remain pertinent in the current travel mediascape. Travel journalists need to be thinking about their specialties, their expertise, and even their voice, in order to make them seem credible and attractive not only to editors but to readers as well. This chapter will highlight some practices that journalists should be aware of, by opening up a dialogue with travel bloggers on how they engage in creating their own distinct brands.

Personal branding and the journalist

In its simplest form, branding involves distinguishing the goods or services of one producer from those of another, allowing consumers the freedom to choose (Murphy, 1987, p. 1). In a networked society, with countless websites available online, it is no stretch to imagine why branding within a specific niche of media, like travel publications, would be important. There is no one way to travel, and those with special interests or needs – budget, adventure, luxury, family, solo, culinary, etc. – no longer need to wait for a travel magazine to publish something that touches upon their specific area of tourism. What the internet has created, however, is an environment where much of this branding, previously established on the level of the publication, is now occurring on the level of the journalist, leading to personal or self-branding of the individual professional as a source of information. *Lonely Planet*, once a more alternative guide, is arguably producing similar content to most other mainstream travel websites. It is falling to individuals to become specialists, to brand themselves online where the publications can't afford to limit themselves.

As Gandini describes in his work on branding and social capital, self-branding is a way to enable 'new practices of sociality that do not remain limited to the branding of the self but act as marketing work that combines networking with the management of social relationships' (2016, p. 126). Extensive research on the idea of personal branding has flourished in recent years, as the norms associated with career advancement have begun to destabilize in an era of late-industrial capitalism (Lair et al., 2005, p. 317). Freelancing and the gig economy are increasingly prevalent choices for the millennial generation, as well as the rising 'Generation Z'. Working digitally, especially on social media, is becoming more commonplace among this workforce. For journalists, this tendency towards freelance work is clearly evident in the UK, where the number of freelancers increased by 67 per cent between 2000 and 2015, from 15,000 to 25,000 (Spilsbury, 2016). Early research into self-presentation online looks at Erving Goffman's 1959 work on stage theory applied to web pages (Papacharissi, 2002). More recent work has applied similar approaches to Twitter and social networks as stages for presentation for journalists. While Chapter 7 underscores many of the questions surrounding social media and journalism, I reiterate here that this evolution is neither new nor ceasing – it's a constant in journalism that the way practitioners function and their professional boundaries will shift relative to the technological, societal, and cultural changes that occur in their time, among countless other factors (Carlson, 2015, p. 8).

What's interesting for journalism is that self-branding remains a contentious concept. As one older travel journalist interviewed stated, 'I've often noticed that too many of today's young writers, travel or otherwise, spend more time fashioning themselves as a brand than they do any writing. There are exceptions, of course, albeit few and far between.' Little research looks directly at the relationship between travel journalists and how they self-brand, partly due to the already powerful branding of publications like *Condé Nast Traveler* or *National Geographic*, which supersedes any personal brand, at least according to interviewees. In the early twenty-first century, however, social media has pushed journalists to think of themselves more as a brand than ever before, even if such practices are adopted more by younger, digitally-savvy journalists (Hedman and Djerf-Pierre, 2013). One group of researchers looked at the differences between employed and freelance journalists, asserting that both groups 'present themselves in a moderated way to their social media audience and in that perspective, they perform a role-play' (Brems et al., 2017, p. 446). In their study, these researchers explained that professionals use Twitter to network, but struggle with sharing personal details as well as explicitly promoting their work. There were notable differences in how employed journalists use Twitter as opposed to freelancers, who 'used Twitter significantly more in an interactive and personal way: they argued more often with other users and shared more non-professional details' (p. 456).

As I'll explain, the travel journalists interviewed deal largely with similar questions when positioning themselves on these networks. Some see it as a positive thing to embrace, while others are less convinced. The idea of personal branding comes with its critics. Authors have commented on the topic generally, without specific reference to journalism, writing,

> Although a certain kind of communication is offered by the personal branders as the solution to economic disadvantage and dislocation, that communication itself may contribute to social alienation as well as to a delay in the necessary structural changes of the society.
>
> *(Lair et al., 2005, p. 337)*

While alienation is just one of many possible critiques, a larger issue of branding techniques boils down to a lack of direction. One study looks at how health journalists struggle with branding themselves, accepting the now commonplace need to feed their identity online, embrace audiences, and risk tension with their publications (Molyneux and Holton, 2015). A central issue, however, is a lack of guidance for these journalists when it comes to branding themselves online. The authors suggest that journalists are looking beyond their profession for how to engage more with branding online, but should proceed cautiously. 'Some may argue, however, that journalism risks losing its professional identity (already under assault, by some estimations) by adopting practices not central to journalism's democratic watchdog function' (2015, p. 237).

For the increasingly precarious career choice of travel journalist, however, self-branding is a necessary part of their routine. Researchers point to the potential to capitalize on one's image, functioning as a curated CV of interests, writing ability, and previous work experience among other attributes. These freelancers, researchers explain, 'might benefit from social media platforms to become self-branding entrepreneurs who can get or stay on the radar of potential media clients. Social media platforms offer an apt environment for designing a potentially lucrative image of the self' (Brems et al., 2017, p. 444). Where alternatives to full-time employment are becoming more commonplace, freelance workers are embracing new possibilities.

Creating a brand

In travel journalism, as stated, word of mouth recommendations are important. All writers interviewed stressed that it is important for the reader to know that the author actually experienced something that they are describing. Online word of mouth still adheres to some of these principals, and having a more transparent persona online contributes positively to establishing trust and credibility (Litvin et al., 2008).

Self-branding is a way to conceive of this relationship building, to participate actively in designing how audiences view the journalist – or blogger for that matter. How, concretely, can information providers do this? Mark Briggs provides a fairly comprehensive guide for journalists and describes how blogging, live-blogging, and even micro-blogging, can all be useful tools for entrepreneurial endeavors (2012). Much work has been done on how blogs and social media can be used as marketing tools (Xiang and Gretzel, 2010; Hays et al., 2013; Hudson and Thal, 2013). Little research looks into how journalists should – or at least, could – be using them to enhance their online identities as travel and tourism experts.

Several journalists interviewed do blog, but mostly for personal reasons. Few revealed that they see their blogs as an extension of their journalism. Concretely, however, blogs can highlight a travel journalist's specific niches or interests that could help editors assess their suitability for a job. While most journalists have some sort of website, highlighting their professional work, few engage in proper blogging, preferring instead to microblog on Twitter. What these websites do, instead, is showcase the work that journalists have already done, much more like a digital CV than a narrative outlet. For journalists with other talents or skills, these websites also let them highlight photography, video, audio, or other publications that they might be working on beyond their journalism. Blogging, however, isn't considered vastly important to their jobs or to establishing who they are as much as microblogging and, increasingly, Instagram.

Most journalists are begrudgingly on these social networks, and while these outlets may not feature prominently in their news gathering processes, they do function to build their brand. Most journalists, however, are not consciously building up a brand, but rather creating their identity more organically or even accidentally as they share and interact with online content that they find important or interesting. A look at their Twitter accounts reveals that most are simply retweeting content from other outlets or sharing their own articles and stories. They aren't using it to dialogue as much as to share their content with audiences. What remains unclear, and where further research could help highlight some of these practices, is how expat journalists act differently from those who live in their home country. One could argue that the fact that they are expats living in Paris or France already gives them a beat to follow, but a look at how bloggers in the same situation reflect upon their work reveals that travel journalists – expats or not – need to think beyond the brand and the destination to understand what their personal brand is offering readers.

Bloggers: branding from the beginning

Part of the problem that travel journalists face is that many of these self-branding techniques have already been mastered – if not originated – by social media natives, specifically bloggers and other influencers. These individuals, never initially supported by a media brand, have based their activity solely on the creation of a personal brand. They understand the nuances of producing this online persona. Molyneux and Holton discussed how some journalists are looking beyond their profession to see how other content producers are engaging with this branding phenomenon, which is both educative and dangerous, as it may erode their underlying journalistic principals (2015). These non-professionals shared their practices, which revealed a varied, but nuanced look at what they do and how they construct their identities online. These practices are helping to create writers and content creators who are attractive to media brands because, among other reasons, they come with an audience that is both engaged and attentive, which means ultimately more traffic for websites.

Bloggers have been engaged in self-branding essentially since blogs began. Recent studies look at how bloggers work towards emitting a certain image or message, be it in lifestyle blogs or even video blogs (Sepp et al., 2011; Duffy and Hund, 2015; Van Nuenen, 2016). A sample of Estonian bloggers revealed how they obtain different types of gratification from their work, such as in promoting or advertising products that they like (Sepp et al., 2011). The researchers explain further, 'Bloggers use their blog to present a desired image to readers, omitting information that might lead readers to take the blogger less seriously, and instead emphasising competences' (p. 1496). Such branding efforts also extend to Twitter, a microblogging platform, where in one study, journalists 'talked about the importance of tending to their personal brands, noting they want to maintain a reputation that is portable and not just linked to one newspaper' (Swasy, 2016, p. 70).

Bloggers I interviewed, mostly expats who cater to a travel audience, reveal an array of practices that contribute to their self-branding. Among them, they try to maintain a focused message in their content while also engaging their audiences in various ways. Responses varied among bloggers who were engaged in more self-serving missions – selling a book, offering concierge services, or writing freelance articles. These bloggers have an overwhelmingly more organized strategy for curating their image, which, 'built on quality content that is narrowly targeted to a specific niche, creates a stronger base for a business' (Briggs, 2012, p. 45). They aren't just blogging about Paris as a destination. They are offering a more nuanced, or even curated view of their experiences in order to define the utilitarian value for their readers. A common theme among all of these bloggers, however, is a clear and focused approach to their content. Unlike journalist who can cover a broad array of topics, bloggers stress the importance of staying on message in a variety of ways. One blogger attributes her focus to her personality, which guides her content, which leads her readers to expect a certain type of post from her, but also allows them to contextualize her travel advice:

> I feel like the people who have been reading my blog for a long time now have an accurate sense of my personality as I display it on the blog and so I guess that is my primary responsibility to my readers, to present a consistent perspective and personality. Then if I do recommend something in a blog post, then that's a good context for understanding that recommendation.

Other bloggers echo this idea that a personality-driven approach to their content, emphasizing style and voice over actual choice of topics. As Gillmor points out, the best blogs have a voice, demonstrating that 'they are clearly written by human beings with genuine human passion' (2006, p. 29). One blogger declared: 'They want to see me. Personal stuff. I can relate because when I read blogs I want to know more about the person and you become a bit obsessed, find out more, learn more.' Another blogger agreed, stating that her blog is a portfolio of her as a person, free and unfiltered:

> No one is editing you, it's your voice. Having a blog is really a great way to find your voice and not be afraid to share it with other people. Then they get to know you through your natural style of writing. Versus writing in a journal, this is actually going into the world.

Whereas journalists may have to adapt to their publications, limiting their ability to brand in situ, bloggers' work is dependent on them creating their own voice. One blogger sums it up, saying, 'My writing is me. It's not separate from me. What I say, how I say it, that's the brand. It's the written expression of the brand and I have to be very clear on what that brand is.'

At the same time, while style and voice seem to be the first layer of branding, the focus of the blog is also important to most bloggers. Some are very practical, like a blogger who shares the most up-to-date happenings in Paris for tourists, shunning topics that are likely to be found in a classic travel guide. As someone who also works as a BBC travel contributor, it's important for her blog to highlight that she is in-step with the city. 'My blog is very much about contemporary Paris,' she said. 'It's whatever is relevant now.'

A book author blogging about Paris shares more anecdotes about her family, echoing the themes in her books. A blogger who also runs a personal concierge service shares practical information in her posts. The content and choices they make are not so much driven by some grandiose idea of travel, but instead they seek to attract audiences to their site, ideally to convert them into customers of whatever service they provide. The blog on a website like Eurocheapo.com focusses on budget activities in European cities, with content that clearly reflects the financial core of the site, allowing readers to book low-cost hotels through it. It would be naive to say that all blogs have content that reflect some sort of financial goal, as many blogs do not bring any direct revenue to bloggers whatsoever.

A minority of bloggers are less practical in their approach, seeking to share a more ethereal vision of Paris as a destination. One blogger said, 'It's to inspire people. It's to inspire, to appeal to that romantic, to that cliché of what Paris is. I am a romantic who idealizes.' In the same way, another blogger only chooses the most positive aspects of her life to highlight, carefully curating an idyllic vision of the city. She said she writes often for armchair travelers for whom she is providing an escape, and explains:

> So this facet of myself I tend to portray on my blog is the American girl living the dream in Paris even though some days it doesn't feel like that … It gives me an opportunity to go to fashion shows and to review Champagne. Who the hell wouldn't want to do that? It's a way for me to express that facet of myself.

Here, the focus is not so much one type of traveler – budget, expat, foodie, etc. – but on inspiring and motivating travelers, like the aforementioned armchair travelers who may not actually have the resources or ability to reach a destination like Paris.

Social networks and self-branding

To advance these aims and to complement their blogs, all bloggers are engaged on social networks to varying degrees. Some bloggers look at social networks as alternative platforms for their work, and even essential for their work, but as one blogger explained, they are possibly two distinct audiences. 'Now Instagram, where I have quite a following but I don't get the sense that those people are necessarily those who read the site. They are finding me because I'm posting things about Europe and Paris.' This inability to know if they are catering to one audience or to two separate ones complicates blogging for those who seek to profit from it, leading to more investment in Instagram accounts where influencers have arguably more impact.

Social networks, however, are still practical for bloggers, even the most casual ones. One blogger, who has little financial investment in her blog, said,

> I use Twitter, Facebook, and Instagram as a way to diffuse my blog's aura, my blog's image, that facet that I keep talking about. To draw people in and hopefully they'll realize I have a blog and if they like reading blogs they'll come on it.

Methods for employing social networks vary from individual to individual, with no one-size-fits-all solution. Another blogger explained her approach:

> I use different ones for different things. I use Tumblr for random stuff I like, what I do for Pinterest as well. Instagram is more personal, like things that make me happy. Whereas Facebook, my page, is to put posts on, and then I share it on my personal one. I tweet when I have new posts, but I use Twitter mostly to consume – I read the news, follow other blogs.

There is no systematic way to brand oneself on these networks, but bloggers do in general maintain some consistency across them, using the same names and photos of themselves when possible. Where they differ is in their approach to engaging readers on social networks – or even in the comment sections of their blogs. One blogger is diligent, almost detrimentally, in responding to her readers' emails and Instagram comments. She said:

> A lot of emails. I need to figure it out, but it takes me three or four hours to respond to all of the emails. Before I became a blogger, I was a blog reader and I wrote to bloggers. So, I want to get back to them the way I wanted to be responded to. I'm so annoyed with some of the questions but I still want to be nice and give them a reply and say look at this post.

Other bloggers are not so altruistic, responding casually or not at all, like one blogger who said, 'I just let people comment and that's about it. I don't gather this intimacy because you can be hurt.' Comparing the bloggers who responded that they engage more with their readers with those who do not reveals some interesting points. Those who do interact tend to attract higher followings, but also report more professional opportunities linked to their blogs. For example, the above blogger who responds to all of her emails also contributes to *Condé Nast Traveler* online, while the less altruistic one reported dreaming of writing for the *New York Times* but with no success. Of course, engagement is just one of many factors affecting how these bloggers brand themselves, but it appears to be one that relates to the overall success of the individual in their endeavors.

All of these strategies are just the beginning. Understanding how bloggers position themselves, however, can help travel journalists identify how they can better brand themselves. For example, one blogger interviewed has adopted a designated hashtag that she uses across her social networks, a way of labelling herself and her work. While perhaps not the most practical thing for a journalist working across multiple publications, it's an example of how travel journalists need to rethink their strategies, develop a clear voice, a set of interests, and a public image that transcends the publications they are writing for online. Perhaps travel journalists need to revisit many of the values ascribed to the typical Romantic travel writer of the late eighteenth and early nineteenth century who 'records not only a literal journey but also a metaphorical "inner" journey of self-discovery and maturation' (Thompson, 2011, p. 117). The destination is important to any travel story, yes, but in a digital world, the journalist's identity might be equally important.

Convergence: when bloggers become journalists

While it may seem trivial to compare bloggers to journalists at all, with one creating its own ideology as it goes along and the latter adhering to a staid yet continually evolving professional identity, it's important for a concrete reason. Perhaps more than political or current affairs bloggers who may never make the leap from amateurism to professionalism, many travel bloggers are slipping into roles formerly filled by travel journalists. While journalism is a career based on a fight for its recognition through the normalization of routines and creation of a professional identity, it has never fully excluded anyone who has adapted to its standards (Ruellan, 2007). It is no surprise then that, with the rise of blogging and the mastering of self-branding techniques by social media users, that these individuals would step into roles formerly filled predominantly by journalists. Several travel bloggers discuss how they have used their blogs as springboards to successful careers working with media brands like BBC Travel and Condé Nast.

Journalists, first and foremost, are critical of those who compete with them for well-paid writing jobs. One professional said:

> I'd think logically that a newspaper would like to have someone who is a very experienced journalist but instead they are just taking whomever. It's frustrating because many experienced journalists can't find work. I don't want to close the door to people who want to get into journalism but it's unfair that people who have experience and studied can't make a living.

This frustration is echoed by several journalists who see bloggers as subverting them, accepting smaller fees for lesser quality work, in their view. Such critiques became particularly salient when the publication *L.A. Weekly* fired much of its staff in 2017, opting instead to solicit unpaid contributions from citizens (Dessem, 2017). Is the future of travel journalism likewise a purely citizen-run activity? One glance at TripAdvisor and it becomes clear that as citizens, we are not all up to that task. Not yet, at least.

While journalists view it as an assault on their profession, bloggers see it as an opportunity to segue into paid, professional work, though they tread lightly. One blogger is cautious about playing up her professional writing, aware that there are higher standards and potentially larger audiences involved. Still, she acknowledges an added layer of credibility to her professional profile. She said, 'Yes the people who know I do it maybe take me more seriously because it's not just the blog anymore. When I write about things for Condé Nast, I get nervous.' Her trepidation is based in part on early experiences with writing for the brand. She wrote a 2013 article about Paris that erroneously announced a firework celebration on New Year's Eve in the French capital, eliciting stinging remarks from readers in the comments section below the article. Such experiences are not surprising given the lack of veracity or fact-finding that bloggers engage in, but perhaps these stumbling blocks are necessary to learn about writing on a professional level.

Additionally, these professional experiences have an effect on how these bloggers approach their blogs. As one blogger, who has subsequently written for numerous publications, said: 'Once I began writing for publications, there is a form, a way of phrasing things, of approaching certain thoughts and that started to seep into my blog posts.' Another blogger used her site to springboard into professional media, and said that her blog and professional experiences feed off each other. She explained,

> It's cyclical. I started the blog, then BBC contacted me, and it gave me a bit of authority to say I work for the BBC, so I felt legitimate. My work at BBC informed how I work on my blog from a psychological point of view.

While these transitions are not happening all of the time, the potential is slowly being exploited by media brands who are harnessing the power of these self-branded individuals to bring their audiences to the professional publication.

Embracing branding

In travel media, it's becoming clear how generic information from legacy media or professional online sites is not enough. Consumers are sifting through countless websites and need a way to distinguish one from the other. To that end, travel journalists should likely be thinking more about their online persona, their unique contributions, and their self-branding techniques. They should be thinking of a well-defined Twitter profile explaining their interests. They should have a blog that gives a behind-the-scenes look at their travels. They should think about sharing photos of their trips on Instagram. All of these factors help create a more complete image of the writer, offering a human face to their audiences.

Journalists currently rely on their branded publications, avoiding too much self-promotion. Bloggers rely almost exclusively on branding themselves, and journalists could look to them to understand better how to engage with these practices online (Molyneux and Holton, 2015). Beyond developing a clear voice in their writing and a unified presence on social media, travel journalists need to be aware of promoting their specialisms beyond 'tourism', which is too broad a topic in today's fragmented mediascape. Being versatile in their writing is a useful skill that they can always apply wherever they work, but an increasing number of freelancers need to be thinking of how to distinguish themselves from the other freelance journalists and increasingly competitive bloggers who are vying for similar professional opportunities.

Clearly, further research will be able to shed more light on how the concept of self-branding affects travel journalists, especially as a generation of more social media savvy individuals replaces the older generation. What emerging tools or practices will allow travel journalists to continue establishing themselves as trusted purveyors of travel information, as entities independent of media brands? Having a distinct voice and curated social media presence is the first step, but these professionals will have to prepare to evolve with whatever comes next.

References

Brems, C., Temmerman, M., Graham, T., and Broersma, M. (2017). Personal branding on Twitter. *Digital Journalism*, 5(4), 443–459.

Briggs, M. (2012). *Entrepreneurial journalism: How to build what's next for news*. Thousand Oaks, CA: CQ Press.

Carlson, M. (2015). The many boundaries of journalism. In M. Carlson and S. Lewis (Eds.), *Boundaries of journalism* (pp. 1–18). Abingdon: Routledge.

Dessem, M. (2017, Dec. 6). L.A. Weekly's new owners fired the staff in favor of unpaid contributors, so I contributed. *The Slate*. Retrieved from www.slate.com

Duffy, B. E., and Hund, E. (2015). 'Having it all' on social media: Entrepreneurial femininity and self-branding among fashion bloggers. *Social Media and Society*, 1(2).

Gandini, A. (2016). Digital work: Self-branding and social capital in the freelance knowledge economy. *Marketing Theory*, 16(1), 123–141.

Gillmor, D. (2006). *We the media: Grassroots journalism by the people, for the people*. Sebastopol, CA: O'Reilly Media.

Goffman, E. (1959). *The presentation of self in everyday life*. Garden City, NJ: Doubleday.

Hanusch, F., and Bruns, A. (2016). Journalistic branding on Twitter: A representative study of Australian journalists' profile descriptions. *Digital Journalism*, 5(1), 26–43.

Hays, S., Page, S. J., and Buhalis, D. (2013). Social media as a destination marketing tool: Its use by national tourism organisations. *Current Issues in Tourism*, 16(3), 211–239.

Hedman, U., and Djerf-Pierre, M. (2013). The social journalist: Embracing the social media life or creating a new digital divide? *Digital Journalism*, 1(3), 368–385.

Hudson, S., and Thal, K. (2013). The impact of social media on the consumer decision process: Implications for tourism marketing. *Journal of Travel and Tourism Marketing*, 30(1–2), 156–160.

Kusumasondjaja, S., Shanka, T., and Marchegiani, C. (2012). Credibility of online reviews and initial trust: The roles of reviewer's identity and review valence. *Journal of Vacation Marketing*, 18(3), 185–195.

Lair, D. J., Sullivan, K., and Cheney, G. (2005). Marketization and the recasting of the professional self. *Management Communication Quarterly*, 18(3), 307–343.

Litvin, S. W., Goldsmith, R. E., and Pan, B. (2008). Electronic word-of-mouth in hospitality and tourism management. *Tourism Management*, 29(3), 458–468.

McGaurr, L. (2015). *Environmental communication and travel journalism: Consumerism, conflict and concern*. Abingdon: Routledge.

Molyneux, L. (2015). What journalists retweet: Opinion, humor, and brand development on Twitter. *Journalism*, 16(7), 920–935.

Molyneux, L., and Holton, A. (2015). Branding (health) journalism. *Digital Journalism*, 3(2), 225–242.

Murphy, J. M. (1987). *Branding: A key marketing tool*. London: Macmillan.

Olins, W. (2000). How brands are taking over the corporation. In M. Shultz, M. J. Hatch and M. H. Larsen (Eds.), *The expressive organization: Linking identity, reputation, and the corporate brand* (pp. 51–65). New York: Oxford University Press.

Papacharissi, Z. (2002). The presentation of self in virtual life: Characteristics of personal home pages. *Journalism and Mass Communication Quarterly*, 79(3), 643–660.

Peters, J. D. (2001). Witnessing. *Media, Culture and Society*, 23(6), 707–723.

Ruellan, D. (2007). *Le journalisme ou le professionnalisme du flou*. Grenoble: Presses universitaires de Grenoble.

Sepp, M., Liljander, V., and Gummerus, J. (2011). Private bloggers' motivations to produce content: A gratifications theory perspective. *Journal of Marketing Management*, 27(13–14), 1479–1503.

Spilsbury, M. (2016). Exploring freelance journalism. UK: National Council for the Training of Journalists. Retrieved from www.nctj.com

Swasy, A. (2016). *How journalists use Twitter: The changing landscape of U.S. newsrooms*. Lanham, MD: Lexington Books.

Thompson, Carl. (2011). *Travel writing*. Abingdon: Routledge.

Van Nuenen, T. (2016). Here I am: Authenticity and self-branding on travel blogs. *Tourist Studies*, 16(2), 192–212.

Wagemans, A., Witschge, T., and Deuze, M. (2016). Ideology as resource in entrepreneurial journalism: The French online news startup Mediapart. *Journalism Practice*, 10(2), 160–177.

Xiang, Z., and Gretzel, U. (2010). Role of social media in online travel information search. *Tourism Management*, 31(2), 179–188.

Yannopoulou, N., and Moufahim, M. (2013). User-generated brands and social media: Couchsurfing and AirBnb. *Contemporary Management Research Pages*, 9(1), 88.

PART III

New interpretations and opportunities

10

A CONSTRUCTIVE APPROACH TO TOURISM REPORTING

Travel journalism in crisis

When terrorists attacked Paris in November 2015, news coverage in the following weeks announced that tourists were afraid to come to the city, hurting local tourism in France. A headline in the *Guardian* read, 'Billions Wiped off European Travel Shares after Paris Attacks', while *Quartz* ran an article under the title, 'The Paris Attacks Will Cost the French Economy more than $2 billion'. Through 2016, the press reported that the tourism industry did lose some 750 million euros due to fearful travelers cancelling their plans, showing how the attacks took their toll financially. While business and economic reporters focused on the numbers related to business losses, travel journalists, immediately after the attacks, took a different approach to their reporting. Many journalists in travel media urged tourists not to cancel their trips, to support Paris by maintaining their plans, to show resilience. Other events in Western tourist destinations – London and Madrid to name two – yielded similar reporting in the early years of the new millennium. The events in Paris, however, came at a time when online media – including both brand name websites and social media – were more widespread than during those earlier attacks, making it easier for travel journalists to reach larger audiences more quickly than ever before.

While just one example of travel journalism responding to a twenty-first-century crisis, the reactions to the attack on Paris can allow us to rethink the travel journalist's role in a digital age. When it comes to devastating events such as the Paris atrocities, can travel journalism function in a way that goes beyond simply offering information and advice to consumers? In this chapter, I'll introduce the idea of constructive journalism and apply it to travel journalism. This unique interpretation of two emerging fields will allow practitioners to challenge and expand their definition of what travel journalism actually is.

From crisis to constructivism

There exists ample research on crisis communication and its relationship to the tourism industry. In a study of tourism boards after 9/11, Fall and Massey discuss the 'crisis recovery phase' of management, writing that 'the organization focuses its efforts at reputation management and returning the organization to a sense of normalcy' (2008, p. 4). Journalists, however, are not necessarily part of an organized crisis management team. Studies look at how destinations can prepare for crisis events (Sönmez et al., 1999). Avraham discusses how tourism boards use the media to rehabilitate the image of Middle Eastern countries during times of crisis, but, again, these studies do not address how travel journalists, specifically, play a role in mediating a crisis, and how they address their publics (2013, 2015).

Instead, perhaps travel journalism can find common ground with another type of journalism, namely advocacy journalism, which also adopts a less objective approach than traditional hard news reporting (Janowitz, 1975). Can travel journalism, then, overcome the traditional journalistic gatekeeping role in favor of something more akin to the advocacy role described by Janowitz, whereby the journalists call upon 'the active intervention of the mass media' to achieve certain objectives (1975, p. 620)? Charles suggests that 'advocacy journalism is a proactive approach that does not just report facts as they are, it seeks ways of improvement, solution and resolution' (2013, p. 388). While taking less of a socio-political angle and more of a cultural or lifestyle approach, travel journalism could, hypothetically, advocate for a cause when needed, be it during a crisis or some other conflict. McGaurr (2015) in her book describes the relationship between travel journalism and environmental conflict and discusses how elite sources possess an advantage in the tourism industry, preventing environmental issues making their way into the foreground of travel reporting (2015). Ultimately, however, she is discussing a form of advocacy in travel journalism, a role that is not often fulfilled by practitioners.

Whereas advocacy journalism seems too charged with notions of social or political change, the idea that travel journalism might take more of a *constructive* approach to reporting could be a more convincing notion for travel journalists to address in the future. As Cathrine Gyldensted proposes, constructive journalism 'investigates opportunities, looks at dilemmas from all sides, and indicates remedies', ultimately leading to solutions to current problems (2015, loc 132). I argue that what travel journalists can do – and were doing during the Paris attacks – was just that, engaging in a form of constructive journalism, a unique way of interpreting the work of journalists beyond simply reporting information or telling stories. Instead of waiting for tourism bureaux to begin campaigns to attract tourists back to France, travel journalists began their own efforts to reframe the crisis and allay the fears of tourists cancelling their trips. Constructive journalism, as I'll discuss, is about promoting solutions and creating knowledge. Applied to travel journalism, its principles can help inform how travel journalists could interpret their work – though such practices are hardly yet on their radar. This chapter seeks to propose situating travel journalism within a constructivist framework, examining how it can work to solve problems and promote opportunities for its readers who are organizing and planning their own travel experiences (Gyldensted, 2015, loc 132). The two fields, constructive and travel journalism, have never been put into conversation, which means that this attempt is just a first step in understanding how travel journalists might also be able to act constructively.

Constructive journalism in focus

To suggest ways of interpreting travel journalism as constructive journalism, it is imperative to understand what academics and practitioners mean by constructive journalism. First, constructive journalism, a relatively new interpretation of journalism in academia, is not altogether novel. Chalmers evokes the idea of constructivism when discussing the muckrakers in the United States, describing how they believed 'they were contributing to the progress of society' (1959, p. 304). Nico Drok and Liesberth Hermans in their discussion of 'slow journalism' evoke the idea of constructivism, writing that it 'should not only be investigative, but inclusive, co-operative and constructive as well' (2016, p. 551). At its core, constructive journalism as we identify it today is about offering stories that are positive and uplifting, but more than just 'feel-good' anecdotes – it should not simply be confused with positive news, advocacy journalism, or solutions journalism. As Gyldensted proposes, 'a new potential in journalism is to facilitate a more future-oriented debate on social issues' (2015, loc 1638). Applied to hard news reporting, the relationship is straightforward. Whereas the press often focusses on negative angles and stories, constructive journalism, according to Haagerup, offers an alternative approach:

> The consequences of media focus on things that do not work, on the maladjusted, and on the negative, are comprehensive, not only to dropping circulation figures, advertising revenues and declining reach. It also changes the mental condition for those who get their picture of reality through the press. It defocuses politics and prevents the changes and the progress, which should have been to the benefit of society. The development threatens the political process and democracy itself.
>
> *(Haagerup, 2015, p. 14)*

We can also extend this concept to lifestyle topics. Constructive journalism seeks to empower readers, to raise the bar and create knowledge and not just awareness. Its practitioners ask the basic questions – who, what, where, when, and why – as well as a sixth 'w', 'what now?' In this manner, the reporter seeks 'to identify a path forward instead of leaving readers with a dead-end street narrative' (Gyldensted, 2015, loc 1784).

The media has illustrated trends towards constructive journalism, with a magazine titled 'Positive News' appearing as early as 1993. Even the *Huffington Post* initiated a 'Good News' section that focusses on more uplifting stories. In April

2016, the UN called for a more constructive approach to journalism to address those who felt 'disempowered' by the news, as the *Guardian* reported (Jackson, 2016). An article in the *Columbia Journalism Review* points out, however, that critics are wary of focusing too heavily on positive reporting, and that it is not the solution to 'bad-news fatigue' that plagues journalism today (Sillesen, 2014).

Constructive journalism, however, goes beyond simply reporting feel-good stories, like a list or round-up of the best cafés in Paris. Gyldensted proposes applying Seligman's five elements of well-being to reporting to arrive at a constructive angle for a story. These elements include positive emotions, but also engagement, relationships, meaning, and accomplishment (2015, loc 820). Gyldensted suggests asking, 'What is the societal importance of your story idea?' to steer away form a simple upbeat story to create more constructive journalism (2015, loc 855). How can such frameworks be used to interpret niche journalism, such as travel journalism, which does not necessarily work under the same constraints or with the same audiences as the civic or 'hard news' reporting that these authors address?

Travel journalists as constructivists

Based on the above questions surrounding constructive journalism, I argue that it is not only possible, but important to consider travel journalism in this light. The internet has facilitated these changes. Whereby *Lonely Planet* used to have only monthly magazines and yearly guides, it now has a website with blogs and articles that can be published immediately, giving a trusted travel brand power to respond quickly, unlike ever before. While not all travel media will be acting constructively all the time, the scope and reach of travel-related stories require practitioners to consider their work beyond instructing consumers where and how to travel. Everyone can theoretically do that now on blogs and social media. Looking deeper into destinations, especially in times of crisis, may be a way forward for travel journalists to situate themselves among all of the travel content available to audiences.

I begin the conversation between travel and constructive journalism by speaking directly with journalists. I'll describe, for example, to what extent travel journalists remain positive in their coverage, and what that signifies to them. While Gyldensted declares that positive reporting is not the only goal of constructive journalism, it remains a component (2015). How then, do travel journalists embrace this positivity while working in a more constructive direction? I'll also explore why travel journalists write in the first place, focusing on print and online journalism for the moment. What are their goals for their publications and how do travel journalists articulate their personal motivations for travel? With varying tastes and experiences, are they seeking to do more than just produce accurate stories, or are there other motivations behind their writing in line with constructive leanings?

Second, I'll show what constructive travel journalism might actually look like in practice. Based on a case study involving travel articles produced directly after the 2015 Paris attacks, we can observe some of these ideas played out in the mainstream travel media, with articles in the *New York Times* and *Travel+Leisure* magazine, for example. As Zelizer and Allan pointed out, during 9/11, journalists were subjected to trauma as much as the people of the United States, and 'there were no detached vantage-points situated "outside" the crisis from which they could objectively observe' (2011, p. 1). The Paris attacks, I argue, had a similar effect, with social media profiles portraying the French flag after the attacks and an outpouring of support from around the world. Journalism has changed since 9/11, as the authors argue throughout Zelizer and Allan's collective work, but none adopt the perspective of the lifestyle journalist. A framing analysis of these articles will illustrate how some travel journalists embrace a constructive approach in travel journalism by framing their stories in very particular ways.

To answer these questions, both interviews and framing analysis were employed to analyze the journalists' practices as well as to understand how travel journalism responded to a particular crisis situation. The results of the interviews revealed several interesting points that could lead to a constructive interpretation of travel journalism if we can be flexible with its initial definition. While not trying to inform their readers as a citizenry, travel journalists do perceive their audiences as needing guidance and assistance when navigating the tourism industry. In this way, travel journalists are fulfilling a constructivist role by pushing their readers forward through the travel process and helping them solve problems as they arrive, rarely dwelling on the negative or uncomfortable aspects of travel. Journalists revealed a strong sense of professional identity, but they fall short of mirroring political and hard news journalists who are often at the heart of journalistic research. Instead, they have their own set of ideals and practices based on their particular audiences and the specific conditions under which travel journalism is produced (Hanusch, 2012). Furthermore, the framing analysis illustrates how travel journalists break from traditional news frames, offering up news coverage that responds more directly to a crisis and its effects on tourism and travelers. Their unique framing of the Paris attacks illustrates again how travel journalism can engage in constructive practice.

Positivity, empowerment, and the travel journalist

One major result that responds to the first question is that journalists are generally positive in their work. They are keenly aware that readers want to know what they *should* do and what they *should* see when they travel, and dwelling on negative aspects does not push their stories forward. This is a key underpinning of constructive journalism, according to Gyldensted (2015, loc 528). Part of this positivity may traditionally be due to insufficient space in magazines and newspapers to waste words on negative commentary, but part of it is also simply understanding the subjective nature of travel. As one journalist put it, there is always a positive spin to put on a topic. 'If I don't like something, there are people who will like it. Somebody likes it, so why?' she said. Another journalist also discussed writing about experiences that may not have been to her taste. She said, however, that her goal is always 'sticking to the truth but making that truth beautiful to read'.

Not all journalists saw positivity as a key element of good travel journalism. One journalist was critical of how remaining positive can sometimes hinder the location and the reader's perception of it. In her mind, remaining positive relates to projecting the truth about a place and combatting stereotypes. She explains, when discussing coverage of Paris:

> In the travel and features pages you have this perfect vision of Paris. In the same newspaper, in the news pages, it's almost xenophobic where they show the French as arrogant and stupid. You don't have to do the fairy cake thing to please your readers If you're working for a newspaper or magazine, it's the editors who are at fault. You need to change them.

This argument leads to a clearer understanding of constructivist reporting. The desire to be positive, but also to promote the truth, is fundamental to travel journalism and contributes to a constructivist interpretation. In this example, the journalist wants to push forward and break from the simplistically positive view of Paris to a more realistic view that contextualizes and nuances those people who are elsewhere treated as stereotypes. The journalists, as we see, go beyond simple positive statements that lack the societal significance that Gyldensted requires of constructive journalism (2015, loc 198).

A broader look at travel media, however, can better situate travel journalism as constructive, especially with online review sites. While the positivity of journalists – and bloggers, as further research has also demonstrated – is appreciated by readers, these writers are the yin to the yang of review sites like TripAdvisor. Never before have so many individuals been able to voice so publicly their opinions about their experiences As research shows, TripAdvisor's website has the 'capacity to give "voice" to the authentic opinion of independent travelers' (Jeacle, 2011, p. 31). These opinions, however, are largely critical, and often wantonly negative, as in one study of complaints on TripAdvisor (Vásquez, 2011). Numerous reviews seek to assess the impact of these reviews on travelers and, moreover, on businesses within the tourism community, to see if they can actually alter perspectives (e.g. Vermeulen and Seegers, 2009). While the debates continue over TripAdvisor's impact, it is interesting to consider travel journalism's role as a potential watchdog of these sites which are growing in prominence. The positivity and truth embraced by journalism seems to counter the negativity and opinionated nature of review sites – though we can easily argue for the necessity of both when making travel decisions. These multiple viewpoints echo Robinson's ideas on journalism as process, whereby individual posts or articles may not be verified or trustworthy on their own, 'but the process itself can achieve the journalistic goal of informational empowerment' (2011, p. 190). This empowerment is a major component of constructive journalism, and travel journalists need to engage actively to promote such empowerment for readers.

Where travel journalists appear to embrace constructive journalism more fully is in their desire to empower and to embolden their readers during their travels.

While the motivations varied from journalist to journalist – some write for money, some for themselves – many journalists claim that they are writing for their audiences, but beyond that they want to inspire and empower them. This is a key element of travel media that recognizes that all readers are not active tourists – some are known as 'armchair travelers' and may be moved to travel based on the media they consume (Damkjoer and Waade, 2014).

The travel journalists interviewed were keenly aware of this potential. One journalist said her motivation to become a travel journalist was altruistic to this effect. 'Being up to speed, being able to share news and information. I think that is probably the main motivation and to get people excited to travel', she said. In a similar fashion, another journalist said that she wants to help readers discover something new. 'In general, in journalism, it's to bring something interesting or new that people didn't know of. Even if it's a topic that's generally known but to bring out a part that people didn't know about', she said.

What these statements also reveal is that travel journalists hold their work to a higher standard than may often be found in travel media. For example, several journalists point to the trend for top ten lists and other such formats popularly used in travel media. McGaurr discusses the popularity of lists, and says 'The tendency of travel journalism lists to condense place image into one photograph and a single paragraph of brand-aligned text, together with their very strong propensity to be shared on social media, makes them exceptionally valuable branding tools' (2015, p. 167). Journalists interviewed, however, are less interested in providing lists to their readers. One journalist suggested that journalism can be more than just reductive lists, saying, 'I think travel writing can be [inspiring] like that, instead of just the top ten list, and where the flock is going next'. Another journalist criticizes lists for completely failing to justify their assertions. She said, 'Travel writing is so easy to use clichés – but why can't you leave Paris without doing this thing? You can get French food anywhere, why do you need to get it here?' The volition of these journalists to go beyond the lists, to give their readers more, is another example of how future journalists should think about embracing constructive ideals. These functions are pushing the reader forward, as Gyldensted suggests, albeit in a very specific way relating to travel and tourism.

One journalist said,

> [My motivation is] a good combination of being helpful and not just giving tips for the secret entrance … but also helping people discover something lesser known or really unique about the city. And giving them the courage to do that.

This statement and its reference to courage is at the heart of constructive journalism, at least in a travel context. While not seeking social change or trying to better society on the whole, travel journalists can still move their audiences forward in many ways. Such an effect could be as simple as booking their first international trip, applying for a passport, or going somewhere they have never heard of before. While the UNWTO projects that 1.8 billion people will be traveling internationally by 2030, many people are still unable to travel at all. Developing countries like China and Brazil are sending increasing amounts of tourists worldwide, but at the same time recent terrorist events in major destinations such as Paris and London have also hurt growth. Travel journalists mediate between these events and travelers, helping to encourage them to travel and to reassure them, playing the role of 'first aid', a journalistic role described by Morgensen (2008).

Constructive travel journalism in crisis situations

To understand why these positive, empowering interpretations of travel journalism are increasingly relevant, we can look at a brief case study to illustrate these points. Consider Paris in 2015, following the attacks carried out by the Islamic State that killed 130 civilians. While not the first attack on a western city benefiting from tourism – think of New York in 2001 and London in 2005 to name just two – the Paris attacks were especially brutal and visible to the world, with reports and images circulating online and through Twitter at a rate that they had never been able to before. Following the attacks, news coverage focused on the incident and its ramifications. Travel journalists, however, writing for established and online media sites, shared a more unique, constructive narrative.

Tourism often pivots around tragedy, though usually many years after the event, as is the case of the 9/11 memorial in New York or the Nazi concentration camps. A rare study on so-called 'dark' travel journalism reveals a complicated interplay between history, culture, and locations marked by tragedy or atrocity (Creech, 2014). The study's author suggests that 'as a cultural form, travel journalism is implicated in the practices that help American and Western audiences make sense of foreign atrocities' (p. 252). Furthermore, in an analysis of the media after 9/11, Morgensen writes that 'the challenge for national television is to provide coverage that at the same time stimulates rational thinking and limits the negative stimulus of the feelings and senses' (2008, p. 36). Such studies help explain the rapport between journalism and terror events, but both fall short of fully explaining how travel journalism online might respond to crises, mostly because mass-mediated terror attacks on Western tourist destinations are, arguably, a newer phenomenon. Dark tourism journalism looks to the past, but the Paris attacks were hardly historical events in the following weeks when travel journalists published dozens of articles about the city. Furthermore, where Morgensen positions basic news coverage as 'first aid', I propose thinking of travel journalism as a form of 'rehabilitation', going beyond the who, what, and where, and asking, as Gyldensted proposes, 'What now?' While travel journalism will not always fulfil this role, following crisis situations, the argument may become especially salient as publication delays shorten and travel journalists – often living in the destination in question – are needed to respond more quickly than before.

Framing and the media

In this final part of the chapter, I explore an analysis of travel articles culled from a sample of fifty-three articles published predominantly in the month following the attacks in Paris. This case study exposes how journalists frame their reporting on the attacks, using methods described by de Vreese (2005) and Entman (1993), as well as research from the 1998 Project for Excellence in Journalism that identifies specific frames used in news media. Through framing, news 'transforms mere happenings into publicly discussable events' (Tuchman, 1978, p. 2). Framing analysis, according to Entman, is the power 'to select some aspects of a perceived reality and make them more salient in a communicating text, in such a way as to promote a particular problem definition, casual interpretation, moral evaluation, and/or treatment recommendations for the item described' (1993, p. 52). This definition is especially pertinent when talking about constructive journalism, where treatments for problems are a central issue. News framing can be discussed within the context of agenda setting, as described by McCombs and Shaw, who suggest that, for example, the news does influence attitudes during elections (1972). They echo Bernard Cohen's assertion that the media 'may not be successful much of the time in telling people what to think, but it is stunningly successful in telling its readers what to think about' (1963, p. 13).

Within framing analysis, there are both issue-specific and generic news frames that researchers can use, and many scholars argue for having 'concise, a priori defined operationalizations of frames in content analysis' (de Vreese, 2005, p. 53). The problem, however, is that many news frames, such as the eleven identified in a 1998 study by the Project for Excellence in Journalism, do not necessarily apply to the travel articles produced after the Paris attacks. While one of the articles examined did fit into the straight news story frame, others were largely framed by emotions and reactions that are not characteristic of more normative news frames. I suggest here three potential frames that travel journalism adopted in this crisis event and argue that the unique position of travel journalists as mediators of experiences allows them to report more constructively than journalists normally might, appealing to their specific audiences.

I propose these frames to help future professionals think outside the box, to embrace alternative views of what travel journalism can be. To do this, I applied framing analysis using fifty-three articles, paying specific attention to their headlines. The texts were selected from online travel sections of broadsheets and tabloids, including *USA Today* and the *Daily Mail*, as well as from online travel sites of various legacy media including *CNN, Fox News, Condé Nast Traveler*, and *Travel +Leisure*. The only condition was that the article had appeared clearly in a travel context, either within a designated travel section or in a dedicated travel publication, and discussed the 2015 Paris attacks. I therefore manually searched leading publications and their travel sections online, narrowing the search to November and December 2015 in the weekends immediately after the attacks, before any formal push to rehabilitate Paris's image had been initiated by the city. I also used

Google News to search news items mentioning keywords like 'Paris' and 'tourism' between the attacks and the end of 2015. Tankard's 'list of frames' approach (2001, p. 100) allowed me to explore how various elements of the articles including headlines, lead sentences, and source selections all helped construct specific frames. The result was that, overwhelmingly, frames used in travel media exhibited constructive elements, especially in that time of crisis.

The results demonstrated that not only did travel journalism respond in a similar fashion across various media outlets during the Paris attacks, but much of the coverage can easily be interpreted using a constructive approach, counteracting the fear that often leads to risk aversion after a terror attack (Huddy et al., 2003, p. 257). In their study on the psychological reactions following 9/11, the authors described how Americans were highly concerned about future terrorist attacks in the United States. They highlighted the role of television news and its impact on how citizens supported national policies after 9/11 (p. 273). Their study was part of a large collection of articles that address the framing of terrorism incidents, but none of the researchers broke away from the pack to explore how lifestyle journalism might play a role in crisis situations.

Travel journalists frame the Paris attacks

The first, and most prevalent frame at work in these articles was one that I identify as 'resilience and solidarity'. Where much of the business coverage on the tourism industry focused on how much money would be lost, travel reporters focused on the ability of the industry and the city to bounce back. CNBC ran the headline, 'Paris Tourism To Be Hurt in Near Term, but not for Long' while the *Telegraph* published '33 Reasons Why You Must Keep Visiting Paris', mimicking a popular type of article after the attacks. This call to action, an act of solidarity with the French, was also found in *Travel+Leisure* and the *Los Angeles Times,* among others. Of the fifty-three articles, twenty-one seemed to fit this category. Travel journalists were arguably adopting a constructive approach here, in line with Gyldensted's principles.

Not all of the solidarity articles were focused on the tourism industry. Several adopted a more personal essay approach, still aimed at travel audiences. On the website for *Travel+Leisure* magazine, an article entitled 'La Vie en Bleu: An Expat Experiences Paris in Mourning' focusses on the day after the atrocities, sharing the author's personal struggle with the attacks. Neither fully negative nor fully uplifting, these personal essays, like those in the *New York Times* feature, 'After Attacks, the Soul of Paris Endures', frame the attacks as an emotional event for the writers, who each adopt their own coping methods. While not necessarily providing practical information for tourists, the essays can be read as examples of constructive journalism that discuss how each author finds their own way of dealing with the attacks. One journalist describes finding comfort in food and the vibrant market scene in Paris, writing, 'I can't wait for Saturday morning this week, since the market will be a celebration of the city itself, unvanquished, animated and always hungry.' Another in the same feature writes about finding solace in her local community café, writing, 'It's here, among Parisians and foreigners embracing, sipping coffee and sharing stories, that I could breathe again.' These are subtle, yet decidedly constructive ways to discuss the attacks that fall within a framework defined by resilience and solidarity.

The second most popular frame is what I identify as 'reassurance'. Like the 'resilience and solidarity' frame, the 'reassurance' frame operates positively and constructively, giving tourists the information that they need to continue visiting Paris, despite the crisis. Many of these articles simply contained information pertinent to tourists, treating them as consumers, albeit consumers in a much-altered environment from the guidebooks and magazines before November 2015. Paris had changed, and so had tourism, so travel journalists were providing the necessary knowledge for tourists to change with it. The *Independent* ran a headline that read, 'Despite the Terror Attacks on Paris We Are Safer Travelling now than ever before' and the *Washington Post* declared 'After Paris Attacks, State Department Says Travel but Be Alert – and Call Home'. The content of the articles reflected their headlines, providing practical information needed for travelers to visit Paris confidently and securely.

For instance, a travel article on the *Fox News* website discussed closures and openings in Paris, but ended its article quoting travel expert Rick Steves, who said, 'the best way for Americans to fight terrorism is to keep on traveling'. An article in *USA Today* highlighted all of the security measures put in place and told its readers, 'For now, travelers were being advised to expect the unexpected – both in France and elsewhere.' On an even more uplifting note, the *Independent*'s Steven Calder wrote that travel is safer than ever, citing statistics that contextualized the Paris attacks, telling readers, 'Don't be intimidated. Don't live in fear. Joie de vivre will return to Paris, and so must we.' As any reading of these articles will reveal, there is plenty of overlap between articles framed by resilience and solidarity and those framed by reassurance, and many can be classified as both. The main distinction I make is that the first set speaks more generally about the attacks and their effects, while the second set addresses readers more directly as consumers, offering them the practical information necessary for reassurance.

A minority – just three articles – fell into a frame that I identify as 'despair', where the journalists were overwhelmingly negative in their reporting, offering no constructive journalism and no solutions. These articles were tabloid in nature, simply reporting on the negative aspects of the attacks and their effect on tourism. Published in the travel section of the *Mail Online*, these articles took a more forlorn look at the attacks' consequences for the travel industry, highlighting how the hotel and transportation industries were badly affected by the terrorist attacks. More straight news reporting, focusing on the negative, than constructive approaches, these articles underline the fact that not all travel journalism will invariably adhere to constructive norms. The publications involved may have been focused more on attracting clicks, as in the three tabloid articles published by the *Mail Online*, or simply in sharing emotional narratives as in the case of the other. Such articles illustrate that not all travel journalism can be – or need be – constructive during a crisis situation. Positivity, reassurance, and solidarity are not hallmarks of travel journalism, but they can be if journalists are to take a more constructive approach to their work.

While an abbreviated look at this content analysis reveals alternative frames for travel journalism in a time of crisis, I do not pretend that these are the final words on the matter. Instead, I want simply to illustrate how travel journalism can operate with a constructive framework under specific conditions – namely that of a crisis such as a terrorist attack like the one on Paris discussed here.

A way forward?

While some journalists do think about their work as benefiting their readers in some way beyond simply informing them, the framing analysis demonstrates that travel journalism can operate in a more multifaceted way. It inspires audiences to push further, to visit in the face of adversity, to somehow stand strong in the case of a terror attack. While this is part of the consumer aspect described by Hanusch, I argue for an interpretation that permits travel journalism to go beyond consumerism and towards constructivism when needed (2010; 2012). This chapter attempts to point out is that constructive journalism can exist beyond current affairs and can deal with audiences other than a democratic citizenry. At the heart of journalism, as Kovach and Rosenstiel point out, all professionals perform the same fundamental tasks (2007). But the context in which they carry out these duties, how they do it, and for whom they do it, is susceptible to change depending on the specific conditions. Travel, in this case, is one such condition. As shown above, in a limited but coherent fashion, travel journalists are living up to constructivist ideals in a sense, though not universally. They are aware of a need to remain positive, and not just by publishing feel-good stories but by providing truth and context for larger issues. They are pushing forward, as Gyldensted suggests, motivating and inspiring their readers to do more and to push further afield. Such attitudes are especially important in situations like the Paris attacks, when a tourist destination can continue to be harmed until the events have faded or been forgotten (Avraham, 2013).

Such actions may seem trivial, but they are important in a digital era when travel journalism is faced with challenges from user-generated content like TripAdvisor, where questions of trust are rife. Travel journalists, working for established and often trusted brands, are able to provide trusted consumer-oriented information with a constructivist angle when needed. Naturally, not all works of journalism will be pushing travelers forward, looking for some greater good. Still, that travel journalists understand their role in the travel media and the potential they have for stimulating change, among readers or even industry actors, is an important realization.

This study is just the first step in discussing lifestyle journalism in a more constructivist manner. For the moment, I hope to have introduced the possibility of looking at travel journalism through a constructivist lens, and realizing the potential of this genre to open itself it up to new interpretations.

References

Avraham, E. (2013). Crisis communication, image restoration, and battling stereotypes of terror and wars: Media strategies for attracting tourism to Middle Eastern countries. *American Behavioral Scientist*, 57(9), 1350–1367.

Avraham, E. (2015). Destination image repair during crisis: Attracting tourism during the Arab Spring uprisings. *Tourism Management*, 47, 224–232.

Chalmers, D. (1959). The muckrakers and the growth of corporate power: A study in constructive journalism. *American Journal of Economics and Sociology*, 18(3), 295–311.

Charles, M. (2013). News, documentary and advocacy journalism. In K. Fowler-Watt and S. Allan (Eds.), *Journalism: New challenges* (384–392). Poole, Dorset: Centre for Journalism and Communication Research, Bournemouth University.

Cohen, B. (1963). *The press and foreign policy*. Princeton, NJ: Princeton University Press.

Creech, B. (2014). The spectacle of past violence. In F. Hanusch and E. Fürsich (Eds.), *Travel journalism: Exploring production, impact, and culture* (pp. 249–266). Basingstoke: Palgrave Macmillan.

Damkjoer, M. S., and Waade, A. M. (2014). Armchair tourism: The travel series as a hybrid genre. In F. Hanusch and E. Fürsich (Eds.), *Travel journalism: Exploring production, impact, and culture* (pp. 39–59). Basingstoke: Palgrave Macmillan.

Deuze, M. (2005). What is journalism? Professional identity and ideology of journalists reconsidered. *Journalism*, 6(4), 442–464.

De Vreese, C. H. (2005). News framing: Theory and typology. *Information Design Journal and Document Design*, 13(1), 51–62.

Drok, N., and Hermans, L. (2016). Is there a future for slow journalism? *Journalism Practice*, 10(4), 539–554.

Entman, R. M. (1993). Framing: Toward clarification of a fractured paradigm. *Journal of Communication*, 43(4), 51–58.

Fall, L., and Massey, J. E. (2005). The significance of crisis communication in the aftermath of 9/11: A national investigation of how tourism managers have re-tooled their promotional campaigns. *Journal of Travel and Tourism Marketing*, 19(2–3), 77–90.

Gyldensted, C. (2015). *From mirrors to movers: Five elements of positive psychology in constructive journalism*. Hershey, PA: G Group.

Haagerup, U. (2015). *Constructive news: Why negativity destroys the media and democracy-and how to improve journalism of tomorrow*. New York: InnoVatio.

Hanusch, F. (2010). The dimensions of travel journalism: Exploring new fields for journalism research beyond the news. *Journalism Studies*, 11(1), 68–82.

Hanusch, F. (2012). Broadening the focus: The case for lifestyle journalism as a field of scholarly inquiry. *Journalism Practice*, 6(1), 2–11.

Huddy, L., Feldman, S., Lahav, G., and Taber, C. (2003). Fear and terrorism: Psychological reactions to 9/11. In P. Norris, M. Kern, and M. Just (Eds.), *Framing terrorism: The news media, the government, and the public*. New York: Routledge.

Jackson, J. (2016, April 25). UN to urge media to take a more 'constructive' approach to news. *Guardian*. Retrieved from https://www.theguardian.com

Janowitz, M. (1975). Professional models in journalism: The gatekeeper and the advocate. *Journalism Quarterly*, 52(4), 618–626.

Jeacle, I., and Carter, C. (2011). In TripAdvisor we trust: Rankings, calculative regimes and systems trust. *Accounting, Organizations and Society*, 36(405), 293–309.

Karaian, J. (2015, Nov. 26). The Paris attacks will cost the French economy more than $2 billion. *Quartz*. Retrieved from https://qz.com

Kovach, B., and Rosenstiel, T. (2007). *The elements of journalism: What newspeople should know and the public should expect.* New York: Three Rivers Press.

McCombs, M. E., and Shaw, D. L. (1972). The agenda-setting function of mass media. *Public Opinion Quarterly*, 36(2), 176–187.

McGaurr, L. (2015). *Environmental communication and travel journalism: Consumerism, conflict and concern.* Abingdon: Routledge.

Morgensen, K. (2008). Television journalism during terror attacks. *Media, War and Conflict*, 1(1), 31–49.

Project for Excellence in Journalism. (1998). Framing the news: The triggers, frames, and messages in newspaper coverage. Retrieved from www.journalism.org

Robinson, S. (2011). Journalism as process: The organization implications of participatory online news. *Journalism and Communication Monographs*, 13(3), 137–210.

Sillesen, L. B. (2014). Good news is good business, but not a cure-all for journalism. *Columbia Journalism Review.* Retrieved from www.cjr.org

Sönmez, S., Apostolopoulos, Y., and Tarlow, P. (1999). Tourism in crisis: Managing the effects of terrorism. *Journal of Travel Research*, 38(1), 13–18.

Tankard, J. W. (2001). The empirical approach to the study of media framing. In S. D. Reese, O. H.GandyJr and A. E. Grant (Eds.), *Framing public life* (pp. 95–106). Mahwah, NJ: Lawrence Erlbaum.

Tuchman, G. (1978). *Making news: A study in the construction of reality.* New York: Free Press.

Vásquez, C. (2011). Complaints online: The case of TripAdvisor. *Journal of Pragmatics*, 42(6), 1707–1717.

Vermeulen, I. E., and Seegers, D. (2009). Tried and tested: The impact of online hotel reviews on consumer consideration. *Tourism Management*, 30(1), 123–127.

Wearden, G., and Allan, K. (2015, Nov. 16). Billions wiped off European travel shares after Paris attacks. *Guardian.* Retrieved from https://www.theguardian.com/

Zelizer, B., and Allan, S. (Eds.). (2011). *Journalism after September 11.* Abingdon: Routledge.

11

CULTURAL REPRESENTATION AND UNDERSTANDING IN A GLOBALIZED COMMUNITY

A website I wrote for had a recurring series on how citizens of a given city view the rest of their nation – how Londoners see the rest of the UK, how New Yorkers see the rest of New York State, and so on – leading my editor to ask for a similar piece about Paris. How did Parisians view the rest of France? I had no idea. I wasn't born in France. I lived in Paris, so I was technically a Parisian, but I did not have enough insight or experience to know what Parisians might think of inhabitants of Marseilles or Lyon. The piece leaned heavily towards the entertainment aspects of travel journalism, with little useful information or critical perspective attached to it, but it was part of the job. I began my research and trod lightly, unsure of how to proceed.

I began by looking at what other people have written about the various regions of France, googling stereotypes, speaking with Parisian friends who came from other parts of the country. I began to pull together images of what characterized each of these areas – the food in Lyon, the beaches of the Riviera, the giant cheeses of the mountains. But it became increasingly clear that it was an impossible task to boil down the identity of the main regions of an entire country, not least in a country like France that has such a long history and patchwork of local culture. The editor took my final list of descriptions and produced a map with images illustrating the various stereotypes I had put together. Far from the pinnacle of my journalistic career, it was no less a statement on globalization that I, an American, was categorizing French national stereotypes for an editor sitting in an office in New York. It felt horribly reductive, but fortunately it was clearly just meant for entertainment and was not to be taken seriously, or so I justified to myself.

Still, the experience highlighted for me the role of a travel journalist in representing place, and how important this task is. Being honest and truthful is difficult when there is potential harm, when you could risk offending a whole group of people. Would the people of Grenoble find it off-putting that I labeled them as 'nerds', referencing its reputation as a university and scientific town? Probably not. And were the people of the Basque region insulted by the title of 'filthy separatists', a nod to the region's nationalist tendencies? If they were reading the website, maybe. It was all in jest, but promoting these stereotypes reinforced how little the outside world knew about the people of France beyond Paris, and how little contemporary information was available to us to help us really understand them beyond the stereotypes.

While much travel journalism has been reduced to lists and how-to guides, it is important to remember one of its core functions: bridging cultures and peoples (Fürsich, 2002a). The cultural representation function of journalists is not to be ignored, and is, I argue, more important than ever in today's globalized society (Cocking, 2009). In this chapter, I want to discuss the representational role of travel journalism, which has already been set within a cosmopolitan framework by researchers. From there, I want to look at examples of how journalists rely on certain tropes when writing about Paris in order to open up a discussion about the role of cliché and stereotypes in travel writing. As we've seen in previous chapters, disparities between what travel writers promote and what the realities are can lead to problematic situations for tourists – think back to wearing stilettos on cobblestones. How can we confront these stereotypes more systematically as both journalists and audiences?

Again, returning to user-generated content, I will argue that the plurality of opinions available on sites like TripAdvisor allows for more open discussions about these issues, and I will compare TripAdvisor forum threads to travel articles dealing with similar topics in order to demonstrate how travel journalism does not have the final word. UGC is ultimately allowing for the possibility of a richer conversation about foreign places by allowing for more viewpoints than ever before. Journalists, however, have yet to fully embrace this opportunity. Duffy has already laid groundwork for the collaborative potential of travel journalists and social media, and this chapter will explore this potential in terms of representation in a globalized age (2016). These new realities, I argue, can contribute positively to travel journalism by functioning as a watchdog of travel media, forcing travel journalists to think more critically about their representations and their role as mediators of culture.

Traveling among *them*

Historically, from its earliest iterations to today's TripAdvisor reviews, travel writing has dealt almost systematically with some notion of the 'Other' (Hanne, 1993). MacCannell defines sightseeing as 'effort based on desire ethically to connect to someone or something "other" as represented by or embodied in an attraction' (2011, p. 7). This concept has been well explored in Edward Said's seminal work, *Orientalism*, which deals with postcolonial representations of the Orient by the West as a way to speak to larger issues of representation in our world (Said, 1979). Much has been written on the topic, especially regarding how Western travel writers have historically capitalized in various ways on those they meet on their travels. As Youngs explains, the idea of encountering and explaining the 'Other' is intrinsic to much travel writing, especially where a writer is on a quest. These others will always serve a purpose for the author (Youngs, 2013, p. 159). 'Difference will always be compromised and mediated, however serious the attempts to respect and represent it; even to facilitate its self-representation' (p. 184). Likewise, Islam writes, 'The other is never a difference in kind, but rather a conceptual differentiation set in motion by the subject for its own self-realisation: it is the self that others the other for the mediation of its own unity' (1996, p. 81). Travel journalism doesn't necessarily bend to many of the postcolonial tendencies that travel writing and narratives often do, according to some authors (Lisle, 2006). Still, travel journalism grapples with these ideas of representing foreign cultures even within the simplest article or top ten list.

Recent research on this idea of othering relates often to questions of globalization, which is especially poignant for today's media workers. Globalization itself is linked to yet another concept, that of cosmopolitanism. Schoon discusses this relationship, writing, 'As an analytical concept, cosmopolitanism is a continuation and specification of the term and concept of globalization' (Schoon, 2014, p. 215). Held describes cosmopolitanism more broadly as 'the ethical and political space which sets out the terms of reference for the recognition of people's equal moral worth, their active agency and what is required for their autonomy and development' (Held, 2010, p. 49). In her research, Schoon suggests taking a cosmopolitan perspective, on travel journalism where 'the question of how difference is negotiated and mediated lies at the core of the concept' (2014, p. 220). All of these concepts weigh on the job of a travel journalist, whose professional purpose 'is to come up with a narrative, a well-told story about other cultures, the past or distant places – in short, to package culture' (Fürsich and Kavoori, 2014, p. 29). They are cultural translators, as the authors say, working in an increasingly globalized world where they establish the worth and agency of those they write about, not least in the eyes of their audiences.

What ends up happening, however, is that travel journalism often fails to engage with its globalized/cosmopolitan potential. In a study on representations of the Middle East in the European travel press, Cocking identifies various colonial tropes in the articles, writing that reverts to historical stereotypes instead of engaging with the modern place: 'It would seem any attention given to the present is either passed over in favour of evoking the past or used as a counterpoint to emphasise the possibility of accessing this exotic and other past' (Cocking, 2009, p. 66). And in another study on television travel programs, one researcher underscored how these shows do not engage with more serious questions surrounding travel and foreign lands. Instead, she writes, these programs

> neglect the important political dimension of international and intercultural contacts in a globalizing world by favoring individualized and personalized travel accounts. Moreover, while these shows have the potential to present open and complex representations of Otherness, they often fall back into a us/

them dichotomy because of the intrinsic motivation of travel media to high-light essentialized difference from a privileged position.

(Fürsich, 2002b, p. 206)

This seemingly frivolous, or at least superficial approach to travel journalism, however, makes sense given its commercial and consumer-oriented nature. In highly competitive media markets, Cocking underscores the importance of using recognizable tropes as a financial necessity to attract audiences. Despite all of this, he concludes that, 'whilst of lower status than the "hard" news of political report-ing, travel journalism plays a significant role in the collective European imagining of the Middle East' (Cocking, 2009, p. 66). Superficial or not, travel journalism still has considerable power, if not to create then at least to contribute to the collective image of a place.

These representations, however, are not always balanced, fair, or universally true. Fürsich writes that many travel texts, like those in her sample of TV programs, highlight some exotic foreign people. 'The dominant aspiration of the text is to find, highlight and celebrate the Other. But the strategy of exo-ticizing proceeds beyond that by actively searching out unusual topics for pre-sentation; what is presented is not only the "typical" but the unusual' (Fürsich, 2002b, p. 217). Painting foreign lands as 'exotic,' in the sense of strikingly colorful or unusual, is nothing new, nor is it unique to the written word. Travel photographs, often regarded as real and objective, do not actually represent the complexities of a place and its people, but rather focuses on one aspect. Instead, Urry and Larsen suggest, 'they reflect and reinforce stereotypical western imaginations of these worlds' (2011, p. 169). Travel journalism, sup-posedly produced with similar objective methods, ultimately produces the same sorts of stereotyped realities.

Tourist places, according to Urry and Larsen, are not given or fixed, and repre-sentations or interpretations of them can change all the time (2011, p. 116). An area can become gentrified, attracting new tourists looking for previously unavail-able experiences, while other places can age, decay, and fall out of favor. A doll museum in Paris, for example, opened in the 1990s but closed in 2017 due to a lack of interest and thus resources – after all, how many children are interested in dolls when there are tablets and smartphones to play with instead? Travel journal-ists, therefore, are constantly mediating these destinations, keeping them updated for tourists, rewriting histories as tourism evolves. 'In many cases, tourism's function is symbolic, working to create a map of the nation for both internal and external consumption' (Fürsich and Kavoori, 2001, p. 158). These maps never stop developing, but there remains a struggle between destinations that try to valorize their past while simultaneously trying to modernize. While the authors go on to question how we can study the relationships between developing nations and their representations in the developed world, further questions about reciprocal cultural stereotyping between countries where there is no power disequilibrium, are also relevant.

Discussing ethics could be a way to understand better this interplay between travel media, globalization, cosmopolitanism, and representation. In his work on tourism ethics, MacCannell explains that there is a reticence to engage with questioning our experiences as tourists. 'Psychic resistance may be generic to any interrogation of ethics. This is not merely theoretical. Tourists openly confess to being ethically conflicted. They want to "get away from it all", including, presumably, ethical concerns' (MacCannell, 2011, p. 46). It is impossible, he argues, to avoid ethical dilemmas while sightseeing, citing among other things, the pervasive trend of bucket lists, which allows tourists to visit 'without articulating the meaning or the good of any attraction to their own thinking, personality, or pleasure' (p. 50). Such ethical dilemmas, often propagated by the media, are fertile ground for research into representation by travel journalists. Conversations surrounding the way travel writers choose to represent their topics have bubbled up continually over the years. As Holland and Huggan write,

> Travel writing in the late twentieth century continues to be haunted by the specter of cliché: its catalogs of anomalies are often recorded in remarkably similar terms. The same words and phrases crop up again and again, the same myths and stereotypes, the same literary analogies.
>
> *(2000, pp. 5–6)*

These sorts of clichés can lead to stereotyping of people, such as the locals of a destination, whereby a certain attribute – e.g. 'Parisian' – is associated with other characteristics – fashionable, cultured, rude – and thus these characteristics are attributed to all members (Hinton, 2000). Much of the research on national stereotypes dates back to the early twentieth century when globalization wasn't a household term, leaving us today with a 'museum of the prototypic stereotypes' of early researchers (Schneider, 2005, p. 527). Today, however, many of these stereotypes are still firmly embedded in travel media and its representation of places and people – at least from a Western perspective.

How, then, do these ideas play out concretely for travel journalists? Moreover, what are the advantages and disadvantages of user-generated content when it comes to travel journalism's role as mediator of people, places, and culture? This chapter will look briefly at some samples of articles written by journalists interviewed to analyze the stereotypes or tropes they employ. Then I will look at how user-generated content, in this case TripAdvisor forums, might contribute to breaking down these stereotypes or challenging them, contributing to the idea of a 'conscious and careful consumer of news about the world' that Kovach and Rosenstiel describe, including identifying whether information is complete and if there are alternative explanations or understandings (2010, p. 168). While they are situating consumers as citizens in a democracy, there is no reason that similar questions can't arise for travel media consumers.

Journalism and the Fifth Estate

It now seems hardly surprising that travel journalists rely on certain tropes and often fall back on stereotyped views – though I argue strongly against such practices in Chapter 6. Of course, not all travel journalism is so predictable. More important today is what can be done to tackle these misrepresentations and stereotypes, thanks in part to the internet. While discussions about the legitimacy of a claim in a travel article could be debated at length between individuals in a pre-internet era, now, thanks to forums and other social media outlets, these conversations can happen publicly and remain on record for other consumers to consult (see Gretzel and Yoo, 2008). A look at how TripAdvisor members discuss the issues presented in the journalists' articles I analyzed will reveal to what extent user-generated content can help challenge stereotypes and clichés, theoretically holding travel journalists accountable for their representations.

Journalism has traditionally occupied a role as the Fourth Estate, holding power to account. Today, many authors look at the role of the new Fifth Estate – from bloggers to WikiLeaks to satirical news sites – as challenges to the relevance of professional journalism (McNair, 2013; Dutton and Dubois, 2015; Berkowitz and Schwartz, 2016). These networked individuals are independent of institutions, use the web to enhance their communicative power, and 'hold other institutions accountable, such as government, the press and businesses' (Dutton and Dubois, 2015, p. 53). WikiLeaks is considered a prime example of this putative Fifth Estate, but little research suggests how a site like TripAdvisor could function in a similar fashion if we narrow the focus to travel media instead of the press more generally. Instead of partisan politics and biased reporting, travel journalism is divisive on questions of taste and representation. Consumers rarely take one journalist at his or her word, but instead verify or confirm using a plethora of other stories. If the Fifth Estate allows for critiques and alternative viewpoints on political affairs, can travel media conceive of its own Fifth Estate on websites like TripAdvisor?

Kovach and Rosenstiel call for a new relationship between journalists and the public, 'to provide citizens with the tools they need to extract knowledge for themselves' (2007, p. 247). They later assert that the press is just one vector for informing audiences, but that 'journalists stand sentinel at a gate with no fence surrounding it' (Kovach and Rosenstiel, 2010, p. 171). Accountability is nothing new for journalists, and Schudson writes, 'Vulnerability to the audience (the market) keeps journalists nimble in one direction, vulnerability to sources (the government) in another' (Schudson, 2005, p. 219). Replace *government* with *tourism industry* and the same argument can apply to travel journalists more specifically. The challenge now, however, is that criticism from these entities is no longer restricted to complaints, but can lead to the creation of competing or alternative websites that provide their own content, circumventing the need for journalists who may not be prepared to adapt. User-generated content has become commonplace since the late 1990s, with blogs, review sites, and eventually social networks allowing for more pervasive conversations among individuals and journalists alike. TripAdvisor, for example, was one such website. Since its launch in 2000, it has grown from a simple review site to a thriving business, selling tours and booking hotels worldwide. While not quite the independent entity described by Dutton and Dubois, its forums still remain relatively free of corporate interests. Interviews with several frequent contributors reveal how difficult it is to promote a product or sell anything in the forum, mainly due to the community who will flag any such content as inappropriate, leading to its removal. This sort of self-policing, common to many forums, leads to a much more independent and arguably honest platform than the rankings section of TripAdvisor that are often wrought with dubious reviews (Arsal et al., 2010).

Cliché and stereotypes: Paris case study

Having read – and written – countless articles about Paris over the years, I wanted to illustrate briefly how certain stereotypes about traveling in the French capital play out in the media. Then, in a second breath, I want to explore how social media can intervene to challenge these representations. Clearly Paris is a special case since it is riddled with so many clichés and stereotypes among English-speaking cultures. Still, the findings of this analysis reveal the underlying principle that social media can nuance, challenge, and even correct what were once top-down representations of a destination. To explore these notions, I selected three online articles from a larger content analysis of pieces produced by the journalists interviewed. They are simply examples of recurring clichés or frames found in English-speaking media about Paris, and by no means representative of all reporting in general. Then, using the search function of the TripAdvisor forums, I selected a random thread that intersected with the topic of the article, to explore – all too briefly – how the forum thread built upon, challenged, or otherwise nuanced the original article. The goal is to show how travel journalists can use these social media sites as reporting tools to help more accurately or more completely discuss a destination.

Example 1: crowds

First, one article by a journalist interviewed presents a similar theme found in many articles about Paris: crowds. The article, appearing on the website for *Fodor's*, an American guidebook, details each major site, offering suggestions for how to avoid long lines. The author writes, 'While there's no magic trick for escaping the crowds, the tips below will help ease your way, so you can see the best the city has to offer *and* cherish the memories' (Ladonne, 2014). This idea of over-crowded tourist sites is a common trope in most publications about Paris, which purport to offer insider information to cope with them. While the article, and others like it, aren't necessarily wrong, they do represent the city in an over-whelmingly misleading way, as the vast majority of things to do in Paris don't have long lines or waits.

A look at a TripAdvisor forum about crowds in Paris, however, reveals the type of conversations that happen on social media that challenge these articles. In a 2010 thread entitled 'September crowds', a user asks the community what to expect in September, and the responses are varied, nuanced, and generous in nature. TripAdvisor does what the journalistic article might not necessarily do. It aggregates the knowledge of the online community to paint a more composite picture of crowds, tailoring the information to the reader's specific needs. The two pages of responses to the question reveal many considerations that never appeared in the article. Fashion and trade shows in September increase the number of tourists, according to some users, while others report their own September experiences with crowds. One user even proposed the following: 'What do you want to see that makes you concerned about crowds? Perhaps we can give you strategies for how to maximize your time.' Rather than simply state that there are crowds and there are some possible solutions, TripAdvisor allows users to get the information they need from a community of users. It provides aggregate information, textual commentaries, and also additional components like rankings of users and helpfulness ratings for reviews (Qiu and Le, 2010). Albeit that there are questions of trust regarding these often anonymous users, I would argue these forums still provide more useful information than the article. Instead of just representing the city in one static way, the forum allows for a more dynamic representation, at least as far as crowds are concerned. While not necessarily journalistic in its production, there is value in these forums that travel journalists can tap into when needed.

Example 2: romance

Another familiar trope appears in several of the articles written by the sample of journalists – that of romance. Paris is unequivocally linked to notions of romance and illicit love, and one article in particular reinforces this cliché. Discussing hotels in Paris, the author begins the article with, 'As a destination, Paris is always a good idea for a romance. Ahhh. Romance. That elixir we all deserve now and again and Paris is the place for it' (Donner, 2016). Again, a nefarious cliché to promote, but it remains a cliché nonetheless. The author goes on to discuss hotels, offering up general descriptions of amenities and décor, without really ever explaining what makes them romantic. Instead, the hotel reviews are simply listed within this framework of romantic Paris. As a list, this particular article promises more than it delivers, offering very little justification for why anything is the best. Beyond the dependence on cliché, the format itself is problematic. As MacCannell writes, 'The implication that every attraction on the list has equivalent status as "good" relieves the affluent listmaker of responsibility for choosing among them' (2011, p. 50).

On TripAdvisor, however, there are numerous forums and threads dealing with the same issue that attempt to undertake such responsibility. One user began a thread in 2008, asking for a romantic place to stay in Paris. Before any recommendations appeared, the community immediately began asking questions to clarify. 'What do you consider romantic?' one user responded. Others asked about budget, length of stay, or desired neighborhood for the holiday. Members of the community shared personal experiences, like one man who described his stay in a hotel, writing, 'You can go whole days without seeing another guest,' which may give a bit more insight to potential consumers than a generic description of the décor or amenities, which can easily be found on a hotel's website.

Consistent with these findings, TripAdvisor contributors interviewed about their practices revealed that these sorts of personalized interactions are what they strive to achieve. One explained that he doesn't react immediately to someone's questions in the forums, but takes a more strategic approach. 'I try to size up people's personalities to see what kind of travelers those are', he said. Another forum contributor, a young woman, said that she responds to forum threads where people are discussing issues related to being a woman in Paris. 'I feel like it's my obligation to comment on it if I can help their experience', she said. These nuanced views, previously sequestered to face-to-face conversations, now have a platform online for public consumption. Again, this information and these voices are also available to travel journalists who may have a more singular view of a destination.

Example 3: etiquette

A third popular cliché plays on the stereotype of Parisians as fashion-forward, which of course depends on the social class and financial resources of the Parisian in question. Regardless of whether or not it's rooted in truth, this cliché spans travel media of all kinds, with a style guide in the *Fodor's* guide to Paris explaining how to dress like a particular type of stereotyped Parisian woman. Beyond fashion, moving to etiquette and gestures, this general cliché creates the stereotype of a homogenized society where individuals must act in a certain way in order to be considered locals. One article on the website for *Condé Nast Traveler*, entitled 'How Not to Look Like a Tourist in Paris' takes a serious approach to disguising oneself in Paris, a place where, if the author is to be believed, shuns those who look like tourists. The author describes how Parisians speak softly, and writes, 'Speaking loudly in public is frowned upon, but it can also make you stand out as a tourist and thus lead to unwanted attention, particularly from pickpockets' (Heise, 2014).

This idea of respecting etiquette in France often inspires more fear than is justifiable. One 2017 TripAdvisor forum on Paris featured a thread entitled, 'Not sticking out like a sore thumb as a tourist?' The user was concerned about wearing shorts in the summer and looking like an 'obnoxious tourist' as described by articles that she had researched. The TripAdvisor community immediately rebuked the idea that wearing shorts is problematic. One member, in Paris at the time, described how hot it was and pointed out that many people were wearing shorts. Another nuanced it further, explaining that shorts may not be appropriate in certain situations, like a five-star hotel bar. Overall, however, the community downplayed the fiction that there is a certain 'Parisian' way to dress and fit into society. These sorts of discussions bring numerous opinions to the table that can help nuance oversimplified representations of the destination in question.

Towards better representation

These are short, introductory examples illustrating some common clichés about Paris, but important ones that frame the way people think about its culture and people. What's important is not how Paris is represented, but that many of these representations will rely on stereotypes and clichés that are often outdated and untrue (Schneider, 2005). While travel journalists are not yet systematic in approaching social media, conversations challenging these misrepresentations are happening every day in the forums of TripAdvisor, on Twitter, in blogs, and elsewhere. As Duffy suggests, travel journalists 'should encourage and moderate online conversations among contributors and consumers' (2016, p. 180). This call for more collaboration between travel journalists and social media, however, remains unclear about exactly how it will occur. When it comes to discussing issues of representation in an increasingly digitalized and globalized world, however, the tools at a journalist's fingertips are all waiting to be exploited, as the entire media landscape continues to evolve.

Travel journalists need education and guidelines, first and foremost, on how social media should influence their work. How can they go about using forum contributions and Instagram posts, and what are the ethical issues surrounding these potential methods? For example, reading a TripAdvisor forum is accessible to anyone online, but actually interacting with forum contributors becomes more difficult. A self-policing community flags users who seem to be collecting information for research purposes, making it difficult to interact directly with these local experts who may have information that could help journalists better perform their duties. Collaboration, therefore, between journalists and social media, is a two-way street. As much as journalists need to develop distinct methods to incorporate social media into their research and publications, social media – including TripAdvisor, Facebook, and the wider blog community – should develop their own sort of collaborative process with journalists, allowing users to disseminate ideas and information through professionally curated or edited channels. The more collaborative these actors can be, the more that travel journalism can move away from clichéd and stereotyped descriptions of destinations and towards a more cosmopolitan and globalized vision.

There are, naturally, limits to creating a more representative travel media. Cultural references, lived experiences, and individual circumstances will always lend themselves to biases somewhere in travel narratives and reports. These factors, however, should not hinder travel journalists from embracing the extraordinary potential of social media, to act, as Duffy says, as curators of user-generated content (2016). It's not yet a perfect system, but this question of achieving a more truthful and nuanced representation of foreign peoples and places using social media is an important element in the evolution of travel media. Future research will need to examine if there are actually effects associated with using social media in travel reporting or if there are strides towards developing a more systematic approach to these collaborations.

Social media is not the answer to challenging the stereotypes and clichés that make up much of the travel journalism produced in the twentieth and twenty-first century. It is, however, part of a proposed solution to diversify content, to move away from top-down editorial structures, while simultaneously seeking ways to legitimize the user-generated content that is often taken with a pinch of salt. The Fifth Estate, a concept not typically applied to lifestyle media, seems a valid interpretation of the relationship between social media and travel journalism. More than just remaining accountable to social media, however, professional travel media should be conceiving of innovative ways to collaborate with audience members who are creating content. What these collaborations will look like remains to be seen – though the next chapter on *Airbnbmag* gives some indication – but what is clear is that both sides will need to cooperate to develop mutually beneficial strategies.

As the internet globalizes travel media, we suddenly find American, British, and Australian authors all contributing to the same publications. Journalists are no longer writing for a local or national audience, especially not when it comes to travel. Bloggers and Youtubers of all nationalities produce stories and videos in English. TripAdvisor reviews can be automatically translated online to English from Spanish, Portuguese, or almost any other language. There is no longer a clear cultural framework in which travel media is delivered. A more collaborative, cross-cultural approach to travel media may, therefore, be a way to respond to some of the issues facing travel journalists in this ever-changing environment. All of these new realities need to be taken into account if travel journalism is to deliver something more meaningful than an arbitrary top ten list.

References

Arsal, I., Woosnam, K. M., Baldwin, E. D., and Backman, S. J. (2010). Residents as travel destination information providers: An online community perspective. *Journal of Travel Research*, 49(4), 400–413.

Berkowitz, D., and Schwartz, D. A. (2016). Miley, CNN and The Onion: When fake news becomes realer than real. *Journalism Practice*, 10(1), 1–17.

Chouliaraki, L., and Bolette, B. (2013). Introduction: Cosmopolitanism and the new news media. *Journalism Studies*, 14(2), 150–155.

Cocking, B. (2009). Travel journalism: Europe imagining the Middle East. *Journalism Studies*, 10(1), 54–68.

Donner, P. (2016). When in Paris, celebrate romance at any of these exquisite hotels. *USA Today*. Retrieved from www.10best.com/

Duffy, A. (2016). How social media offers opportunities for growth in the traditional media industry: The case of travel journalism. In V. Beson, R. Tuninga, and G. Saridakis (Eds.), *Analyzing the strategic role of social networking in firm growth and productivity* (pp. 172–187). Hershey, PA: IGI Global.

Dutton, W. H., and Dubois, E. (2015). The Fifth Estate: A rising force of pluralistic accountability. In S. Coleman and D. Freelon (Eds.), *Handbook of digital politics* (pp. 51–66). Cheltenham: Edward Elgar.

Fürsich, E. (2002a). How can global journalists represent the 'Other'? A critical assessment of the cultural studies concept for media practice. *Journalism*, 3(1), 57–84.

Fürsich, E. (2002b). Packaging culture: The potential and limitations of travel programs on global television. *Communication Quarterly*, 50(2), 204–226.

Fürsich, E., and Kavoori, A. P. (2001). Mapping a critical framework for the study of travel journalism. *International Journal of Cultural Studies*, 4(2), 149–171.

Fürsich, E., and Kavoori, A. P. (2014). People on the move: Travel journalism, globalization and mobility. In F. Hanusch and E. Fürsich (Eds.), *Travel journalism: Exploring production, impact and culture* (pp. 21–38). Basingstoke: Palgrave Macmillan.

Gretzel, U., and Yoo, K. H. (2008). Use and impact of online travel reviews. In P. O'Connor, W. Höpken and U. Gretzel (Eds.), *Information and communication technologies in tourism 2008* (35–46). New York: Springer.

Hanne, M. (Ed.). (1993). *Literature and travel*. Amsterdam: Rodopi.

Heikkilä, H., and Kunelius, R. (2008). Ambivalent ambassadors and realistic reporters: The calling of cosmopolitanism and the seduction of the secular in EU journalism. *Journalism*, 9(4), 377–397.

Heise, L. (2014, July 14). How not to look like a tourist in Paris. *Condé Nast Traveler*. Retrieved from www.cntraveler.com/

Held, D. (2003). *Cosmopolitanism: A defence*. Cambridge: Polity Press.

Held, D. (2010), *Cosmopolitanism: Ideals, realities, and deficits*. Cambridge: Polity Press.

Hinton, P. R. (2000). *Stereotypes, cognition and culture*. Hove: Psychology Press.

Holland, P., and Huggan, G. (2000). *Tourists with typewriters: Critical reflections on contemporary travel writing*. Ann Arbor: University of Michigan Press.

Islam, S. M. (1996). *The ethics of travel: From Marco Polo to Kafka*. Manchester: Manchester University Press.

Kovach, B., and Rosenstiel, T. (2007). *The elements of journalism: What newspeople should know and the public should expect*. New York: Three Rivers Press.

Kovach, B., and Rosenstiel, T. (2010). *Blur: How to know what's true in the age of information overload*. New York: Bloomsbury.

Ladonne, J. (2014, May 16). How to manoeuver Paris's top tourist attractions. *Fodor's Travel*. Retrieved from www.fodors.com/

Lisle, D. (2006). *The global politics of contemporary travel writing*. Cambridge: Cambridge University Press.

MacCannell, D. (2011). *The ethics of sightseeing*. Berkeley: University of California Press.

McGaurr, L. (2012). The devil may care: Travel journalism, cosmopolitan concern, politics and the brand. *Journalism Practice*, 6(1), 42–58.

McNair, B. (2013). The rise of the Fifth Estate. *Journalism Practice*, 7(6), 772–774.

Qiu, L., and Li, D. (2010). Effects of aggregate rating on eWOM acceptance: An attribution theory perspective. *PACIS 2010 Proceedings* (p. 147). Retrieved from http://aisel.aisnet.org

Said, E. W. (1979). *Orientalism*. New York: Vintage.

Schneider, D. J. (2005). *The psychology of stereotyping*. New York: Guilford Press.

Schoon, W. (2014). Representations of interconnectedness: A cosmopolitan framework for analyzing travel journalism. In F. Hanusch and E. Fürsich (Eds.), *Travel journalism: Exploring production, impact and culture* (pp. 213–230). Basingstoke: Palgrave Macmillan.

Schudson, M. (2005). Autonomy from what? In R. Benson and E. Neveu (Eds.), *Bourdieu and the journalistic field* (pp. 214–223). Cambridge: Polity.

Urry, J., and Larsen, J. (2011). *The tourist gaze 3.0*. London: Sage.

Youngs, T. (2013). *The Cambridge introduction to travel writing*. Cambridge: Cambridge University Press.

12

TRAVEL JOURNALISM AND THE SHARING ECONOMY

The case of *Airbnbmag*

Dragging my suitcases across the cobblestones in Naples, I wondered why I hadn't taken a taxi, and was angry that in 2018 Italy still didn't embrace Uber. I followed Google Maps to the piazza where my host had left the key to an apartment in a bar. The old Italian man behind the counter, not understanding why I was asking him for keys, looked at me with a bit of pity behind his scowl. I used WhatsApp to call my host, who spoke to the barkeep in Italian, eventually discovering that there was, indeed, a set of keys in the register. I suddenly realized how utterly dependent I was on technology for my travels, despite being able to function easily without it. It was only in 2006 that I slept on the floor of Rome's Termini station when every hostel I showed up at had no room for me. You learn to make do. In 2018, however, my smartphone was a tool I leaned on, and it got me the keys. I spouted a few *grazies* and made my way across the piazza to my new home for a few months that I organized through Airbnb.

Staying in someone else's home is hardly a novel experience, with *chambres d'hôtes* in France and bed and breakfasts in the UK existing long before the internet (Stringer, 1981). Airbnb, however, established in 2008, changed the way the masses travel. The change wasn't immediate, nor was it revolutionary, but its inception started a more widespread trend towards experiential travel that, after a decade, continues to grow. Recent research points to this desire to differentiate one's travels in order to achieve what one perceives as a more prestigious experience (Chan et al., 2016). Airbnb has been just one such twenty-first-century tourism innovation that allows travelers to go beyond hotels to achieve a more unique lodging option. It was born as part of the sharing economy, whereby individuals could rent or sell unused possessions – like spare rooms – through new websites that embrace Web 2.0 technology (Guttentag, 2015). It has shifted into a more commercial offer where professional operators can also hire out their properties, but the idea of staying in a local's apartment instead of a hotel remains a guiding force behind the company. Ample research on this phenomenon, including older websites like Couchsurfing.com and VRBO.com, detail the challenges, changes, and concerns surrounding house sharing and apartment renting in a digital travel environment. More recently, Airbnb has segued into offering activities it calls 'experiences', allowing customers to book tours, cooking classes, and other events with local hosts, complementing their hospitality services. Having moved into experiences, Airbnb has greatly expanded its potential market.

Taking its expansion one step further in 2017, Airbnb merged with journalism when, partnering with publishing house Hearst, it printed the first edition of *Airbnbmag*, a glossy magazine dedicated to the travel ideals espoused by Airbnb. This publication arguably marked an important moment in travel media history, when such a consequential online company branched out into traditional print media. As an example of brand journalism, Airbnb and Hearst have curiously created a print publication for a digital native company. Andy Bull detailed strategies for brand journalism, which he labels a hybrid of traditional journalism, marketing, and public relations (2013). While it is easy to criticize a simple vector for advertising, *Airbnbmag* demonstrates possibilities for travel journalists as well as an acknowledgement that travel media and its production can – and should – change along with the industry, as I have already suggested. As Hearst Magazines' chief content officer, Joanna Coles, said in an interview, 'There is a new travel consumer whose needs and interests weren't being served in the current media landscape' (Stiehm, 2017). Brand journalism, as described by Bull, is also constantly evolving, and its validity constantly being challenged (2013, p. 1). It seems imperative, therefore, to examine how these two concepts have intersected.

In this chapter, I take a closer look at the first two issues of *Airbnbmag* published in 2017 to understand how the title developed curiously in a culture that is increasingly moving towards digital-only publications. Through a content analysis of the two issues, I'll reveal to what extent journalistic practices are at work, looking at how sourcing and curating still require a journalistic eye, even in the framework of a branded magazine. Of course, this magazine does present several challenges to travel journalism that I will highlight. My goal is not to endorse *Airbnbmag* as an exemplary version of travel journalism, but rather to see how this sort of model can still require the journalistic work that has been described in the previous chapters. Travel journalism, linked to the tourism industry, can never truly be free of economic considerations, and just because a travel company sponsors a publication doesn't mean that the content is entirely self-serving.

Airbnb and the tourism industry

Much discussion about remixing and convergence culture has dominated the early twenty-first century as web users find new ways to engage with literature, cinema, music, and other cultural productions. Lessig discusses at length the rewriting practices that have opened up new possibilities and challenge read-only culture, spawning new communities (2009, p. 80). We can consider Airbnb as one such community, rewriting the rules of the dominant top-down tourism industry. For Lessig, this read-only, or top-down culture is professionally-oriented. It grants authority and promotes culture in a controlled, deliberate way. Rewrite culture, however, requires participation and feedback by readers. 'In a culture in which it is common, its citizens develop a kind of knowledge that empowers as much as it informs or entertains' (p. 85). Airbnb is a brand that has thrived off this sort of participating, with reviews of hosts and guests forming an important part of the website's success. Such examples of the sharing economy are, at least initially, founded on exchange, but a true sharing economy cannot be centered on financial exchange. Lessig writes, 'Thus, no distinction between 'sharing' and 'commercial' economies can be assumed to survive forever, or even for long' (2009, p. 150). Airbnb, therefore, is not as much emblematic of the sharing economy as inspired by it, with sites like Couchsurfing.com exemplifying more of a true sharing economy, where financial goals are secondary.

Most internet businesses, like Airbnb, are ultimately hybrids. As Lessig explains, the commercialization of the sharing economy cannot include a simple buyout (p. 178). You need to preserve the ideals of the sharing economy while switching to a commercial economy – a difficult balancing act that Airbnb has seemingly mastered. To that end, three responsibilities help make the hybrid work. These include giving respect, responsibility, and a sense of belonging to something that has meaning – not unlike at Wikipedia where people believe they are doing useful, meaningful work (pp. 184–185). Airbnb, by giving an outward-facing, printed outlet to its community, has done just that. It has created an outward facing product created for and by its users, with help from an editorial team, in the form of *Airbnbmag*.

The magazine was designed, as its CEO and co-founder Brian Chesky said in the editor's note of the first issue, because existing travel magazines, in his estimate, had no people in them. 'We found that strange, because in our experience, the real magic of travel comes from meeting and connecting with people' (*Airbnbmag* issue 1). Airbnb thrives on promoting activities that users won't find in guidebooks, often touting the word 'authentic', as discussed in Chapter 5. As Gilmore and Pine emphasize, however, all authenticity is inherently fake. 'Individuals long for authenticity, but struggle with how to gain it. Businesses long to fulfil that need by selling authenticity, but cannot really provide it' (2007, p. 89). Through *Airbnbmag*, however, the company is trying to tap into some human element, to go beyond the reviews and into deeper stories, engaging in more journalistic storytelling than the reviews that users will find on the website.

This focus on human voices in the travel industry is something that Gilmore and Pine underscore. While suggesting strategies for engaging with audiences, they write,

> Also be sure to focus your remaining live person-to-person interactions on turning every seemingly mundane encounter into an engaging experience. Amidst today's sea of technological mediation, handing this human remnant

well sends a powerful message to your customers and should inform the design of all other interactions.

(Gilmore and Pine, 2007, p. 16)

While Airbnb engages in such person-to-person interactions via its internal messenger, the magazine offers a tangible, more illustrative way to reach consumers. More than just telling stories, *Airbnbmag* is taking information from its site and creating an edited product with 'curated material – in this case, material which has been professionally evaluated according to standards of technical polish or commercial potential' (Jenkins et al., 2013, p. 243). Editors and journalists are performing this work, giving the polish to otherwise non-professional contributions from hosts and guests on the site.

Airbnbmag and journalism

While brand magazines, like airline publications *easyJet Traveller* or *N by Norwegian*, are not a new concept, few, if any, are available on newsstands. *Airbnbmag*, however, was designed to be available at kiosks and in airports, to the general public. It's not something that readers will only find in Airbnb accommodation. It is a media text that mixes a mass media model, published by Hearst, with the niche interests of Airbnb consumers. In *Spreadable Media*, the authors describe the differences between the two, writing:

> People use media texts both to enjoy shared cultural experiences and to differentiate themselves from mass tastes. Mass-media content often becomes spreadable because its relative ubiquity provides common ground for conversation with a wide variety of people. Niche content, on the other hand, spreads because it helps people communicate their more particular interests and sensibilities, to distinguish themselves from most others.
>
> *(Jenkins et al., 2013, p. 242)*

By bringing *Airbnbmag* into existence, the company has brought a niche market of consumers to traditional media, while Hearst helps expose Airbnb to a larger public. As such, 'niche cultural production is increasingly influencing the shape and direction of mainstream media' (Jenkins et al., 2013, p. 36). This phenomenon is not unique to *Airbnbmag*. Also in 2017, French newspaper *Le Monde* helped finance a health magazine, *Doctissimo*, an online health forum that has become a popular resource in the French-speaking world. A previous print edition of *Doctissimo* appeared in 2013, but the new version, backed by *Le Monde*, carries the credibility described by Lessig (2009). Axel Bruns described the segue of online citizen journalism to print editions in German publications, but *Airbnbmag* doesn't just reprint user content, as the *Fodor's* guides once did with TripAdvisor reviews (2009). Instead, it is using the website and its individuals as material for a sort of spin-off, creating original content independent from but inspired by the website. It will be interesting to watch how other websites in the future may expand from web-only existences into other forms of media like print, radio, or television.

While online and pre-web media do sometimes collide, such convergence is fairly new territory for travel journalism. It is important to understand how traditional practice still fits into this new branded niche-yet-simultaneously-mainstream content. A look at the Airbnb magazine reveals ample opportunities for journalists to adapt their practices to this particular type of publication. A few studies have already looked at how audiences react to brand journalism. As Cole and Greer discuss, audiences respond negatively to messages that are framed commercially (2013, p. 684). Their study analyses the effects of framing, sourcing, and product involvement on the perceived credibility among audiences. Before even beginning to discuss public perceptions, I want to take a look at *Airbnbmag*'s content to point out a few key elements of journalism inherent in the magazine. By understanding how journalistic practice manifests itself in this branded magazine, perhaps future travel journalists will better see the possibilities in these new types of publications.

It is important to understand that the magazine has all of the trappings of a traditional magazine. It has a masthead, a table of contents, advertisements, a letter from the editor and sections that have changed slightly between the first two issues. The first issue is divided into 'the Local', 'Stay', 'Roam', and 'Belong'. The second issue kept the 'Stay' and 'Roam' headings but lost the other two, adding 'Discover'. Both also feature an editor's letter and a section called 'Not yet trending'. It has longer features in addition to smaller articles, lists, profiles, and a calendar of events around the world. There are a few product reviews as well as indications of how to book certain Airbnb services clearly denoted by the company's logo. There is also an interactive feature that brings the magazine back to the website. By downloading a specific app and scanning the page, readers can be directed back to Airbnb.com on their smartphones, creating a publication that is in conversation with and not independent from the website. The stories themselves mimic traditional travel journalism, often incorporating first person narratives along with reporting about a destination. *Airbnbmag*'s creators – editors, journalists, writers – also produced a fair amount of original reporting, sourcing, and curation that reflects a clear tendency towards journalism.

Original reporting

Obviously, and understandably, *Airbnbmag* runs stories related to destinations that are linked to their properties. The first issue features a story about food in London, while the second issue highlights the already popular Paris on its cover – the company's two largest markets (Bishop, 2017). Many of the stories are simply round-ups or lists that feature local voices or Airbnb hosts. The longer features, however, do contain some really interesting reporting that is not immediately linked to any Airbnb property or activity. The first issue takes an in-depth look at Cuba through the eyes of locals. And while, yes, much of the story pivots around an Airbnb 'experience' of cycling with that local, it still offers some solid journalism. The second issue does a similarly good job looking at the LGBT and queer scene in Beirut. The story actually does not link back to any Airbnb content in the writing, though a special app on a smartphone will take readers to discover additional content from Beirut hosts on the website when it scans the page.

What is notable about these stories is that Airbnb, partnered with Hearst, has the money to send writers on these excursions, or remunerate them substantially – at least in theory, as no public information is available regarding salaries or pay scales. To the reader, it is unclear how the stories are produced and who pays what – unlike *Condé Nast Traveler* or other legacy media who are forthcoming about not accepting sponsored travel – but ultimately it doesn't matter. Journalistic transparency is less of an issue because, due to the fact that it is a brand-sponsored magazine, readers don't expect Airbnb to be absent from each story. We expect them to have financed or supported the content. Airbnb's endorsement of the stories, in fact, lends to a certain level of trust between the reader and the writer. As Jenkins et al. write,

> In current Web 2.0 business rhetoric, 'transparency' refers to the degree to which brands and audience members alike are forthcoming about their ties to one another, ensuring that potential customers have access to all the information needed to assess the credibility of a recommendation. Meanwhile, in the recent parlance of marketing, 'authenticity' represents the overall assessment of the credibility of a brand or audience member.
>
> *(2013, pp. 76–77)*

Both of these ideas help to establish trust for a tourist who may engage in an activity described in *Airbnbmag* (p. 77).

Finding these stories, achieving some notion of authenticity, is what travel journalists always need to do, regardless of the publication. Journalists – like any product or service provider – always want to appeal to the exceptional, as Gilmore and Pine write. They stress, 'It is not just being different, but different in a way that comes across as authentic by exemplifying a certain attitude of accepting nothing but the utmost in excellence and demonstrating that attitude via individual, extraordinary acts' (2007, p. 63). Reporting on niche, surprising, and unreported topics is one such way to demonstrate excellence, instead of simply peddling Airbnb's own interests and experiences. These possibilities have not faded away simply because *Airbnbmag* is branded content.

Sources

One of the notable fortes of *Airbnbmag*, as Brian Chesky insisted, is the amount of people presented in its pages. A host of local voices, restaurateurs, shopkeepers, students, and tour guides share their recommendations and favorite spots in their various locations. The writers in the longer feature stories – of which there are four of five per issue – incorporate a host of sources from both within and beyond the

Airbnb community. Another part of the magazine includes round-ups of local voices addressing various themes. The first issue has a page of interviews with writers about why they travel. There is also a spread on how to visit Los Angeles through the eyes of a shopper, an adventurer, a foodie, and a family. The second issue has a profile on a novelist and her bookstore in Brooklyn. There is a series of mini profiles of influencers in Shanghai, ranging from a cocktail maker, an art gallery director, and a trendspotter. There are also short interviews with celebrities about their travels. Few if any of the sources are necessarily experts, but are framed mostly as peers, though whether or not that matters remains difficult to discern empirically (Cole and Greer, 2013).

All of these interviews are similar to what audiences can find in most travel journalism, but aside from the few celebrities, most sources are regular people and not elite individuals. As news sources, they still relate back to the traditional relationship whereby the journalist requires material and the source requires access to audiences (Franklin and Carlson, 2011, p. 2). The difference is that the sources inherently have an audience on the website, while the magazine exposes them to new offline audiences, to potential future customers. The magazine shows its commercial roots in the profiles of Airbnb hosts who tell the stories behind their properties, but they are still regular people. While on one hand this sort of journalism borders advertorial, it is also catering to the target audience. Airbnb mimics classic competitive market values, giving customers what they want. 'The new part is to recognize a wider range of wants, some me-motivated, some thee-motivated, and the way technology can help serve them' (Lessig, 2009, p. 224). For Airbnb users, these wants include going behind the scenes, living among locals, and hearing the histories behind unusual properties.

The idea of personal recommendations, discussed throughout previous chapters, is what drives Airbnb, despite much debate over their authority and validity.

> We all take the recommendations of trusted sources over strangers, experts over neophytes. However, that influence typically is contextual and temporal, depending on the subject, the speaker's credibility, and a variety of other factors. Sure, there are influencers, but who those influencers are may shift substantially from one situation to another.
>
> *(Jenkins et al., 2013, p. 81)*

In the pages of *Airbnbmag*, the journalists remove these influencers from the context of the website and situate them journalistically into a larger story. This requires all of the interviewing and fact-finding skills that journalists have in their toolbox. In the magazine, they aren't just copying reviews from the website, but creating fresh content, telling new stories, and going deeper into the lives of people who provide only short biographies and a photo online. While intimately linked to the financial interests of Airbnb, there is still plenty of journalistic work going on within the pages of this magazine. This publication provides opportunities for travel journalists to exercise their professional skills in a new environment.

Curation

Airbnbmag also allows editorial teams to stretch their curatorial muscle. Since so much of the magazine's content depends on the hosts and travelers of the Airbnb community, the magazine writers have to learn to identify potential sources and stories from the website. This requires reading reviews and understanding what experiences or properties deserve coverage inside the magazine.

Curation goes back to the notion of Axel Bruns' 'gatewatching' (2005). Guerrini builds on these notions, writing that Web 2.0 tools allow one person to now do the work of a whole editorial team (2013, p. 8). In *Airbnbmag*, such curation is evident in several spreads. Both issues, in their 'Stay' section highlight several interesting or unique properties, with photos and links to the property on the website. Whether they be castles, jungle bungalows, tiny houses, or tree houses, these properties have been selected by the writers for multiple reasons – uniqueness, popularity, newness, etc. Travel journalists already perform this kind of work when recommending hotels, but Airbnb adds another layer to such curatorial processes, as they must look at the reviews for a certain host and property, to understand the nuances of home sharing. Similarly, in a feature about Shanghai, the writer selected seven female hosts to highlight, creating a one-page spread for each individual. Such curatorial skills require the writer to be familiar with the website and its source material and to make a judgement call on the most interesting characters to profile and how to approach the piece. In this case, the journalist justified the piece by identifying 60 per cent of Airbnb hosts in Shanghai as women, exhibiting some sort of editorial judgement needed to make sense of all of the noise on the Airbnb website.

The magazine takes these collective discussions full circle, spreading them from the internet to the printed page. 'At the heart of our spreadable media model is the idea that audience members are more than data, that their collective discussions and deliberations – and their active involvement in appraising and circulating content – are generative' (Jenkins et al., 2013, p. 176). By curating content from the site, the magazine's editors are engaging with their readers in a unique way, bringing their conversations to a new venue. Travel journalists working with a brand like Airbnb still need to engage in the curatorial and gatewatching practices that have become mainstays of twenty-first-century journalism. While there are still many conversations to be had about how these writers assemble their stories, the basic curatorial process is still at work.

Challenges for *Airbnbmag*

While the magazine does allow for a certain amount of journalistic work to be performed, it is not a perfect model. The reporting, sourcing, and curating that editors and journalists engage in will be guided ultimately by the interests of the company, which is neither reproachable nor unexpected. While Airbnb community members may not balk at that, we may wonder how such a publication, with such advertorial leanings, will fare in the long-term. The problem is in distinguishing the content clearly enough from straight advertising so that consumers will want to buy this magazine as it perches among legacy titles like *Travel+Leisure* or *National Geographic Traveller*. The features on LGBT culture in Beirut and on the opening up of Cuba, however, may illustrate how *Airbnbmag* is aware of these issues. It is doing more than just advertising its own products.

Throughout the magazine, however, the reader is rarely allowed to forget that this is a commercially produced magazine, which brings into question the authenticity espoused by Airbnb. Many of the stories feature activities or hosts with links to the Airbnb site where users can find these services. Again, this is to be expected, but the constant consumerism – however strongly a facet of travel journalism – is a bit ever-present. Gilmore and Pine suggest that consumers seek authenticity as it relates to the larger portrait of human history. 'People tend to perceive as authentic that which refers to some other context, drawing inspiration from human history, and tapping into our shared memories and longings; not derivative or trivial' (2007, p. 50). Reading about a nineteenth-century chateau with a gorgeous photo and then having the price tag and website right next to it makes it difficult to feel that the item is something unique, or at least anything more than a commodity. Of course, the goal is to sell these properties and experiences to travelers, but the magazine often feels more like a catalogue than a work of journalistic integrity, which may or may not clash with consumers.

This biggest problem facing a publication like *Airbnbmag* is uncertainty. The website and consequently the publication are both too recent to be fixtures of the tourism industry. Many cities like Berlin and Barcelona have passed legislation limiting or prohibiting short-term apartment renting in recent years (Oltermann, 2016). It's possible that this segment of the sharing economy will rapidly disappear, rendering *Airbnbmag* useless. Or, more likely, newer modes of accommodation will crop up to respond to governmental regulations. However it evolves, the point is that the tourism industry *will* change, and these publications will follow suit. The journalistic practice inherent in them, however, will remain fundamentally the same, adapting itself to whatever new media environment develops next.

Journalists and the sharing economy

The goal of this chapter is not to praise or criticize *Airbnbmag*. It is a new player in a new environment, and its editors are still finding their legs. The takeaway message here is twofold. First, the changing face of the tourism industry will have an ever-evolving effect on travel media and journalists, offering new opportunities. This is something that future travel journalists need to embrace, as change comes quicker and quicker with advancing technology and increased internet access. Being prepared to enter this turbulent environment and not relying on stereotypes of travel journalists simply as luxurious jetsetters or adventurers will be key to their success in the future.

Second, the sharing economy, inasmuch as it is still a novelty in the Web 2.0 era, presents a large amount of source material for journalists to use. Why, then, wait for a branded magazine to sponsor its own? Travel journalists can – and do – write stories based on these websites, their offers, and their communities. TripAdvisor, a mainstay of travel and Web 2.0, has been the subject of numerous articles over the years. The *Irish Independent* ran a story on January 8, 2018, about a restauranteur who shot back at a disgruntled client (Gittens, 2018). An online article in *Forbes* discusses how TripAdvisor deals with sexual assault, in part due to all of the discussion around the topic stemming from Hollywood and political scandals (Goldstein, 2017). Airbnb, Uber, and other sharing economy websites, therefore, should also be held to such scrutiny, and articles on them not treated as fluff or secondary pieces. If these actors are major players in the tourism industry – even if only ephemerally – they require the same sort of coverage and scrutinizing, watchdog reporting that travel journalists would perform for any other topic. To put it in context, Airbnb saw rising profits in 2017, hitting 1 billion dollars, up from 500 million dollars in the same quarter a year earlier according to Bloomberg (Zalesky, 2017). Most of the reporting on Airbnb, however, remains focused on regulation and financial performance and not on the cultural or social challenges that this growing entity might present. Equal coverage in the travel media should be able to focus on these experiences, what they offer, and how they fit into the tourism industry more specifically.

There is a lot of potential for travel journalists to tap into these innovations and to exercise their journalistic muscles accordingly. These new beats provide ample material for the original reporting, sourcing, and curating possibilities that are touchstones of the journalistic profession. With *Airbnbmag* channelling all of this online culture into a printed magazine, it seems important – and prudent – to maintain a journalistic handle on such a publication, and any others that may develop in the future.

References

Bishop, J. (2017, April 5). You'll never guess which city has the most Airbnb properties. *Forbes*. Retrieved from www.forbes.com/

Bull, A. (2013). *Brand journalism*. Abingdon: Routledge.

Bruns, A. (2005). *Gatewatching: Collaborative online news production*. New York: Peter Lang.

Bruns, A. (2010). Citizen journalism and everyday life. In B. Franklin and M. Carlson (Eds.), *Journalists, sources, and credibility: New perspectives* (pp. 182–194). Abingdon: Routledge.

Chan, W. Y., To, C. K. M., and Chu, W. C. (2016). Desire for experiential travel, avoidance of rituality and social esteem: An empirical study of consumer response to tourism innovation. *Journal of Innovation and Knowledge*, 1(1), 24–35.

Cole, J. T., and Greer, J. D. (2013). Audience response to brand journalism: The effect of frame, source, and involvement. *Journalism and Mass Communication Quarterly*, 90(4), 673–690.

Franklin, B., and Carlson, M. (Eds.). (2011). *Journalists, sources, and credibility: New perspectives*. Abingdon: Routledge.

Gilmore, J. H., and Pine, B. J. (2007). *Authenticity: What consumers really want.* Boston: Harvard Business Press.

Gittens, G. (2018, Jan. 17). 'You were the rudest person we ever encountered' – Irish restaurant hits back after customer's 'disgraceful' behaviour. *Irish Independent.* Retrieved from https://www.independent.ie

Goldstein, M. (2017, Dec. 28). Looking back on 2017: TripAdvisor and sexual assault. *Forbes.* Retrieved from https://www.forbes.com/

Guerrini, F. (2013). Newsroom curators and independent storytellers: Content curation as a new form of journalism. Reuters Institute and University of Oxford. Retrieved from http://reutersinstitute.politics.ox.ac.uk

Guttentag, D. (2015). Airbnb: disruptive innovation and the rise of an informal tourism accommodation sector. *Current issues in Tourism*, 18(12), 1192–1217.

Jenkins, H., Ford, S., and Green, J. (2013). *Spreadable media: Creating value and meaning in a networked culture.* New York: NYU Press.

Lessig, L. (2009). *Remix: Making art and commerce thrive in the hybrid economy.* New York: Penguin.

Oltermann, P. (2016, June 8). Berlin ban on Airbnb short-term rentals upheld by city court. *Guardian.* Retrieved from https://www.theguardian.com

Stiehm, C. (2017). Hearst magazine's new Airbnbmag encourages readers to be at home in the world. Hearst.com. Retrieved from www.hearst.com/newsroom

Stringer, P. F. (1981). Hosts and guests: The bed-and-breakfast phenomenon. *Annals of Tourism Research*, 8(3), 357–376.

Zalesky, O. (2017). Airbnb is said to double revenue to $1 billion last quarter. *Bloomberg.* Retrieved from https://www.bloomberg.com

CONCLUSION

By now, traveling to Istanbul or New York and writing a story about it might seem much more complicated and nuanced than you previously thought. It should seem like work. At the end of the day, it is. As much as travel journalism seems frivolous to critics and glitzy to some practitioners, there is something more substantial happening in a travel section. This was likely always the case. Today, with the internet, however, the processes we use to create these stories, the tools at our disposal, and the goals of our work are changing, constantly shifting to respond to the needs of an evolving industry. Everything is moving, and as travel journalists we need to do our best to keep up, even if we might always be one step behind.

Despite all of this, I don't want to suggest that travel journalism is any harder or more complicated than other forms of journalism. Instead, following Hanusch's lead, this book bolsters the argument that travel journalism, as a branch of lifestyle journalism, can and should be taken seriously (2014). Future journalists and researchers need to pay special attention to travel, to recognize its specificities. Political journalists, environmental journalists, health journalists, and the list continues, should be doing the same thing. The digital innovations or adaptations described in the previous chapters, I admit, are not all unique to travel journalism. I hope to have set them, however, firmly enough into a specific context so that future journalists and researchers can discuss the profession in terms unique to travel and tourism, and not to paint all journalism with the same brush.

Instead, I believe – and I'd like to think not too naively after penning this book – that travel journalism will continue to be a trusted resource for consumers. Its many forms, from hotel and restaurant reviews to long form stories, will continue to have a place among the blog posts, Instagram posts, and TripAdvisor reviews that the internet has fostered. All of these sources work together for consumers, but tourists still want some sort of authority, some sort of trust, some sort of face guiding them. While that authority may come from an individual

TripAdvisor user or a favorite blogger, it can continue to come from the *New York Times* or *Travel+Leisure* as well. Travel guides and magazines admittedly no longer have a monopoly on travel media, but travel journalism can happen elsewhere. It happens on blogs. It happens on YouTube. It happens through company publications. We will see where it will happen with the innovations of the future.

Looking no further than *Airbnbmag*, we see the relationship between public service and business interests described by Coddington (2015). He describes the eroding wall between journalism and business interests that has given way to norms of transparency and integrity (p. 79). For travel journalism, however, the idea of a wall, of some boundary between what journalists experience and what they produce, seems fruitless to debate. Travel journalists produce content that is both *about* and *sponsored by* the same industry, so financial liaisons are inevitable. How journalists deal with these liaisons, however, has been discussed throughout this book and remains a central point of concern for the profession.

Travel journalists don't write about travel experiences simply for the pleasure – acknowledging that armchair travelers exist – nor do we write for some greater public good. Instead, we write to help people make informed spending decisions. We write to inform them about the destinations, the people, the accommodations, and the experiences that they may engage in while there. We aren't like Egeria writing letters just to friends who may probably never travel beyond their town. We are writing for people who want to know about Paris, about Naples, about Seattle, about Tehran, about Dakar because they are going there, or they might go there, or they know someone who is going there. Travel journalism is linked to consumerism, and as such, linked to the tourism industry. Above all, if we are being honest, travel journalists write to make money, to earn a living, and so some sort of financial interest is always at play in our work.

As such, a publication by a hotel chain, an airline, or a home share service like Airbnb carries as much journalistic potential than a publication like *Condé Nast Traveler*, which requires independence from its writers. But really, what's the difference between *Condé Nast Traveler* who needs to attract advertisers and *Airbnbmag* which acts as its own advertising? There are always agendas. Consequently, there will always need to be transparency and disclosure. Travel journalism is not likely going to happen in a vacuum by some benevolent professional not seeking any financial remuneration, so let's be clear about that upfront.

Identify, understand, and challenge

Though no one book can tackle all of the intricacies of even this one niche form of journalism, the previous chapters will have at least, ideally, sparked some conversations. Looking at a small sample of actors in travel media – from journalists to review site contributors – I have attempted to highlight the differences, to help future practitioners identify what their unique contributions are, where there is crossover, and what alternative routes may exist. The studies are by no means exhaustive and the analyses are not the final word – nor can they be. Travel journalism will confront new challenges the day this book hits your local bookstore or e-reader, and likely every day after.

I have tried to situate these ideas in contemporary academic research on journalism, but the difficulty is to understand how these ideas play out specifically in a travel context. Travel journalism is not uniquely a public service, it does not advance democratic ideals, it does not need to be objective in the traditional sense. Instead, practitioners need to understand how their particular type of journalism relies on their own branded identities, on the consumer aspect, on a very large and consequential industry.

But more importantly, I hope students and future practitioners feel compelled to challenge the norms and ideals attributed to journalism in most of the literature that's out there. Journalism *can* be a more constructive practice – though it need not always be, and good journalism *can* grace the pages of a publication like *Airbnbmag*. To say otherwise would be to trap journalism in some arbitrarily drawn boundaries. Travel journalism can look to social media for inspiration and sources, and arguably should in more systematic ways. These places are where the news is happening, where the trends are being set, and travel journalists need to tap into this information as best they can.

Journalism, as most researchers agree, is not just going to go away. Schudson suggests that the news paradigm – the inverted pyramid, interviews, objectivity, and other practices – that has guided much of journalism for the last century is still intact. He talks about the heavy financial investment in, and moreover, legal ramifications of creating sound journalism, which user-generated content cannot uniformly reproduce (2011). At least not yet. The question here is whether or not there is a travel news paradigm that is functioning in the same way, and whether or not social media actually could replace it

The first few chapters of this book, mapping out a specific sociology and news values that I associate with travel journalism, suggest that, indeed, such a paradigm does exist. By nuancing Hanusch and Fürsich's definition of travel journalism, we could arrive at such a list of practices, however imperfect it would always be. To return to it, they write that travel journalism includes

> factual accounts that address audiences as consumers of travel or tourism experiences, by providing information and entertainment, but also critical perspectives. Travel journalism operates within the broader ethical framework of professional journalism but with specific constraints brought on by the economic environment of its production.
>
> *(Hanusch and Fürsich 2014, p. 11)*

Building upon this base, we can ask further questions of travel journalists to help them understand better what they are actually providing. What do facts and information look like? Are these the factual observations of the journalist, the facts provided by a PR agency, aggregate rankings from a review site, or even quotes from social network users? It may include a mix of all of these, and often does.

When we suggest that travel journalists provide critical perspectives, do they take into account the critical perspectives of the masses on TripAdvisor, as some journalists reported using in their research? In this way, we think of travel journalists more as curators than single voices, sifting through and identifying user-generated content that may be useful for their specific audiences.

What about entertainment? Is this something that journalists provide simply through their narrative or are there other elements? Are travel journalists required to produce Instagram feeds, live Twitter chats, and other media for their audiences to enjoy? I would stress the importance of interactivity and multimedia endeavors for travel journalists in the twenty-first century, but not at the expense of any other element.

What does an ethical framework look like? It involves disclosure and transparency, but it also involves questions of cultural sensitivity, of understanding stereotypes and how to represent others. Naturally, any journalist will have to act in the same way, but these questions need to be highlighted, underlined, and boldfaced for travel journalists who deal with them routinely. It involves thinking more constructively about their reporting, especially during anthropogenic or natural crises, to think about the effect their reporting may have on a destination, as explored in Chapter 10 and the 2015 Paris attacks.

What are the specific constraints brought on by travel journalism and the economic environment of its production? Pickard rightly points out that little research probes this issue thoroughly, that it is one of the blind spots of journalism studies that he highlights in his essay (2017). In lifestyle and travel journalism, there is even less research into these questions, though some research looks at how lifestyle journalists respond to commercial pressures with both resignation and resistance, as I have seen among the travel journalists interviewed here as well (Hanusch et al., 2017). Here, we look to questions related to writing for SEO, self-branding, influencer status, and mixing booking sites with journalistic content. All of these elements provide their own challenges, and travel journalists will likely encounter some or all of them, whether working for a legacy media brand or an online-only platform.

Does all of this lead us to a definition of a travel journalist in a digital age? It leads us to many, but to employ one definition any more specific than what Hanusch and Fürsich have developed risks limiting this profession to something that cannot evolve, stretch, or change as the industry and media landscape demand. Instead, I want readers to look at travel journalism through a broader lens that will allow them to understand how the profession exists at that specific time and place, to be able to apply these ideas as they are pertinent, and to put aside those that aren't.

Values of travel journalism – for now

Ultimately, however, we need to ask what value journalism has at all. Why bother financing these magazines or websites if TripAdvisor and blogs can provide all of the information needed? Journalists aren't doing anything that bloggers can't do, right? Perhaps, but just because bloggers can potentially act like journalists does not mean they will. For individuals booking often costly trips, to rely on a blogger or a faceless forum contributor may not be enough. Hyde reported on the various ways that people research their trips in the twenty-first century, from search engines to travel agents, and as expected, there are many factors that contribute to how an individual books travel (2009). What is clear, however, is that they use lots of sources, cross-checking on the web as they go along (Pirolli, 2016). Trust is a mosaic that individual users put together themselves.

Journalists can, and should, play a role in this process. But as Jeff Jarvis writers, journalists need to practice efficiency, something that user-generated content does not always espouse. He writes, 'If you can't imagine why someone would link to what you're doing, you probably shouldn't be doing' (2009). This leads to a conclusion that journalists, when not creating important content, can also be the ones doing the linking, curating, gatewatching, or whatever we choose to call it. As Jarvis sums it up, 'Do what you do best and link to the rest' (2009). While his quote may reduce journalists to nothing more than simple information providers, in travel journalism the idea carries some weight. As consumers, we don't need travel journalists to provide us with opening hours and addresses. It's fine if they do, but these are the things that anyone can find through a quick Google search. Untold stories, unique perspectives, and engaging narratives, however, are not so easily searchable on Google.

Therefore, if we accept these things to be true, travel journalists add value in two very concrete ways. First, they sift through all of the social media, the user-generated content for us, curating and highlighting the most pertinent stories. Such choices will depend on the publication – Eurocheapo and *Condé Nast Traveler* clearly aim for different audiences, but the principles at work are the same. Journalists are trusted voices that can do the heavy lifting for us, as consumers of travel experiences. Sifting through information and being able to pull out the useful bits is at the heart of journalism, and social media is essentially a source like any other. It just happens to be one that we can also contact and chat with to go deeper if needed.

Second, they can produce the storytelling that bloggers do not engage in systematically. As part of their professional profile – or paradigm – they know how to interview people, get fresh perspectives, and find stories to tell. This is at the heart of any journalist's education – or should be – and in travel is extremely important in order to convey a sense of place to audiences. As Chapter 6 detailed, an attention to writing is paramount, as tourists will often turn away from websites where the writing is anything less than good (Pirolli, 2016). Yes, again, blogs and even forum writers can do these things. But tourists don't typically go to TripAdvisor looking for a 2000-word narrative that will transport them to Lima. There is a quality that journalists, specifically those writing for any sort of trusted brand, can convey instantly. Editorial and quality filters, while maybe less in demand for other types of journalism, still resonate with travel audiences.

Curation and storytelling are not new concepts, but they are two clear examples of the value that travel journalists can still bring to the travel media landscape. These functions recent research suggesting journalists adopt different functions as marketers, service providers, friends, connectors, mood managers, inspirers, and guides (Hanitzsch and Vos, 2018). If professionals begin to adopt, in a more wide-spread fashion, the practices discussed throughout this book, will they be able to add value in different ways? Or will they just become too indistinguishable from the rest of the user-generated content online, eventually fading into the background? Ideally it will be the former, but future research will hopefully answer these questions.

Opportunities for travel journalists

While the future is uncertain, other things are quite clear. There is still a viable future that can emanate from understanding the basics of being a travel journalist. Going forward as a travel journalist, I'd argue that the internet has actually opened up more opportunities for professionals. Realizing how journalistic training and practices can apply beyond traditional publishing is one of the keys to succeeding as a travel journalist. In news writing, we see already how journalists are using their expertise to work with automated, so-called robo-writing (Thurman et al., 2017). Travel journalists, similarly, learn and develop skill sets that they can use across the tourism industry. I do not suggest abandoning the hopes of writing for major pub-lications in order to earn money, but the freelance nature and precariousness of the profession means having to be resourceful. Not all journalism scholars and graduates, after all, are aiming for a job as a reporter (Mellado and Scherman, 2017).

Most of the journalists interviewed discussed their experiences working across travel media, and not just in journalism, to turn their skills into profits. For some, myself included, the options have been numerous over the years. Writing and editing skills can apply easily to creating applications for smartphones, generating content that is as quick and engaging as it is true and factual. Other copywriting opportunities for travel websites, tour companies, and offices of tourism can pro-vide periodic, yet often lucrative work. To that end, as many journalism students do, working in travel PR is also a profitable way to put the professional skills dis-cussed here to work. Writing about travel is a highly transferable skill that extends well beyond journalism.

More entrepreneurial individuals may look to YouTube and other self-publish-ing platforms to create their own brands. I worked with a production company from New York on a video series on YouTube that never earned me a dime, yet, but it gave me the opportunity to stretch my storytelling and research skills while branching out into a new medium. Others might adopt podcasts, creating travel-related content through this developing medium. Personal websites can attract audiences, which in turn can produce profits through online advertising. Without creating high expectations, I merely suggest that, as one of many streams of income, branded websites can contribute. Perhaps the more business-minded can use their travel journalism profiles to become tour operators or tour guides. In the broadest sense, giving a tour face-to-face isn't all that different from taking someone on a trip with you through your written story. Such avenues have worked for me and others in the past, and being a travel journalist helps establish more credibility when walking these alternative paths.

Of course, there is also always the opportunity to teach. My father always said, quoting George Bernard Shaw's play *Man and Superman*, 'Those who can, do; those who can't, teach.' Back in 1903, when Shaw wrote those words, journalists did not yet have professional recognition in most of the world, but the idea might still apply to journalists today. Fortunately, journalism programs often require educators to teach *and* do. In one study, Sarah Niblock proposes various ways of looking at the 'reflective' study of journalism, exploring the tenuous fusion of practice and theory in academia. She discusses the idea of practice-as-research, whereby journalistic output itself could fulfil the research goals of academics. Such approaches, she highlights, are especially problematic for lifestyle journalists – and subsequently travel journalists – who produce work which is still viewed as something less important than 'serious' news (Niblock, 2007, p. 28). While I straddle both worlds, I can attest that this not always easy to do. Still, the possibility is there, as I mentioned at the beginning of this book, as universities are recognizing the academic potential of cultural and lifestyle reporting.

No matter which path, if any, the budding travel journalist goes down, the same skills and challenges discussed through these chapters apply. Understanding how the practices and values of a profession evolve in tandem with the needs of a growing and changing industry, as well as ever-diversifying ways of communicating these needs, is key for a travel journalist. Questions of cultural representation, branding, economics, and emerging markets are all important, whether you are working on a 5,000-word commission for *National Geographic Traveller* or creating content for a new travel app from a start-up out of Berlin.

Final remarks

It should be obvious, but if my students are any indication, it is not: Journalists need to read. Stories, lists, reviews, blogs – it's all helpful even if in different ways. Maybe podcasts fit better into your lifestyle, or you are a fan of travel documentaries. These are all fair game as well, but reading is necessary for understanding the intricacies of travel language. I would suggest, as well, taking advantage of travel journalism's close cousin, the rich and vast world of travel narratives. While eschewing certain journalistic principles, these narratives can help inspire writers to think outside of the box, to understand what works and what doesn't. Narrative accounts like Adam Gopnik's *Paris to the Moon* and George Orwell's *Down and Out in Paris and London* also pushed me to want to work in travel writing in some capacity. Maybe for you it's Elizabeth Gilbert's *Eat, Pray, Love*, or a Bill Bryson novel, or Paul Theroux's *The Old Patagonian Express*. Any writing guide will tell you that good writers are active readers, and the same rings true for travel journalists. How can you hope to produce any sort of story that someone will want to read if you have not, yourself, identified what you appreciate reading?

Finally, travel journalism requires a passion for, above all, travel. I didn't think it necessary to dedicate an entire chapter defining travel. Alain de Botton's *The Art of Travel* and Dean MacCannell's *The Tourist: A New Theory of the Leisure Class* are two books that have inspired me in my research and which discuss the concept at length. The point is that travel journalists need to be travelers. Travel doesn't require spending a year traipsing the world – again, de Botton can discuss this in detail for you. Everywhere is a destination for someone, even if it's your local diner or café, and this sort of attitude is what guides a travel journalist. Travel stories happen everywhere, and as a travel journalist these stories are yours to find and tell.

Without these two passions for reading and traveling, all the lessons in journalistic practice, economy, transparency, and innovation are useless. If you've made it this far, however, chances are you're doing fine. Now, whether you are producing travel journalism or merely researching it – or likely both – the objective is to keep an open mind and be prepared for whatever comes next. Whether it's sifting through Instagram photos, researching the best pizza in Naples on TripAdvisor, or preparing a trek across China's New Silk Road, you'll be thinking like a travel journalist, and that is the most important – and only – credential you'll have or need.

References

Carlson, M. (2015). Introduction: The many boundaries of journalism. In M. Carlson and S. C. Lewis (Eds.), *Boundaries of journalism: Professionalism, practices and participation* (pp. 1–18). Abingdon: Routledge.

Coddington, M. (2015). The wall becomes a curtain. In M. Carlson and S. C. Lewis (Eds.), *Boundaries of journalism: Professionalism, practices and participation* (pp. 67–82). Abingdon: Routledge.

Hanitzsch, T., and Vos, T. (2018). Journalism beyond democracy: A new look into journalistic roles in political and everyday life. *Journalism*, 19(2), 146–164.

Hanusch, F. (Ed.). (2014). *Lifestyle journalism*. Abingdon: Routledge.

Hanusch, F., and Fürsich, E. (2014). On the relevance of travel journalism: An introduction. In F. Hanusch and E. Fürsich (Eds.), *Travel journalism: Exploring production, impact and culture* (pp. 1–18). Basingstoke: Palgrave Macmillan.

Hanusch, F., Hanitzsch, T., and Lauerer, C. (2017). 'How much love are you going to give this brand?' Lifestyle journalists on commercial influences in their work. *Journalism*, 18(2), 141–158.

Hyde, K. F. (2009). Tourist information search. In M. Kozak and A. Decrop (Eds.), *Handbook of tourist behaviour* (pp. 50–67). New York: Routledge.

Jarvis, J. (2009, April 24). Journalists: Where do you add value?BuzzMachine. Retrieved from https://buzzmachine.com

Mellado, C., and Scherman, A. (2017). Influences on job expectations among Chilean journalism students. *International Journal of Communication*, 11, 18.

Niblock, S. (2007). From 'knowing how' to 'being able': Negotiating the meanings of reflective practice and reflexive research in journalism studies. *Journalism Practice*, 1(1), 20–32.

Pickard, V. (2017). Rediscovering the news: Journalism studies' three blind spots. In P. Boczkowski and C. W. Anderson (Eds.), *Essays on the future of journalism scholarship in the digital age* (pp. 47–60). Cambridge, MA: MIT Press.

Pirolli, B. (2016). Travel information online: Navigating correspondents, consensus, and conversation. *Current Issues in Tourism*, doi:10.1080/13683500.2016.1273883

Schudson, M. (2013). Would journalism please hold still. In C. Peters and M. Broersma (Eds.), *Rethinking journalism: Trust and participation in a transformed news landscape* (pp. 191–199). Abingdon: Routledge.

Thurman, N., Dörr, K., and Kunert, J. (2017). When reporters get hands-on with robo-writing: Professionals consider automated journalism's capabilities and consequences. *Digital Journalism* (March), 1–20.

INDEX